Houghton Mifflin
English

Shirley Haley-James   John Warren Stewig

Marcus T. Ballenger   Jacqueline L. Chaparro   Nancy C. Millett

June Grant Shane   C. Ann Terry

HOUGHTON   MIFFLIN   COMPANY   BOSTON

Atlanta   Dallas   Geneva, Illinois   Palo Alto   Princeton   Toronto

Acknowledgments

"Cinquain: An Image" by Carlota Cárdenas de Dwyer. Reprinted by permission of the author.

"Eagle Flight" by Alonzo Lopez from *The Whispering Wind,* edited by Terry Allen. Copyright © 1972 by The Institute of American Indian Arts. Reprinted by permission of Doubleday, a division of Bantam, Doubleday, Dell Publishing Group, Inc.

"Earth and Its Nearest Neighbors," from *The Solar System* by Sue Becklake. Copyright © 1979 Macmillan Publishers Limited. Reprinted by permission of Macmillan, London and Basingstoke.

"An Evening on the River," Chapter XIV from *Stuart Little* by E.B. White. Text copyright 1945, 1973 by E.B. White. Reprinted by permission of Harper & Row, Publishers, Inc., and Hamish Hamilton Ltd.

Haiku: "That duck, bobbing up . . .," by Joso from *Cricket Songs* Japanese haiku translated by Harry Behn. © 1964 by Harry Behn. All rights reserved. Reprinted by permission of Marian Reiner.

"In the Fog," from *I Feel the Same Way* in the compilation *Something New Begins* by Lilian Moore. Copyright © 1982 Lilian Moore. Reproduced with the permission of Atheneum Publishers, an imprint of Macmillan Publishing Company.

"Letter to His Readers" by E.B. White. Reprinted by permission of Harper & Row, Publishers, Inc.

"Lost on a Mountain in Maine," from *Donn Fendler Lost on a Mountain in Maine* by Donn Fendler as told to Joseph B. Egan. Copyright © 1978 by New Hampshire Publishing Company. Reprinted by permission of New Hampshire Publishing Co., PO Box 70, Somersworth, NH 03878.

"Marbles," from *Small Poems* by Valerie Worth. Copyright © 1972 by Valerie Worth. Reprinted by permission of Farrar, Straus and Giroux, Inc.

"Markings: The Comma," from *Finding a Poem* by Eve Merriam. Copyright © 1970 by Eve Merriam. All rights reserved. Reprinted by permission of Marian Reiner for the author.

"New Sneakers," from *Dandelion Wine* by Ray Bradbury. Copyright © 1956 by Ray Bradbury; Renewed 1984 by Ray Bradbury. Reprinted by permission of Don Congdon Associates, Inc.

"Phaethon" from *D'Aulaires' Book of Greek Myths.* Copyright © 1962 by Ingri and Edgar Parin D'Aulaire. Reprinted by permission of Doubleday & Company, Inc.

"Poem," reprinted from *The Dream Keeper and Other Poems,* by Langston Hughes. Copyright 1932 and renewed 1960 by Langston Hughes. By permission of Alfred A. Knopf, Inc., and Harold Ober Associates, Incorporated.

"Poem for Rodney," from *Spin a Soft Black Song* by Nikki Giovanni. Copyright © 1971 by Nikki Giovanni. Reprinted by permission of Farrar, Straus and Giroux, Inc.

"Rascal" from *Rascal* by Sterling North. Copyright © 1975 by Sterling North. Reprinted with permission of the publisher, E.P. Dutton, a division of Penguin USA Inc.

"The Real Robinson Crusoe," adapted from *True Sea Adventures* by Donald J. Sobol. Copyright © 1975 by Donald J. Sobol. Reprinted by permission of E.P. Dutton, a division of Penguin Books USA Inc.

Printed in U.S.A.
ISBN: 0–395–50266–7
LMNO-VH-98765

(Acknowledgments continued on page 580.)

Table of Contents

UNIT 2

Literature and Writing: Personal Narrative

UNIT 3

Language and Usage: Nouns

UNIT 10

Literature and Writing: Persuasive Letter

UNIT 11

Language and Usage: Pronouns

Strategies Handbook

Writer's Handbook

Glossaries

Getting Ready to Write

. . . I write down everything, everything, everything. . . .
Marie K. Bashkirtsteff
from *The Journal of a Young Artist*

1

LITERATURE

What happened to Rascal's treat?

Rascal

By Sterling North

I decided one day that Rascal was clean enough and bright enough to eat with us at the table. I went to the attic and brought down the family highchair, last used during my own infancy.

Next morning while my father was fixing eggs, toast, and coffee, I went out to get Rascal, and placed him in the highchair beside me at the table. On his tray I put a heavy earthenware bowl of warm milk.

Rascal could reach the milk easily by standing in the chair and placing his hands on the edge of the tray. He seemed to like the new arrangement and chirred and trilled his satisfaction. Except for dribbling a little milk, easily wiped from the tray of the highchair, his table manners proved excellent, much better than those of most children. My father was amused and permissive as usual, and even petted the raccoon as we finished our meal.

Breakfast-for-three became part of the daily ritual, and we had no trouble whatsoever until I had the idea of offering Rascal a sugar lump. . . .

Rascal felt it, sniffed it, and then began his usual washing ceremony, swishing it back and forth through his bowl of milk. In a few moments, of course, it melted entirely away, and a more surprised little 'coon you have never seen in your life. He felt all over the bottom of the bowl to see if he had dropped it, then turned over his right hand to assure himself it was empty, then examined his left hand in the same manner. Finally he looked at me and trilled a shrill question: who had stolen his sugar lump?

Recovering from my laughter, I gave him a second sugar lump, which Rascal examined minutely. He started to wash it, but hesitated. A very shrewd look came into his bright black eyes, and instead of washing away a second treat, he took it directly to his mouth where he began to munch it with complete satisfaction. When Rascal had learned a lesson, he had learned it for life. Never again did he wash a lump of sugar.

His intelligence, however, created many problems. For instance, he had seen the source of the sugar—the covered bowl in the middle of the table. And whereas I had previously been able to confine him to his highchair, he now insisted upon walking across the tablecloth, lifting the lid of the sugar bowl, and helping himself to a lump. From that day on, we had to keep the sugar bowl in the corner cupboard to avoid having a small raccoon constantly on the dining room table.

This story is from Sterling North's book *Rascal* about a boy who raises a pet raccoon in a small town.

Think and Discuss
1. How did Rascal lose his sugar lump?
2. What do you think "trilling" sounds like? Explain.
3. Does Rascal learn the same way you do? Explain.

The Writing Process

STEP 1: PREWRITING

How to Get Ideas: Listing

How do you find a topic? One way is to sit down, pen in hand, paper in front of you, and just list anything that comes to your mind. Don't stop to think. Just write!

GUIDELINES FOR LISTING

- Set a time limit for yourself—maybe five minutes.
- List as many ideas as you can. Don't worry about how good they are.
- Don't worry about capitalization, punctuation, or grammar. Just write.
- Evaluate your ideas only after your time is up. Later you can choose the ideas you think will work best and save the others in your writing folder.

When Rob began thinking about writing a paragraph of instructions, he listed every idea that came to mind.

> how to choose your first pet
> how to make a dog house
> how to clean a bird cage
> pet safety – not letting dogs hang out of car windows
> raccoon prints and how to recognize them
> how to train your dog
> balanced diets for pets, or how to feed a dog

n Your Own

st of as many *how-to* topics as you can. Don't
out mistakes. Just write! See how many ideas you
e up with in five minutes!

Write

How to Explore Your Topic: Interviewing

You have your topic now, but what should you include? What will interest your readers? One way to get ideas about what to write is to have a partner interview you.

Here are some things you might ask to help a partner write instructions.

- What do you do first?
- Do you need any special equipment?
- What order do you have to follow?
- How easy is it to do that?

Here are some questions you might ask to help a partner with any kind of writing.

- How did you feel when . . . ?
- Can you explain why . . . ?
- What happened when . . . ?
- Who else was involved?

Rob asked Roy to interview him.

Rob: I'm going to tell my readers how to identify raccoon prints.
Roy: When you find prints, how do you know they weren't made by a cat or dog?
Rob: Raccoons have big hind feet and smaller front feet.
Roy: Don't other animals have feet like that?
Rob: Yes, but you also look at the size of the feet and some other things. I'll write about the differences.

Having an Interview

With a partner, take turns interviewing each other about your *how-to* topics. Do the questions spark some ideas for writing your instructions? Jot down these ideas.

How to Write a First Draft

You've chosen your topic, you've decided what you're going to write about, and now you're ready to write your first draft. This is a *rough* draft. This is not the time to worry about making mistakes. This is the time to get your ideas down on paper.

GUIDELINES FOR DRAFTING

- Keep in mind your purpose and who your audience will be.
- Get your ideas down quickly.
- Don't worry if your paper is messy. Just write.
- Skip every other line. That way you'll have plenty of room to add or to make changes later.
- Don't worry about mistakes. You can fix them later.

Think and Discuss

- How did Rob change his beginning? How did he show this?
- Are his instructions clear?
- Are there any words he should explain?

~~If you want to~~ Here's an easy way to identafy a raccoon's prints. Check the track. The big hind feet should be parellel to the front feet. When a raccoon walks its straddle is 9–13 centimeters, with a stride of 15–52 centimeters. Check the prints. The front feet should be 6.5 centimeters long and wide and the hind feet should be 10.5 centimeters long. The prints should show five toes on each foot.

Drafting on Your Own

Using your ideas from your interview, write the clearest instructions you can. Write on every other line so that you will have room to add or make changes later.

STEP 3: REVISING

How to Have a Writing Conference

Congratulations! You've written your first draft. Where do you go from here? First, reread it. Make whatever changes occur to you at the moment. Then discuss it with a partner. Your conference will help you see how you can revise your writing to make it more effective.

Think and Discuss

- How does Sarah begin the conference?
- What suggestions does she make?
- How can Sarah's comments help Rob?

GUIDELINES FOR A CONFERENCE

- Listen carefully.
- Be positive. Tell the writer something you liked about the writing, or retell what you have heard. That way, the writer will know you were listening.
- Ask questions that begin with *how, why, when, where, who,* and *what*.
- Offer suggestions only when you are asked. Do not tell the writer what to do.
- Be polite at all times.

Questions for a Conference

- What part do you like best?
- What feeling do you want your reader to have?
- Tell me more about . . .
- What happened after . . . ?
- When did that happen?
- Did you mean . . . ?
- How could you *show* instead of *tell* this?
- Could you make that a little clearer?
- How might you put the parts together?
- Which part is most important?

Having a Writing Conference

Work with a partner. Take turns sharing your instructions. Ask each other questions. Offer each other helpful suggestions. Listen carefully, and be polite at all times. Jot down those suggestions that will improve your writing.

How to Revise Your Draft

You are now ready to make changes in your draft. This is your chance to revise—to change the beginning, add details, and make points clearer. Don't worry how your paper looks.

GUIDELINES FOR REVISING

- Write new words and sentences between the lines, in the margins, wherever you have room.
- Draw arrows and circle words, sentences, or even whole paragraphs to show where you want to move them.
- Cross out parts that you want to change or take out.

~~If you want to~~ Here's an easy way to
identafy a raccoon's prints. First, Check the
track, which is a series of prints. The big hind feet should be
parellel to the small front feet. When a raccoon
walks its straddle (the width of the track) is 9-13 centimeters,
with a stride (the distance between prints) of 15-52 centimeters. Next, Check
the prints. The front feet should be 6.5
centimeters long and wide and the hind feet
should be 10.5 centimeters long. and 6 centimeters wide The prints
should show five toes on each foot.

Think and Discuss

- What words did Rob add to make the steps clearer?
- What details did he add?
- Which sentence did he move? Why?

Revising on Your Own

Revise your instructions, making them as clear as possible.

STEP 4: PROOFREADING

How to Proofread Your Writing

The moment has arrived! Finally, you can polish your writing and make it as perfect as possible. Use proofreading marks to correct your paper.

> ~~If you want to~~ Here's an easy way to identⁱfy a raccoon's prints. First, Check the track, which is a series of prints. The big hind feet should be parᵃllel to the ᵃsmall front feet. When a raccoon walks, its straddle, (the width of the track) is 9-13 centimeters, with a stride, (the distance between prints) of 15-52 centimeters. Next, Check the prints. The front feet should be 6.5 centimeters long and wide, and the hind feet should be 10.5 centimeters long. and 6 centimeters wide The prints should show five toes on each foot.

GUIDELINES FOR PROOFREADING

- Make sure you have indented all paragraphs correctly.
- Check that you have used capital letters correctly.
- Check that you have used punctuation as needed.
- Check spellings of words in a dictionary.
- Check your grammar.

Proofreading Marks

- ¶ Indent
- ∧ Add
- ⅄ Add a comma
- ⱽⱽ Add quotation marks
- ⊙ Add a period
- ℓ Take out
- ≡ Capitalize
- / Make a small letter
- ∿ Reverse the order

Proofreading on Your Own

Proofread your instructions. Use the proofreading marks in the box on this page.

STEP 5: PUBLISHING

How to Publish Your Writing

GUIDELINES FOR PUBLISHING

- Copy your paper as neatly as possible on a clean piece of paper.
- Add an attention-getting title.
- Reread your paper to make sure you have not left anything out or made mistakes in copying.
- Share your writing.

Ideas for Publishing

- Read your writing aloud while a classmate acts out an appropriate part.
- Turn your story into a comic strip. Make a frame for each step of your instructions.
- Combine your writing with that of your classmates in a *how-to* book for the classroom library.

Publishing on Your Own

Publish your writing. First, copy your story as neatly as possible. Add a title. Then use one of the ideas on this page or one of your own to share your instructions.

Language and Usage

Stand still.
The fog wraps you up
and no one can find you.
Walk.
The fog opens up
to let you through
and closes behind you.

 Lilian Moore "In the Fog"

The Sentence

Getting Ready You have been speaking in sentences since you were a baby. You use them to ask, tell, explain, command, request, astonish, amuse, share. The more successfully you use sentences, the more successfully you communicate what you want. In this unit, you will learn more about sentences—how to make them do what you want them to do and how to use them to communicate more successfully.

ACTIVITIES

Listening
Listen to each sentence in the poem on the opposite page. What is the poet talking about? In which sentences is she explaining, ordering, describing? With whom do you think she is trying to communicate?

Speaking
Look at the picture. Ask some questions about it. How would you express your surprise if you suddenly came upon this beautiful scene? Make some statements about it. Give an order about it. Now you have used the four basic sentence types!

Writing
Has something already happened or is something about to happen in this picture? Write your ideas in your journal.

1 | Kinds of Sentences

A **sentence** is a group of words that expresses a complete thought. All sentences start with a capital letter.

1. A sentence that makes a statement is a **declarative sentence**. It ends with a period.

   > I bought a package of wrapping paper.

2. A sentence that asks a question is an **interrogative sentence**. It ends with a question mark.

   > What are you going to wrap?

3. A sentence that gives a command or makes a request is an **imperative sentence**. It ends with a period.

   > Help me. Please hold the box.

4. A sentence that shows excitement or strong feeling is an **exclamatory sentence**. It ends with an exclamation point.

   > This is a wonderful gift! How clever you are!

Guided Practice What punctuation mark should end each sentence? Is the sentence declarative, interrogative, imperative, or exclamatory?

Example: Look at the bowl   *period* *imperative*

1. How many pennies are in it
2. The contest deadline is tomorrow
3. Write your answer in the box
4. What an interesting guess you made
5. Do you think I'll win a prize

Summing up

- ▶ A **declarative sentence** makes a statement.
- ▶ An **interrogative sentence** asks a question.
- ▶ An **imperative sentence** gives a command or makes a request.
- ▶ An **exclamatory sentence** shows excitement or strong feeling.

Independent Practice   Copy each sentence. Add the correct end punctuation and write what kind of sentence it is.

Example: What fun this trip will be
           What fun this trip will be!   **exclamatory**

6. I am looking forward to this trip
7. Have you ever climbed this mountain
8. I have new hiking boots
9. Please give me the bug spray
10. Did you pack a map
11. Two pairs of socks will be enough
12. How careless I was to forget my soap
13. Take this shirt with you
14. Will the flashlight fit into your pack
15. These snacks will give us energy
16. Do we have everything
17. What unusual birds I can see
18. Hiking brings us close to nature
19. How fast that stream is flowing
20. Are you thirsty now
21. Hand me the canteen, please
22. This is a spectacular view
23. How high we have climbed
24. What a cool breeze this is
25. I will come back here next summer
26. Will you climb another mountain soon
27. Look at that woodpecker in the tree
28. What a loud noise that bird makes
29. Are you ready to start climbing now
30. We should follow this trail
31. The trail has a very pretty view
32. Stay together, please, along the trail

Writing Application: A Newspaper Report

Your newspaper has sent you out to report on the discovery of a prehistoric dinosaur. Write a report about what you saw. Include a declarative, an interrogative, an imperative, and an exclamatory sentence in your report.

For Extra Practice, see p. 41.   **Kinds of Sentences**

2 | Complete Subjects and Complete Predicates

Every sentence has two parts, a subject and a predicate. The **subject** tells whom or what the sentence is about. The **predicate** tells what the subject does, is, has, or feels.

All the words in the subject make up the **complete subject**. All the words in the predicate make up the **complete predicate**.

COMPLETE SUBJECT	COMPLETE PREDICATE
Green sneakers	are on sale.
Who	wants a pair?
My friend	does.
Everyone in school	is wearing bright shoes.

Two of my friends are wearing red shoes.

Guided Practice In each sentence, what is the complete subject? What is the complete predicate?

Example: Judy Hart visited a computer store.
   complete subj.: *Judy Hart*
   complete pred.: *visited a computer store*

1. She took a bus.
2. The bus stopped at Bill's Computer Store.
3. Bill Woo is the owner of the shop.
4. The salesclerk smiled at Judy.
5. Bright lights glowed.
6. Large screens flashed messages at Judy.
7. Other customers were trying out the computers.
8. Software of all types lined the shelves.

> ▶ Every sentence has a subject and a predicate. A **subject** tells whom or what a sentence is about. A **predicate** tells what the subject does, is, has, or feels.
> ▶ A **complete subject** contains all the words in the subject.
> ▶ A **complete predicate** contains all the words in the predicate.

Independent Practice Write each sentence. Draw a line between the complete subject and the complete predicate.

Example: Fireworks have existed for hundreds of years.
Fireworks|have existed for hundreds of years.

9. Everyone enjoys fireworks.
10. Even little children like them.
11. Celebrations for the Fourth of July include fireworks.
12. The ancient Greeks used them.
13. The Chinese learned the art of firecrackers.
14. Lights of many colors dance in the sky.
15. The fireworks sparkle against the dark sky.
16. Loud pops go with the lights.
17. Crowds roar with pleasure at the sight.
18. Colorful patterns fill the sky.
19. People of all ages applaud the display.
20. The onlookers wait for the next pattern.
21. Brilliant stars fall from the sky.
22. A shower of light bursts above the crowd.
23. Children cry out with pleasure.
24. Even parents sigh with wonder.
25. The whole crowd cheers at the last display.
26. The cheers fill the night.
27. The last of the colors fade from the sky.
28. Small, white stars shine in the sky.

Writing Application: A Description
Pretend that you have just seen a fireworks display. Write a description of what you saw and heard. Be sure that every sentence has a subject and a predicate.

3 | Simple Subjects and Simple Predicates

You have already learned about complete subjects and complete predicates. The *main* word (or words) in the complete subject is called the **simple subject**.

The main word (or words) in the complete predicate is called the **simple predicate**. The simple predicate is made up of at least one verb, a word that shows action or being.

SIMPLE SUBJECT	SIMPLE PREDICATE
The **doorbell**	**rang** .
The frisky brown **puppy**	**jumped** at the noise.
Bob Smith from New York	**was visiting** at the time.
He	**played** with the puppy.
New York	**is** Ann's home too.
Ann's **dog**	**has grown** large.

Guided Practice In each sentence, what is the simple subject? What is the simple predicate?

Example: One child was watching a construction crew.
simple subj.: child
simple pred.: was watching

1. Marty Shaw heard the bulldozer.
2. The bulldozer moved slowly.
3. Its big scoop pushed piles of dirt.
4. Marty's eyes sparkled with delight.
5. Piles of stones disappeared.
6. The dark earth looked moist.
7. A pool of water was evaporating in the sun.
8. Marty noticed everything on the site.
9. He could hear the steam shovel's horn.

> ▶ A **simple subject** is the main word (or words) in the complete subject.
>
> ▶ A **simple predicate** is the main word (or words) in the complete predicate. A simple predicate is made up of at least one verb.

Independent Practice Read each sentence. Write the simple subject and underline it. Then write the simple predicate and underline it twice.

Example: Three customers had entered the bicycle shop.

<u>customers</u> <u><u>had entered</u></u>

10. The owner smiled.
11. The oldest girl studied the bicycles.
12. The best bicycle stood in front of the others.
13. Two blue saddlebags hung on the rear fender.
14. A shiny silver bell decorated one handlebar.
15. The sound of the bell surprised Julie.
16. Julie's sister bought reflectors.
17. A man in overalls was looking at dirt bikes.
18. The man was my Uncle Bert.
19. Uncle Bert rides dirt bikes for fun.
20. Two girls at the door smiled at each other.
21. A woman near the cash register waved to them.
22. Five people were buying equipment.
23. Another customer asked for advice.
24. The salesclerk took some gloves from the shelf.
25. The leather gloves will give the rider a better grip.
26. A young boy was studying a book about bicycle repair.

Writing Application: A Description

Imagine that you are taking a trip through an unexplored country. Write a paragraph describing what you see. Circle the simple subject, and underline the simple predicate in each sentence.

For Extra Practice, see p. 43.   **Simple Subjects and Predicates**

4 | Subjects in Imperative and Interrogative Sentences

You know that an imperative sentence gives a command and an interrogative sentence asks a question. Can you find the subject of this imperative sentence?

Please call a taxi for me.

The subject of an imperative sentence is always *you*. *You* is usually understood rather than stated.

(You) Please call a taxi for me.

You can find the subject of an interrogative sentence by rearranging the question into a statement. Then ask *who* or *what* does the action.

QUESTION: Will the taxi get to the airport on time?

STATEMENT: The taxi will get to the airport on time.

(Simple subject is *taxi*.)

Guided Practice What is the simple subject of each sentence? Is the sentence imperative or interrogative?

Example: Give the bus driver your ticket.
(You) *imperative*

1. Did Paula find her seat?
2. Watch that first step.
3. Can you climb up?
4. Should we sit here?
5. Sit next to me.
6. Please take any seat.
7. Will the driver stop here?
8. Do we get off soon?
9. Please hold this bag.
10. Can you read the sign?

▶ The subject of an imperative sentence is always *you*. *You* is usually understood rather than stated.

▶ To find the subject of an interrogative sentence, rearrange the question into a statement. Then ask *who* or *what* does the action.

Independent Practice

A. Write the simple subject of each sentence.

Example: Does the car need water?   *car*

11. Please test the batteries.
12. Check the oil too.
13. Does the car need oil?
14. Please clean the rear window.
15. Will your helper check the tires?
16. Do the tires need air?
17. Please give me ten gallons of gas.
18. Don't fill the whole tank.
19. How much do I owe?

B. Write the simple subject of each sentence. Then label each sentence *imperative* or *interrogative*.

Example: Buy your ticket at the box office. *(You)* *imperative*

20. Will you see a comedy?
21. Follow the usher to your seat.
22. Wait for the first act.
23. Will the actors speak loudly?
24. Should I ask for a program?
25. Stretch your legs at intermission.

Writing Application: Creative Writing

Imagine that you are a flight attendant on an airplane. Write two imperative sentences that tell your passengers what to do. Then write three interrogative sentences that ask what they want or need.

For Extra Practice, see p. 44.

Subjects in Sentences **21**

5 | Compound Subjects

You already know that every sentence has a simple subject.

The students in the band play well.

Some sentences have more than one simple subject. When a sentence has two or more simple subjects joined by the connecting word *and* or *or,* the subject is called a **compound subject**.

Joan and Carol practice often.

My brother or sister will sing tomorrow.

Parents , relatives , and friends may attend.

Beautiful music and lively dances will be performed.

Guided Practice What is the compound subject in each sentence? What connecting word joins the simple subject?

Example: Suitcases, watches, and boats can be made from plastic.
Suitcases watches boats
connecting word: *and*

1. Handbags and wallets are often plastic.
2. Plastic, steel, and aluminum are building materials.
3. Is aluminum or steel stronger?
4. Coal, gas, or oil can be used to make plastic.
5. Is plastic or glass better for lenses?
6. Cheap plastic and expensive steel can be used together in the same product.
7. Cars and trolleys are made from plastic.
8. Computers and modern typewriters have some very strong and sturdy plastic parts.

Summing up

▸ A **compound subject** contains two or more simple subjects. They are joined by a connecting word such as *and* or *or.*

Independent Practice Write the compound subject of each sentence. Then write the connecting word that joins the simple subjects.

Example: Large companies and small businesses produce plastic.
companies businesses
connecting word: *and*

9. Glass or plastic is used to make bottles.
10. Plastic tools and machines do not break easily.
11. Plastic pots and pans are easy to clean.
12. Plastic containers and kitchen tools are common.
13. Plastic skis, bikes, and snowshoes are expensive.
14. Are plastic counters or wooden tables more practical?
15. Does your watch or your camera have plastic parts?
16. Completely plastic houses and cities do not exist yet.
17. Homemakers, businesspeople, and children use plastic.
18. Do televisions and telephones have plastic parts?
19. Casey and Bea counted the plastic items in their picnic basket.
20. Forks, glasses, and the tablecloth were plastic.
21. Does a plastic thermos or a cardboard carton leak?
22. Is plastic or aluminum cheaper?
23. The sandwiches and the salad were wrapped in plastic.
24. The bowls and the lids were made from plastic too.
25. Bea and her classmates learned more about plastic.
26. A book or an encyclopedia is a good place to find information.
27. Boys and girls in the class divided into teams.
28. Bea and her team watched a film about plastic.
29. Casey, his team, and the librarian searched in magazines.
30. Books, magazines, or films were used by each team.
31. Posters and drawings were made by the teams.
32. Bea, Casey, and their teammates presented the reports to the class.

Writing Application: Creative Writing

Imagine that you and a friend are in a spaceship. Write a paragraph about what you see and how you feel. Use compound subjects. Underline the simple subjects that make up each compound subject, and circle the connecting word that joins them.

For Extra Practice, see p. 45.   **Compound Subjects 23**

6 | Compound Predicates

You have learned that a sentence can have more than one simple subject. A sentence can also have more than one simple predicate. When a sentence has two or more simple predicates joined by the connecting word *and* or *or*, the predicate is called a **compound predicate**.

Children in the park jumped , played , or ran .

Al and I will walk fast <u>and</u> stop at Jim's house.

People opened umbrellas, hopped on buses, <u>or</u> dashed into stores.

splashed and dripped.

Guided Practice

What is the compound predicate in each sentence? What connecting word joins the simple predicates?

Example: Joe took us to a museum and bought us lunch.

      compound pred.: *took   bought*   **connecting word:** *and*

1. Visitors to the museum paid and entered.
2. They toured the galleries or watched slides.
3. A guide wore a suit of armor and told dragon stories.
4. We looked, asked questions, and learned.
5. Children and adults ate lunch or rested.

Summing up

▶ A **compound predicate** contains two or more simple predicates. They are joined by a connecting word such as *and* or *or*.

Independent Practice
Write the compound predicate of each sentence. Then write the connecting word that joins the simple predicates.

Example: Jim went to a science museum and saw everything.
*went   saw   **connecting word:** and*

6. Our group had followed the tour and listened to the guide.
7. We studied coins, saw jewels, or examined tools.
8. Berto watched and listened.
9. A guide held a snake and described it.
10. Everyone touched it or held it.
11. Emily saw and used a television camera.
12. People made faces or danced in front of the camera.
13. Several computers played games and taught arithmetic.
14. One computer talked and sang songs.
15. Water in a tank rocked and splashed.
16. Big waves grew, crashed, and disappeared.
17. Bruce and Ana saw and tried everything.
18. Ana talked into a phone and pushed some buttons.
19. Then she listened and heard her own voice.
20. Bruce walked upstairs and found the animal room.
21. Everyone went to the gift shop and bought postcards.
22. Then Bruce's class planned and held a science fair.
23. People wrote reports, made posters, or built models.
24. Parents and friends came and saw the science projects.
25. Dylan drew pictures and made them into a movie.
26. People looked, touched, or listened all morning.
27. The judges asked questions and made comments.
28. Pablo answered questions and explained his project.
29. The best project won first prize and received a blue ribbon.
30. All the students posed for a picture and received applause.

Writing Application: A Description
Describe a trip to a museum. Write about what you have seen or would like to see. Use compound predicates. Underline the parts of the compound predicate, and circle the word that connects them.

For Extra Practice, see p. 46.   **Compound Predicates**

7 | Compound Sentences

So far you have studied only simple sentences. Sometimes two simple sentences can be combined into one sentence called a **compound sentence**. The simple sentences are joined by a comma and a connecting word like *and, or,* or *but.*

Jo is a scientist.
She travels often.

Jo is a scientist, and she travels often.

Will you go to Peru?
Will you do more research?

Will you go to Peru, or will you do more research?

Ancient people had no alphabet. They drew signs.

Ancient people had no alphabet, but they drew signs.

Do not confuse a compound sentence with a simple sentence that has a compound subject, a compound predicate, or both. A compound sentence has a subject and a predicate on *each* side of the connecting word.

COMPOUND SUBJECT: Ann and I do research.

COMPOUND PREDICATE: We write reports and read them aloud.

COMPOUND SUBJECT AND
COMPOUND PREDICATE: She and I study and work together.

COMPOUND SENTENCE: Ann types the report , and I proofread it .

Guided Practice Which sentences are compound sentences? Which are simple sentences? What is the connecting word that joins the parts of each compound sentence?

Example: Chisels were used for pencils, and stone was used for paper. *compound sentence   and*

1. Pictures on cave walls tell a story, but the story is not in words.
2. Scientists form teams and study the pictures.
3. Pictures and signs tell us about ancient people.
4. Did people draw on clay, or did they chip pictures into stone?
5. The pictures were drawn about a thousand years ago.

> ▶ A **compound sentence** is made up of two simple sentences. The simple sentences are joined by a comma and a connecting word like *and*, *or*, or *but*.

Independent Practice   Copy each sentence. Underline the two simple sentences in each compound sentence. If the sentence is not a compound sentence, write *not compound*.

Example: Huge pictures were drawn, but they are a mystery.
          Huge pictures were drawn, but they are a mystery.

6. Ancient people made long lines, and they drew huge pictures of animals.
7. Some of the lines are forty miles long, and some of the pictures are bigger than two football fields.
8. Dirt, rocks, and stones were scraped away from a dark layer of the earth.
9. The sandy layer showed up clearly, and it still shows today.
10. The pictures are seen best from the air, and now people take photographs of them from airplanes.
11. Ancient people drew these pictures, but they probably never saw any of them whole.
12. Most of these pictures are in Peru, but some have been found in other countries.
13. Are these pictures a giant calendar, or were they drawn for other reasons?
14. We will have to guess correctly, or the meaning of the pictures will be lost.
15. Scientists have studied these pictures, and many books have been written about them.
16. We must protect these drawings against damage, or they will be lost to us forever.

Writing Application: Personal Narrative
Think back to when you first learned to read or write. Write a paragraph about your experience. Use at least three compound sentences. If you can't remember, imagine what it was like.

For Extra Practice, see p. 47.

8 | Conjunctions

The connecting words *and, or,* and *but* are called **conjunctions.** You can use conjunctions to make subjects, predicates, and sentences compound. The conjunction that you use depends on your purpose.

Use *and* to add information: I can swim and dive.
  Use *but* to show contrast: I swim, but Lee sails.
    Use *or* to give a choice: Does he sail or swim?

Guided Practice Choose the better conjunction.

Example: Shall we sail now (but, or) wait until later? *or*

1. The wind is strong, (or, and) the waves are high.
2. We might tip over (but, or) freeze out there!
3. We could water ski, (but, and) the water is rough.
4. Maybe you (and, but) I should shoot baskets instead.
5. I want to swim, (or, but) I am cold.

Summing up

▶ The words *and, or,* and *but* are conjunctions. Use *and* to add information, *or* to give a choice, and *but* to show contrast.

Independent Practice Use *and, or,* or *but*.

Example: Now the weather is better, ____ we can sail. *and*

6. John, Sue, ____ I can steer.
7. Help us raise the sail ____ pull up the anchor.
8. I brought the picnic lunch, ____ I forgot the juice.
9. We can sail to that island ____ stop for a swim.
10. John ____ Sue both want to go there.

Writing Application: A Description
Write about an outdoor activity you enjoy. Use compound subjects, compound predicates, and compound sentences.

9 | Combining Sentences: Compound Sentences

To make your writing more interesting, use sentences of different lengths. You can make a sentence longer by combining two choppy sentences into a compound sentence.

Join the simple sentences with a comma and a conjunction. Use a conjunction that gives the meaning you want.

SIMPLE SENTENCES	COMPOUND SENTENCES
I want to play my guitar. I lost my music.	I want to play my guitar, but I lost my music.
Can you play this song? Is it too difficult?	Can you play this song, or is it too difficult?
I take music lessons. I practice each week.	I take music lessons, and I practice each week.

Guided Practice Form a compound sentence by joining each pair of simple sentences with *and, or,* or *but.* Where does the comma go?

Example: We can practice now. We can wait until tomorrow.
We can practice now, or we can wait until tomorrow.
*The comma goes before **or**.*

1. We could play the piano. We could go to the concert.
2. We played the piano for an hour. Then we went to the concert.
3. I brought my flute home. It is not in my room.
4. I used to like the clarinet. Now I prefer the saxophone.
5. Will Mom drive me to the rehearsal? Should I take a bus?
6. I arrived on time. The band members were not there.
7. I studied my music. I practiced some difficult parts.
8. Should we wait for Rich? Should we start without him?
9. Hans usually plays well. Today he made mistakes.
10. Do you like jazz? Do you listen to classical music?
11. I like classical music. I like jazz too.
12. Louis Armstrong was a famous jazz musician. I like his music.

> ▶ Combine two choppy sentences into a compound sentence to vary sentence length in your writing.
> ▶ Join the simple sentences with a comma and a conjunction.

Independent Practice
Combine each pair of simple sentences into one compound sentence. Punctuate correctly, and use the conjunctions *and*, *or*, and *but* at least once.

Example: Bob plays bass guitar. Lisa plays too.
Bob plays bass guitar, and Lisa plays too.

13. They play in bands. They are not in the same band.
14. Lisa's band must play popular music. People will not come.
15. Lisa plays on Saturday night. She practices after school.
16. She must practice often. She might not learn the songs.
17. Bob likes being a bass player. He is good at it.
18. Some songs are difficult for him. Most are not.
19. Lisa has played bass for three years. She likes nothing more.
20. Does Lisa play well? Does she make mistakes often?
21. People sometimes don't hear the bass guitar. Lisa doesn't mind.
22. She knows how important it is. That's what counts.
23. Some players become nervous. Lisa does not.
24. Lisa is a good musician. She can also sing.
25. She sings well. She does not sing with the band.
26. Bob and Lisa want to write music. They are studying together.
27. Would you like to write music? Do you just like to listen?
28. Bob and Lisa write simple melodies. They play them on their guitars.
29. The melodies sound like songs. They are just practice exercises.
30. Bob and Lisa share their music books. They practice the same drills together every day.

Writing Application: Creative Writing
Pretend that you are a famous person in the world of music. Write a paragraph explaining how you rehearse for a concert. Include some compound sentences in your paragraph.

 For Extra Practice, see p. 49.

10 | Combining Sentences: Complex Sentences

You have learned to form a compound sentence by using *and, or,* or *but* to join two simple sentences. You can also combine two simple sentences to form a **complex sentence.**

SIMPLE: Salmon swim to fresh water. They lay eggs.
COMPOUND: Salmon swim to fresh water, and they lay eggs.
COMPLEX: Salmon swim to fresh water before they lay eggs.

The words *and, or,* and *but* are **coordinating conjunctions.** When you use one of them to form a compound sentence, the two main parts of the new sentence are equal. When you form a complex sentence, however, you use a **subordinating conjunction** to join two simple sentences. Subordinating conjunctions make one part of the sentence subordinate to the other part.

coordinating conjunction
Salmon swim to fresh water, | and | they lay eggs.

subordinating conjunction
Salmon swim to fresh water | before | they lay eggs.

The chart below shows some subordinating conjunctions you can use to form complex sentences.

Conjunctions in Complex Sentences

after	because	since	when
although	before	unless	whenever
as	if	until	while

Guided Practice Form a complex sentence from each pair of simple sentences. Use the conjunction in parentheses.

Example: Dolphins are easy to train. They are very smart. (since)
Dolphins are easy to train since they are very smart.

1. Dolphins swim near the surface of the water. They need to take in air often. (because)
2. Stingrays are gentle. They are disturbed. (unless)

3. The eyespot on a starfish's arm can see a shadow. A fish swims above the starfish.   (if)
4. The killer whale can be thirty feet long. The white-sided dolphin is about nine feet long.   (while)

Summing up

▶ A **complex sentence** is made up of two simple sentences joined by a subordinating conjunction.

Independent Practice

A. For each sentence write *simple, compound,* or *complex.*

Example: Pythons are scary because they are so large.   *complex*

5. Pythons can grow to a length of thirty feet.
6. Many people shiver when they see a picture of a python.
7. Some pythons change color, and they become very colorful.

B. Combine each pair of sentences into a complex sentence. Use the conjunction in parentheses.

Example: There are many legends about pythons. They are such unique snakes.   (since)
There are many legends about pythons since they are such unique snakes.

8. A python may be thirty feet long. Smaller species might grow to only three feet in length.   (while)
9. Perhaps you can admire the python's colorful skin. You don't particularly care for its size.   (if)
10. Some pythons change from yellow to green. They grow.   (as)
11. A python's skin might look colorless. It is time to shed its skin.   (whenever)
12. The snake rubs its nose against something rough. The old skin begins to peel off.   (until)

Writing Application: Riddles
Describe five different animals, using a complex sentence for each description. Use at least three different conjunctions.

For Extra Practice, see p. 50.

11 Correcting Fragments and Run-ons

You know that a sentence must have a subject and a predicate. A **sentence fragment** is missing one or both of these. A fragment does not express a complete thought. You can correct sentence fragments by supplying the missing sentence parts.

INCORRECT: I wanted to talk to you. About a summer job.

CORRECT: I wanted to talk to you about a summer job.

A **run-on sentence** is two or more sentences that are run together into one sentence. Often you cannot tell where one thought ends and the next one begins.

INCORRECT: Uncle Frank is a writer Aunt Jill is one too.

INCORRECT: Ann read their book and she loved it and she will read it again and then she will give it to me.

You can correct a run-on sentence by separating each thought into a sentence of its own.

CORRECT: Uncle Frank is a writer. Aunt Jill is one too.

Sometimes you can combine the parts of a run-on sentence into a compound subject, a compound predicate, or a compound sentence.

CORRECT: Ann read their book and loved it. She will read it again, and then she will give it to me.

Guided Practice

A. How would you correct each fragment?

Example: My dad works on a pit crew. At a dirt track.
My dad works on a pit crew at a dirt track.

1. I love to stand in the pit. And watch races.
2. Once I waved. The checkered flag.
3. Cars stop at the pit. For repairs.
4. The pit crew fixes the cars. As fast as possible.
5. I want to work on automobiles. As a mechanic.

B. How would you correct the run-on sentences in each item?

Example: I have a different job every summer it is fun.
I have a different job every summer. It is fun.

6. Last year Al and I walked dogs and we fed them and we bathed them also.
7. Once Al walked three big dogs together their leashes became tangled they tripped him.
8. This summer I am working in a pet store the customers laugh at the puppies I laugh at the puppies.
9. By next year I will have a lot of experience with animals I want to work for a veterinarian.
10. Veterinarians are usually kind and they are helpful and sometimes they work long hours.

Summing up

▶ A **sentence fragment** is a group of words without a subject or a predicate or both.
▶ A **run-on sentence** is two or more sentences that are run together into one sentence.
▶ Fragments and run-ons can be corrected in several ways.

Independent Practice

A. Rewrite these sentences, correcting the fragments.

Example: The world is full. Of interesting careers.
The world is full of interesting careers.

11. My uncle builds skyscrapers. In large cities.
12. He studied engineering. In college.
13. Cousin Rose is a different kind. Of engineer.
14. She designs machines. For a manufacturing company.
15. My uncle's last building. Was built of granite.
16. Tons of stone were used. For the outside walls.
17. Workers drove enormous cranes. At the building site.
18. My uncle was so proud. Of the new building.
19. He received an award. At the opening.

B. Rewrite these run-on sentences correctly.

Example: Yesterday was an exciting day my class visited a college we learned some interesting things.
Yesterday was an exciting day. My class visited a college and learned some interesting things.

21. All of us in the class went together I sat next to Susan on the bus.
22. A professor escorted us into an auditorium people with different careers talked with us it was fascinating.
23. Susan enjoyed the forest ranger's discussion I was interested in the detective's lecture.
24. One speaker planned the diets for zoo animals she brought a lion cub she let us pet a chimpanzee.
25. We got a special treat from the last speaker the gourmet chef gave us baked apples for dessert they were great!
26. We are planning a similar class trip next month we will tour a hospital a doctor will speak to us.

C. (27–35) Rewrite the paragraphs below. Correct the fragments and the run-ons.

Example: I paint funny pictures on sweatshirts and I give them to friends, or I sell them. At craft fairs.
I paint funny pictures on sweatshirts. I give them to friends, or I sell them at craft fairs.

My brother is interested in landscape design. As a career. My father is a floral designer my mother is a photographer all three careers are similar. In some ways. Each occupation requires an artistic ability the person should also have a good eye for color. And balance.

My brother enjoys planting colorful flowers he likes to clip shrubs into unusual shapes. He has been reading a variety of books about different trees, there is so much to learn About landscaping.

Writing Application: A Paragraph

Write a paragraph of at least five sentences about a career that you think would be interesting or fun. Check your paragraph. Repair any sentence fragments or run-ons.

For Extra Practice, see p. 51.   **Correcting Fragments and Run-ons**

Grammar-Writing Connection

Combining Simple Sentences

Good writers avoid unnecessary repetition. One way you can avoid repeating words and ideas is by combining simple sentences. You can combine short simple sentences in several different ways.

The Sahara is a large region. It is hot. It is too dry for farming. > The Sahara is a large region, it is hot, and it is too dry for farming.

The Sahara is a large region. It is hot. It is too dry for farming. > The Sahara is a large, hot region that is too dry for farming.

Notice that the first combined sentence repeats some words. The second combined sentence contains fewer unnecessary words. The meaning is clearer.

Revising Sentences

For each item, write the sentence that best combines the simple sentences.

1. Irrigation is a farming practice. It is ancient. It brings water to dry lands.
    a. Irrigation is an ancient farming practice, and it brings water to dry lands.
    b. Irrigation is a farming practice, it brings water to dry lands, and it is ancient.
    c. Irrigation is an ancient farming practice that brings water to dry lands.

2. Antarctica is a desert. It is large. It is cold.
    a. Antarctica is a desert, it is large, but it is cold.
    b. Antarctica is a large desert that is cold.
    c. Antarctica is cold, and it is a large desert.

Creative Writing

This could be a photograph of a river or a road or a piece of ribbon. Actually, it shows a strip of neatly plowed farmland. Margaret Bourke-White took this picture in 1954 for *Life* magazine. It is one of many clear, direct photographs that Bourke-White took of people and places around the world.

- Why would this photograph be hard to identify without a title?
- What shapes, patterns, and textures can you find in the photo?

Contour Plowing
Margaret Bourke-White
Life magazine, © 1954, Time Inc.

Activities

1. **Write a photo caption.** Imagine that this picture has been handed to you without any explanation. What would you think it is? Write a caption, or description, to go along with the photograph.
2. **Make up a story.** Suppose you were to follow this curving path. Where do you think it would lead you? Write a story about what happens and where you end up.
3. **Write a poem.** How would it feel to walk barefoot through the plowed soil? Write a poem about the imaginary experience.

Check-up: Unit 1

Kinds of Sentences *(p. 14)* Copy each sentence, and add the correct punctuation. Then write *declarative, interrogative, imperative,* or *exclamatory* to identify each sentence.

1. Has a circus come to your town
2. A small circus visited us in June
3. What a sight the tent was
4. Our seats were near the center ring
5. Go to the circus next week

Complete Subjects and Complete Predicates *(p. 16)* Copy each sentence. Draw a line between the complete subject and the complete predicate.

6. My best friend collects posters.
7. Her large collection includes twenty horse posters.
8. A poster hangs on her door.
9. Posters cover her bedroom walls.
10. A cousin from Texas gave her a giant poster of a sunset.

Simple Subjects and Simple Predicates *(p. 18)* Write the simple subject, and underline it once. Write the simple predicate, and underline it twice.

11. Dan Jones read a travel folder.
12. He has discovered Jamaica.
13. He calls it the "Wooded Isle."
14. His cousin rode on a bamboo raft.
15. Many tourists like the shops.
16. Jamaica has great natural beauty.

Subjects in Imperative and Interrogative Sentences *(p. 20)* Write the simple subject. Then write *imperative* or *interrogative.*

17. May we see your new dog?
18. Step into the yard.
19. Would Jed like a puppy?
20. Look in the doghouse.
21. Please hold the leash.

Compound Subjects *(p. 22)* Write the compound subject and the connecting word that joins the simple subjects.

22. Will Fran or Joe rebuild the bike?
23. Joe's brother and sister sketched a new design.
24. Orange paint or reflectors will glow in the dark.
25. Mirrors and horns will be added.
26. Mike, Pam, and Chris will paint the bike.

Compound Predicates *(p. 24)* Write the compound predicate and the connecting word that joins the simple predicates.

27. A ship appeared and raised a flag.
28. Crew members grabbed the helm and worked the sails.
29. The ship outran the clouds and escaped the storm.
30. The crew shivered or sweated.
31. The waves rose and fell.

Compound Sentences *(p. 26)* Label each sentence *simple* or *compound*. Copy the compound sentences. Underline the simple sentences that make up each compound one.

32. Buses and planes bring tourists to Washington, D.C.
33. Spring is here, and it is breezy.
34. I see cherry trees and smell their sweet blossoms.
35. The Capitol has Saturday tours, but the FBI is closed then.

Conjunctions *(p. 28)* Write the conjunction in parentheses that fits the sentence better.

36. Paris (and, but) London are both capital cities.
37. Either London (and, or) Paris is a wonderful place to visit.
38. You can speak English in both cities, (or, but) it is more fun to speak French in Paris.
39. The Seine River runs through Paris, (and, or) the Thames River runs through London.

Combining Sentences: Compound Sentences *(p. 29)* Combine each pair of simple sentences into a compound sentence. Use commas correctly.

40. The air is cool. The sun is warm.
41. They went to the beach. We picnicked on a hill.
42. We had fun. Everyone stayed late.
43. Nora had borrowed a bike. One of the tires was flat.

44. Should we walk home with her? Should friends drive her home?

Combining Sentences: Complex Sentences *(p. 31)* Combine each pair of simple sentences into a complex sentence. Use the conjunction in parentheses.

45. Giant pandas could become extinct. Bamboo is growing scarce. (because)
46. Pandas can't stay healthy. They eat large amounts of bamboo. (unless)
47. Scientists must plant new bamboo. Many bamboo forests are dying. (since)
48. Pandas can depend on the new bamboo. One kind of bamboo dies. (if)

Correcting Fragments and Run-ons *(p. 33)* Label each group of words *sentence*, *fragment*, or *run-on*. Rewrite fragments and run-ons correctly.

49. Packed the moving van.
50. Last week was exciting we moved to a new house on Monday my sister came home from college too.
51. Our lawn was full of people no one minded cars were everywhere.
52. Then my brother and I.
53. Our friends will help paint and then we'll put down the rug and later everyone will unpack boxes.
54. New furniture for the living room will arrive next week.

Enrichment

Using Sentences

Design a Card

Imagine that you work for a greeting card company. You are asked to design a new birthday card. First, fold a piece of construction or typing paper in half. Then write a birthday message, using the four sentence types—declarative, interrogative, imperative, and exclamatory. Punctuate these sentences correctly. Illustrate your card with original drawings or pictures from magazines.

Silly Sentences

Players—2. **You need**—20 index cards. Each player labels 5 cards *simple subject* and writes a simple subject on the back. Then each makes 5 simple predicate cards. **How to play**—Players exchange both sets of cards. They mix the new subject cards, place them face down, and do the same with the predicate cards. One player takes a card from each pile and writes a sentence, using those words. The other player does the same. Sentences may be silly but must have subjects and predicates. Play ends when all cards are gone. The first person to write 5 correct sentences wins.

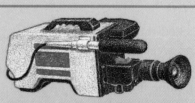

Among Friends

Your local cable television station is doing a special program for young people called *Among Friends*. Write a dialogue, giving a typical conversation between two friends your own age. Use as many interrogative and imperative sentences as possible. Write the simple subject of each sentence.

1 | Kinds of Sentences (p. 14)

● Copy each sentence. Add the correct end punctuation.

Example: Where do crickets live   *Where do crickets live?*

1. Some crickets live outdoors
2. How do crickets chirp
3. They rub their front wings together
4. Did you hear that cricket
5. How cheerful it sounds
6. It is chirping quickly
7. Field crickets chirp quickly in hot weather

▲ Copy each sentence. Add the correct end punctuation, and label each sentence *declarative, interrogative, imperative,* or *exclamatory.*

Example: Look at those horses   *Look at those horses.*   **imperative**

8. They are draft or work horses
9. Watch them pull the heavy plows
10. Why doesn't the farmer use a tractor
11. Tractors and fuels are very expensive
12. Draft horses start up on cold mornings
13. Can't tractors pull more weight than horses
14. How beautiful those big horses are

■ Follow the directions in parentheses to write each new sentence.

Example: Was 1816 a strange year?   (change to exclamatory)
         What a strange year 1816 was!

15. Was it a year without a summer?   (change to declarative)
16. The weather was very unusual.   (change to interrogative)
17. Can you find out about it?   (change to imperative)
18. What a summer frost the South had!   (change to declarative)
19. A blizzard hit New England in June.   (change to exclamatory)
20. A volcano caused the odd weather.   (change to interrogative)

2 | Subjects and Predicates (p. 16)

● Copy the underlined words. Then write either *complete subject* or *complete predicate* beside each group.

Example: Some wonderful toys are made at home.
Some wonderful toys   complete subject

1. Kim and her father made a track for marbles.
2. They looked at different materials.
3. Kim's father had some pieces of pipe.
4. Kim and her brother found some paper tubes.
5. The children taped the tubes and pipes together.
6. Everyone took turns holding up one end.
7. Dozens of marbles rolled from one end to the other.
8. The marbles rolled out into a bucket.
9. All the children dropped the marbles back into the tubes.

▲ Copy each sentence. Draw a line between the complete subject and the complete predicate.

Example: Many people play dominoes.
Many people|play dominoes.

10. The game of dominoes is very old.
11. Early settlers in this country played dominoes.
12. My little brother makes domino snakes.
13. He arranges the dominoes in rows.
14. The dominoes stand on their narrow ends.
15. One good push knocks them all down.
16. I like the real game instead.
17. The pieces in the game are black with white dots.
18. Each piece has two squares.

■ Write a sentence, using each word group.

Example: friend writes   *My friend writes stories and poems.*

19. train climbed
20. people need
21. quarterback threw
22. light shines

23. Mike was
24. soup boiled
25. boy watched
26. girl heard

3 | Simple Subjects and Predicates (p. 18)

● Copy the underlined words. Write either *simple subject* or *simple predicate* beside each word.

Example: My <u>family</u> travels each summer.   *family   simple subject*

1. Sometimes we <u>sleep</u> in a tent.
2. Last summer we <u>stayed</u> in hotels.
3. One <u>hotel</u> was really special.
4. Every <u>room</u> was a railroad car.
5. My sister's <u>bed</u> was huge.
6. All of us <u>were enjoying</u> ourselves.
7. I <u>slept</u> on a train for the first time.

▲ Write the simple subject and simple predicate of each sentence. Underline the simple subject.

Example: Ms. Brown has taught art for three years.
       <u>Ms. Brown</u>   *has taught*

8. She helped my class.
9. The whole class presented a play.
10. The class play needed sound effects.
11. The art teacher filled a can with paper clips.
12. A boy in the band shook the can.
13. The roar of a train filled the room.
14. Everyone in the audience enjoyed our play.

■ Complete the following sentences. Underline each simple subject. Draw two lines under each simple predicate.

Example: Three tired passengers ____.
       Three tired <u>passengers</u> <u>boarded</u> the train.

15. The two women ____.
16. The man with the package ____.
17. The train ____.
18. ____ fell to the floor.
19. ____ stopped suddenly.
20. ____ searched through the luggage.
21. The startled passengers ____.
22. ____ continued on its way.

4 | Imperatives and Interrogatives (p. 20)

● Write the simple subject of each sentence.

Example: Look at this new bike.   *(You)*

1. Do you have one?
2. Is your bike blue also?
3. Hold this wrench, please.
4. Are the handlebars straight?
5. May I ride your bike?
6. Look at me.
7. Shall we go to the park?

▲ Write the simple subject of each sentence. Then label each sentence *imperative* or *interrogative*.

Example: Does this bus go to First Street?   *bus*   ***interrogative***

8. Is the stop near us?
9. Put on your sneakers.
10. Can we walk that far?
11. Take the map along.
12. Wait for the green light.
13. Does the sign say *First Street*?
14. Look for Alan's house.

■ Rewrite each sentence. Make your sentence imperative or interrogative, as shown in parentheses. Then write the simple subject of the new sentence.

Example: I would like you to hold my camera.   (imperative)
          Hold my camera, please.   (You)

15. I wonder why we are stopping here.   (interrogative)
16. Perhaps something is blocking traffic.   (interrogative)
17. Someone will have to look out the window.   (imperative)
18. A car broke down at the traffic light.   (interrogative)
19. Everything has stopped.   (interrogative)
20. You should ask the bus driver for more information. (imperative)
21. The bus will be moving soon.   (interrogative)
22. You should sit down in your seat again.   (imperative)

5 | Compound Subjects (p. 22)

● Give each sentence a compound subject by adding a simple subject. Use each word from the box only once. Write the new sentence.

Example: Linda and ____ went to the park.
Linda and Pat went to the park.

| friends |
| Erin |
| pitcher |
| Pat |
| girls |
| foul lines |
| spectators |
| glove |

1. Erin and her ____ met near the baseball field.
2. Teen-age boys and ____ were warming up.
3. Linda and ____ were on the same team.
4. The catcher's mask and ____ were new.
5. The batter's box and the ____ were marked.
6. The batter and the ____ faced each other.
7. The team and the ____ cheered.

▲ Write the compound subject. Then write the connecting word.

Example: Arts and crafts are often found in museums.
arts   crafts   **connecting word:** *and*

8. Hopis and Navajos make silver jewelry.
9. Pottery and sculptures have been found in Mexico.
10. Ornaments and fine metal objects come from Peru.
11. Plates and utensils are carefully made.
12. Even snowshoes or moccasins can be beautiful.
13. Colors, shapes, and figures decorate the objects.

■ Write compound subjects to complete the sentences below. Use connecting words to join the simple subjects.

Example: ____ make good pets for children.
Gentle dogs or cats make good pets for children.

14. ____ live in a fishbowl.
15. ____ are dangerous and should be kept in cages.
16. ____ are very unusual pets.
17. ____ must be kept in birdcages.
18. ____ sleep all day and play at night.
19. ____ require a great deal of space to run and play.
20. ____ often have huge appetites.

6 | Compound Predicates (p. 24)

● Copy the sentences. Underline the compound predicates.

Example: The Clock Museum shows clocks and sells them.
The Clock Museum <u>shows</u> *clocks and* <u>sells</u> *them.*

1. Leon walked inside and looked around.
2. Many clocks stood on the floor or hung on the walls.
3. They ticked, hummed, or turned.
4. A tall clock told time and rang bells.
5. Water clocks and sand clocks splashed or dripped.
6. Leon liked the sand clock best and studied it carefully.
7. He bought a picture of one and took it home.

▲ Write the compound predicate of each sentence. Then write the connecting word that joins the simple predicates.

Example: Steam engines can move ships or pull trains.
can move   pull   **connecting word:** *or*

8. A fire boils water and creates steam.
9. Steam turns wheels or heats buildings.
10. We visited a museum and saw a steam engine.
11. People can see, hear, and smell the boilers.
12. My mother and father heard a steam whistle and smiled.
13. Mom had worked in a factory and knew that sound.
14. Some people covered their ears or left the room.

■ Complete each sentence, adding a compound predicate. Write the completed sentences.

Example: The ticket taker _____.
The ticket taker greeted us and tore our tickets.

15. A large wheel _____.
16. The whole crowd _____.
17. The strange machine _____.
18. Pat and a friend _____.
19. Several small boats _____.
20. A group of children and a teacher _____.
21. Dozens of different voices _____.
22. All the children _____.

7 | Compound Sentences (p. 26)

● Write *compound* or *not compound* to describe each sentence.

Example: You know the English alphabet, but do you know any others? *compound*

  1. There are many different alphabets today.
  2. Our alphabet has twenty-six letters.
  3. Some of the letters are consonants, and some are vowels.
  4. Some alphabets are read from right to left.
  5. We read from left to right, and we write that way too.
  6. Alphabets are interesting, and I want to learn more about them.

▲ Write *compound* or *simple* to describe each sentence. Remember that a simple sentence may have a compound subject or a compound predicate.

Example: The Chinese language is different from the Japanese language, but the writing is similar. *compound*

  7. Chinese and Japanese are written from right to left.
  8. People speak different forms of Japanese, but most people understand each other.
  9. There are nine forms of Chinese, but they are very different from each other.
  10. The earliest Chinese writing dates from some time in the fourteenth century B.C.
  11. Is it harder to read Chinese and Japanese, or is it harder to read English?

■ Write compound sentences, using the subjects and predicates given below. Use commas correctly, and use *and, or,* and *but* at least once.

Example: subjects: Kate, Ben
predicates: prints, types
Kate prints her stories, but later Ben types them.

  12. subjects: my sister, she
predicates: is, teaches
  13. subjects: Jim, he
predicates: writes, sings
  14. subjects: mother, I
predicates: builds, paint
  15. subjects: Jo, we
predicates: plays, watch

8 | Conjunctions (p. 28)

● Write the conjunction in each sentence.

Example: My sister Jane and I went to summer camp.   *and*

1. We met other campers and made friends quickly.
2. The camp was on a lake, and the setting was beautiful.
3. Mountains and forests surrounded the lake.
4. Few people lived or worked in the area.
5. The lake was ice cold, but we swam every day.
6. We hiked and rode horses on trails through the woods.
7. It was a great summer, but finally it ended.
8. We'll go back and climb our first mountain next year.

▲ Write *and, or,* or *but* to complete each sentence.

Example: My brother Joe ____ I have a sailboat.   *and*

9. One person can sail the boat, ____ two can take turns.
10. Today Joe ____ I sail together.
11. We can sail to an island ____ stay near the coast.
12. I like the island, ____ Joe likes the coast better.
13. We put the sails up ____ sail toward the island.
14. At first, a strong wind blows, ____ then it dies down.
15. The boat ____ the sails must both be in the right position.
16. The wind must fill the sails, ____ we will not move.

■ Write a conjunction to complete each sentence. Then write *compound subject, compound predicate,* or *compound sentence.*

Example: High diving takes courage ____ demands great skill.
         and   **compound predicate**

17. A diver leaps off a surface ____ plunges into deep water.
18. A brave person can jump, ____ a skillful diver must also control every movement of the dive.
19. Judges study the dive ____ give points to the diver.
20. All positions ____ motions must be done the right way.
21. Are the diver's feet ____ hands pointed?
22. Is an arm ____ a leg held at the wrong angle?
23. Does the diver's body twist ____ roll correctly?
24. Is the diver's back arched enough ____ turned too far?

9 | Combining: Compound Sentences (p. 29)

● Each compound sentence needs the conjunction *and, or,* or *but.*
Write the conjunction that makes the most sense.

Example: I need sheet music, ____ I can't afford it.   *but*

 1. I played the first solo, ____ I cannot play the second solo.
 2. Leroy plays the trumpet, ____ he sings well too.
 3. Kate takes lessons for an hour, ____ then she rests.
 4. Do you practice here, ____ do you practice at home?
 5. I like classical music, ____ I'm not in the orchestra.
 6. I went to a rehearsal, ____ I had to leave early.
 7. The musicians warmed up, ____ the conductor raised his baton.

▲ Join each pair of simple sentences to write a compound sentence. Use *and, or,* or *but,* and punctuate correctly.

Example: Cheryl may buy the record. She may borrow mine.
          Cheryl may buy the record, or she may borrow mine.

 8. She wanted to record the concert. It was not allowed.
 9. Cheryl heard the violins first. Then she heard the oboes.
10. The woodwinds were out of tune. The audience didn't notice.
11. The conductor did notice. She waved her hands furiously.
12. The musicians responded quickly. They played in perfect harmony.
13. Was the conductor pleased? Was she just relieved?
14. The symphony ended. The audience applauded loudly.

■ Write compound sentences by completing the beginnings below.

Example: Most people like music, ____.
          Most people like music, but we like different types.

15. Rock concerts are popular, ____.
16. Lucia likes country music, ____.
17. Carol plays jazz flute, ____.
18. Peter sings in a trio, ____.
19. Is rock music the best, ____?
20. Harlan has a compact disc player, ____.
21. Do most people prefer stereos, ____?
22. Good speakers are important, ____.

10 | Combining: Complex Sentences (p. 31)

● Write the conjunction used to form each complex sentence.

Example: Where does your pet stay when you go away?   *when*

1. Don't take your pet on vacation unless you plan ahead.
2. A veterinarian should check your pet before you leave.
3. Allow time for water whenever you make a stop.
4. Select a comfortable carrier if you plan to fly.
5. Some airlines allow pets on board while others do not.
6. Give your pet water after you reach your destination.

▲ Write each pair of sentences as a complex sentence. Use the conjunction in parentheses.

Example: There are many stories about the unicorn. It is an imaginary animal.   (although)
There are many stories about the unicorn although it is an imaginary animal.

7. The stories were told in the Orient. They traveled to Europe.   (before)
8. Explorers described animals. They spotted them.   (as)
9. The descriptions were often wrong. There were no binoculars then.   (since)
10. Some stories told of the unicorn's magical powers. Others described its strength and speed.   (while)
11. A unicorn horn was considered valuable. People thought it could make water clean.   (because)

■ Write each pair of sentences as a complex sentence. Use a subordinating conjunction to combine the sentences.

Example: Penguins couldn't survive. Their bodies were special.
Penguins couldn't survive unless their bodies were special.

12. Penguins can live in the cold. There is a layer of fat under their feathers.
13. Penguins have wings. They can't fly.
14. Their short wings are used as flippers. They swim.
15. Penguin eggs won't hatch. They are kept warm.
16. Males sit on the eggs. Females return from feeding.
17. Then females warm the eggs. The males are away.

11 | Fragments and Run-ons (p. 33)

● Label each word group *fragment* or *run-on*.

Example: fixes old cars.   *fragment*

1. His hammer.
2. That car is old, it is pretty.
3. Tom wants a car my sister just got one.
4. Rides like a new one.
5. One day the morning bus.
6. I once rode the train I liked that.
7. Every person in our family.

▲ Label each group of words as a *fragment, run-on,* or *sentence.*

Example: Is my friend and neighbor.   *fragment*

8. She has roller skates I have skates too.
9. We skate at the park it has a rink the rink is free.
10. We go for an hour after school on Fridays.
11. Sometimes my older brother.
12. He is a good skater we skate together.
13. I have never skated on ice I think I could.
14. Ann ice-skates she even dances on skates.

■ Rewrite each run-on correctly. Rewrite each fragment to make it a complete sentence.

Example: Sal was hungry he wanted a snack he loved baked apples.
   Sal was hungry and wanted a snack. He loved baked apples.

15. Luckily, a large bag of apples.
16. Tony offered his help he turned on the oven.
17. Sal got a pan he put the apples in it he waited.
18. The smell of apples and cinnamon.
19. Would take at least an hour.
20. Checked the apples.
21. The apples were perfect Sal and Tony shared them.
22. Sal ate two baked apples he saved one for another time.
23. Put the dishes in the sink.
24. Sal washed the pan he also washed the dishes.

Literature and Writing

It was hot that afternoon. But I came racing home with my final report card all folded up in my pocket. The weather was dry as dust, and I was glad to be walking across pasture on the soft green meadowland, instead of kicking rocks the long way round which was by the dirt road.

Robert Newton Peck
from *A Day No Pigs Would Die*

Personal Narrative

Getting Ready In this unit, you will be writing about one of your favorite people: you! You have in your own life the raw material for many good stories. You could write about your accomplishments (or your failures), your projects, your ideas, your funny experiences, your frightening ones. What happened that you *want* to write about? What details would you include to make the story complete? Who else was involved? How would you describe them?

ACTIVITIES

Listening   Listen to the story segment on the opposite page. Explain why it would make a good beginning for a narrative. Do you think the report card was good or bad? Why?

Speaking   Look at the picture. What kinds of things might happen here? Share your ideas with your classmates.

Writing   If you were to write a story about yourself that took place in this picture, what would happen? List some ideas in your journal.

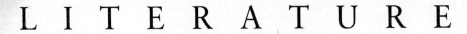

When did Donn know he was lost?

Lost on a Mountain in Maine

Donn Fendler, as told to Joseph B. Egan

Donn Fendler, twelve years old and a Boy Scout from Rye, New York, thought the few steps down from the rocky summit of Mt. Katahdin would take him to his father and brothers.

Here is the beginning of Donn's story.

THE TOP of Katahdin was just ahead. We could see it through a break in the cold, misty clouds that whirled about us. Henry wanted to race for it, but I shook my head. Those last hundred yards were heavy ones and, in spite of the stiff, rocky climb, I was cold and shivery.

Just as we reached the summit, the mist closed in around us and shut off our view of the mountain below. I was disappointed. Who wouldn't be, after such a climb? We waited, shivering in the icy blasts that swept around us, for another break in the clouds. Dimly, just like a ghost, we saw a man standing over to the right, on a spur leading to what is called the Knife Edge.* He saw us, too, and waved to us, then started towards us.

Henry is the son of a guide and he seemed pleased. "Let's wait here until he comes over," he said, "then we can start back together—that's the best thing to do."

But I was cold and shivery. I never was good at standing cold, anyway. Nights, when Ryan and Tom slept with only a sheet over them, Dad always came in with a blanket for me. I thought of that, and of Dad somewhere back on the trail behind us.

"Let's get out of here now," I said. I remember that my teeth were chattering as I said it, but Henry shook his head. He wanted to wait for the man.

I think Henry was just a little bit nervous and who wouldn't be, with all that big cloud-covered mountain below us and clouds rolling like smoke around us? But Henry was wise. I can see that now. He *knew* Katahdin.

I was nervous, too, and maybe that is why I decided to go right back and join Dad and the boys. Maybe I was sorry that I had gone on ahead of them. Maybe *that* had been a foolish thing to do. Such thoughts run through a fellow's head at a time like that. Anyway, they ran through mine and made me more and more anxious to get back to the folks below.

I had on a sweatshirt under my fleece-lined jacket. When I made up my mind to start back, I peeled off the jacket and

---

*The Knife Edge is a curving granite wall with sheer drops of up to 1500 feet. It connects Baxter Peak and Pamola.

55

gave the sweatshirt to Henry. "That'll keep you warm while you're waiting," I said, "But I'm going *back, right now.* I'll tell Dad you and the man are coming down soon."

Henry said I was foolish and tried to stop me, but I knew I was all right. I guess I thought I knew more than he did, for I only shrugged my shoulders and laughed at him. Just then, an extra heavy cloud rolled in around us. I thought of people being lost in clouds and getting off the trail—and maybe that hurried me a little as I pulled up my fleece-lined reefer about my neck and started down. Boy, I can see now what a mistake *that* was! A fellow is just plain dumb who laughs at people who know more than he does.

The clouds were like gray smoke and shut Henry from me before I had gone a dozen yards. The going was very rough, and the trail wound in and around huge rocks. It hadn't seemed so awfully rough on the way up—I mean the last hundred yards, but *then* you climbed slowly—while going down, you could make better time. I hadn't gone far before I noticed that the trail led me up to rocks that I had to climb over like a squirrel. That seemed funny to me, but I went on just the same, because a fellow forgets easily, and I figured going down was different, anyway.

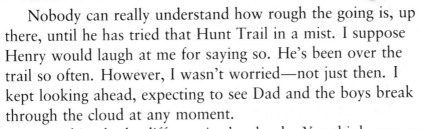

Nobody can really understand how rough the going is, up there, until he has tried that Hunt Trail in a mist. I suppose Henry would laugh at me for saying so. He's been over the trail so often. However, I wasn't worried—not just then. I kept looking ahead, expecting to see Dad and the boys break through the cloud at any moment.

Everything looks different in the clouds. You think you see a man and he turns out to be only a rock. It kind of scares a fellow, especially when you are alone and awfully cold.

When I had gone quite a distance over the rocks—far enough, I thought, to be down on the plateau—I stopped and looked around. I couldn't see anything that looked like a trail.

57

I couldn't find a single spot of white paint.* I thought I *must* be down on the plateau, but could not be sure. There are plenty of huge rocks on the plateau, but the trail winds in and out around them. The going is fairly level and the rocks don't bother as long as you are on the trail, but *I* was in the middle of the worst mess of rocks you can imagine. I began to worry a little. Boy, it's no fun getting off the trail, when the cloud is so thick you can't see a dozen yards ahead!

One thing helped me not to worry too much. I knew that if Dad and the boys were still on the way up they must be nearing the place where I stood. At least they must be within hearing distance. I shouted several times. Not a sound answered me. My voice seemed hollow. I had a feeling it didn't go far through that heavy cloud. I waited and then I shouted again and again. At last, I just stood and listened for a long time. No answering shout—nothing but the noise of the wind among the rocks. Boy, I felt funny when I started on.

I couldn't see far on any side of me and I had a feeling I was right on the edge of a great cliff. The way the clouds swirled scared me. The rocks about me looked more like ghosts than rocks, until I tried to climb over them. Besides, sleet was beginning to fall. It formed slick, thin ice on the sleeves of my reefer, and I had to wipe it off my face. I didn't like that I was wearing a pair of blue dungarees and I could feel the water seeping through and getting cold about my legs.

"Maybe," I thought, "I ought to sit down and wait for Henry and the man. They'd be along now any moment." But when I stood still, the cold, wet cloud seemed to wrap me

---

* In hiking language, a "trail" does not necessarily mean a path. The Hunt Trail, for instance, is marked by daubs of white paint on trees and rocks.

in an icy blanket. I started an Indian war dance to warm up.
"Christmas!" I finally said to myself. "No use in this. Might
as well go on. I'll be sure to find Dad a little farther down!"
But I didn't find him, and the going grew rougher and rougher.

Donn did not know he was about to begin a journey that
would bring him close to death.

Fighting off hallucinations, he crawled and stumbled on
bleeding numbed feet for days along a stream he knew would
lead downhill to civilization. He had no equipment and only a
few berries and water for sustenance. His shoes and clothing
became torn and lost. By night he huddled in empty tree trunks
or mossy shelters. Nine days later he crawled from the forest
half naked and starving.

You can read his story in the book *Donn Fendler Lost on a
Mountain in Maine.*

Think and Discuss

1. When did Donn realize that something was wrong? What
   clues did he have?
2. Some stories are told by a person in the story—like Donn.
   When a story is told by one of the story characters using *I*,
   the story is told from the **first-person point of view**. If someone outside the story were telling about Donn and Henry being lost, using *he* and *they*, the story would be from the
   third-person point of view. How would Donn's story be different if it were told from the third-person point of view?
3. Donn mentioned a number of worries about being lost, such
   as the cold, the edge of the cliff, and the clouds. What do
   you consider his most important concern? Why?

Whatif

By Shel Silverstein

Last night, while I lay thinking here,
Some Whatifs crawled inside my ear
And pranced and partied all night long
And sang their same old Whatif song:
Whatif I'm dumb in school?
Whatif they've closed the swimming pool?
Whatif I get beat up?
Whatif there's poison in my cup?
Whatif I start to cry?
Whatif I get sick and die?
Whatif I flunk that test?
Whatif green hair grows on my chest?
Whatif nobody likes me?
Whatif a bolt of lightning strikes me?
Whatif I don't grow taller?
Whatif my head starts getting smaller?
Whatif the fish won't bite?
Whatif the wind tears up my kite?
Whatif they start a war?
Whatif my parents get divorced?
Whatif the bus is late?
Whatif my teeth don't grow in straight?
Whatif I tear my pants?
Whatif I never learn to dance?
Everything seems swell, and then
The nighttime Whatifs strike again!

"Whatif" from *A Light in the Attic* by Shel Silverstein. Copyright © 1981 by Snake Eye Music, Inc. Reprinted by permission of Harper & Row, Publishers, Inc., and Jonathan Cape Ltd.

Think and Discuss

1. Were any of the nighttime Whatifs real fears? Explain.
2. When the lines in a poem end with words that have the same last sounds, the lines **rhyme**. Which lines rhyme in this poem? Is there any pair that does not quite sound alike?
3. How is the poem humorous? Is it serious in any way?

RESPONDING TO LITERATURE

The Reading and Writing Connection

Personal Response Donn was hiking in the mountains with no supplies. If you were to take a mountain hike, what would you take with you? Explain why you would need each item. Remember, what you take, you have to carry.

Creative Writing Read the poem "Whatif." Use the following beginnings to write your own "Whatif" poem. Remember, make every two lines rhyme.

Whatif I'm   Whatif they've

Whatif I   Whatif there's

Whatif my   Whatif nobody

Creative Activities

Design There are a number of ways to mark trails for others to follow. Trail markers can be stacked rocks, bent twigs, or signs with words, symbols, or numbers. Use words or pictures to design some trail marker signs.

Choral Speaking Form small groups. Discuss the ways that your group can present the poem "Whatif" as a choral reading. Choose the way that you like best and present your choral reading to the class.

Vocabulary

The weather on Mt. Katahdin was very important to the hikers. Recheck the story for all the descriptive weather words. Then write a television weather report about the mountain area for that day.

Looking Ahead

Personal Narrative Later in this unit, you will be writing a story about yourself. Begin making a list of some of your experiences. You will use it later.

VOCABULARY CONNECTION

Borrowed Words

The English language contains words borrowed from almost every language.

> I didn't like that I was wearing a pair of blue **dungarees** and I could feel the water seeping through. . . .
> *from "Lost on a Mountain in Maine" by Donn Fendler*

The word *dungarees* is borrowed from the Hindi word meaning "trousers made of coarse cotton cloth."

Explorers and traders brought back to England words from around the globe. Early settlers in the United States borrowed words from the Native Americans. Later the language of the Spanish settlers mixed with that of the English settlers.

sofa (Arabic)   garage (French)
ranch (Spanish)   piano (Italian)
chipmunk (Algonquian)   elastic (Latin)

We still add new words to English. Sometimes we use the ancient Greek and Latin languages to name inventions, such as *stereo, photography,* and *television.*

Vocabulary Practice

A. For each of these words from "Lost on a Mountain in Maine," write the meaning and the language in which the word originated. Use your dictionary.

1. mistake   **2.** anxious   **3.** guide   **4.** plateau   **5.** squirrel

B. The state of Maine is named after a French province. Most state names are borrowed from Native American, Spanish, French, and Dutch words. Choose five states and look up their origins in an encyclopedia. Share your information.

Prewriting
Personal Narrative

Listening and Speaking: Sequence

A story's **sequence** is the order in which the events occur. A listener or reader is able to follow a story only when the sequence is clear. In "Lost on a Mountain in Maine," this was the sequence of events.

> 1. Donn and Henry reached the top of Katahdin just as a mist shut off their view of the mountain below.
> 2. Anxious to begin the trip down, Donn set off alone.
> 3. He soon noticed that the trail was unfamiliar.
> 4. Later, Donn realized that he was off the trail.
> 5. Cold and now worried, Donn continued down the mountain as the way grew rougher and rougher.

• What words give you clues about the order of events?

When you listen to a story or when you plan one to relate to others, be sure that the sequence is clear. These guidelines will help you.

Guidelines for Sequencing

1. Picture each event as it is described.
2. Think about how each event leads to the next one.
3. Listen for or use order words such as *just then, while, later, when,* and *by the time.*
4. Ask questions if you don't understand the sequence.

Prewriting Practice

A. Listen as your teacher reads another passage about Donn Fendler's experience. List the main events in order.
B. Choose a partner. Take turns telling each other everything you did yesterday. Tell the events in order.

Thinking: Recalling

> The clouds were like gray smoke and shut Henry from me before I had gone a dozen yards. The going was very rough, and the trail wound in and around huge rocks.
>
> *from "Lost on a Mountain in Maine" by Donn Fendler*

Donn's experience on the mountain became real for us because he recalled so many details. Recalling is important when you are writing or telling about an experience.

Guidelines for Recalling

1. **Brainstorm.** Think very quickly and broadly about a topic or an experience. Search for every fact or detail and jot down lists of words or phrases that come to mind. Write as quickly as you can.

2. **Freewrite.** Think of a topic or an experience as you push a pencil without stopping. Write quickly for a certain amount of time. If you can't think of any new details to write, just write the same thing over and over until something new comes to mind.

3. **Do a memory search.** Pretend to be watching a movie of your experience as it runs backward. Run the film over and over as you list details of the event.

Prewriting Practice

Think of a personal experience that you have already told someone about. Answer the questions below. Use the recalling guidelines.

1. What did the scene look like? Do a memory search and take notes on all the visual details.

2. What did people say? What sounds did you hear? Brainstorm about what you heard and list words and phrases that pop into your mind.

3. What were your thoughts and feelings during the experience? Freewrite about them.

Composition Skills
Personal Narrative

Writing a Good Beginning ☑

A good beginning invites the reader to come into the story. It gets the reader's interest right away. It may also leave your reader with the questions *who? what? where?* or *why?* Read the beginning of Donn Fendler's story.

> The top of Katahdin was just ahead. We could see it through a break in the cold, misty clouds that whirled about us. Henry wanted to race for it, but I shook my head. Those last hundred yards were heavy ones and, in spite of the stiff, rocky climb, I was cold and shivery.
>
> *from "Lost on a Mountain in Maine" by Donn Fendler*

- How does the writer catch your attention?
- What questions do you have after reading the opening?

Some stories, like Donn's, start with a description of the setting. Some stories start with dialogue. Other stories will give you a hint about the plot or the characters.

> "Psst!" I whispered as I poked Wendy. "Did you hear that?" I hated to wake her up, but I had a shivery feeling that we were not alone in her attic bedroom. What could be creeping around up here in the darkness?

Prewriting Practice

Select a partner. Together write three good beginnings for each of the following story ideas.

1. You hear a strange sound deep in the forest while you are sitting around a campfire.
2. Odd messages keep showing up on your computer while you are using it to write a composition.

Supplying Details ☑

Have you ever read something so interesting that you could not put it down? Most writers want their readers to feel this way.

The right details can let your reader know how the things you are describing feel, sound, taste, and smell. The weather was very important in the story "Lost on a Mountain in Maine." Donn became lost because of the weather. Donn lets you experience the clouds and the sleet by providing details about them.

Read this paragraph, paying close attention to the details provided by the author.

> I couldn't see far on any side of me and I had a feeling I was right on the edge of a great cliff. The way the clouds swirled scared me. The rocks about me looked more like ghosts than rocks, until I tried to climb over them. Besides, sleet was beginning to fall. It formed slick, thin ice on the sleeves of my reefer, and I had to wipe it off my face. I didn't like that. I was wearing a pair of blue dungarees and I could feel the water seeping through and getting cold about my legs.
>
> *from "Lost on a Mountain in Maine" by Donn Fendler*

• What details show you how Donn felt about the clouds?
• What words help you imagine what the sleet felt like?

You can also make your stories lively and interesting by including the right details. Don't just say how the character feels; let the details show the feelings.

Read the following two paragraphs. Which paragraph does a better job of making the situation and the characters seem real?

> 1. My best friend was moving away. We had been classmates and friends for many years. I would miss her. When it was moving day, I went to her house. I had a farewell present to give her. I thought it would remind her of some of the fun times we had spent together.

2. Talia's moving day had arrived. Unfortunately, so had the movers! As I raced to her house, I thought back on all the years since kindergarten. How would school seem without my best friend? I tightened my fingers around the "good-by and good luck" token—the sand dollar we'd found two summers ago at Sea Gull Cove—and I blinked hard.

- How do the two paragraphs differ?
- Which one is better? Why?
- Which one lets you know the writer's feelings? How?
- Which one gives a clearer picture of what happened? How?

Prewriting Practice

A. Suppose Donn Fendler had been lost in a desert. What details could he have used to show how hot it was?

B. Rewrite the following paragraph as if it were your own. Make up details so that the reader can feel what it was like to be in the situation. Do not try to tell everything, but tell enough to hold a reader's interest.

> This was the day my friend and I were going horseback riding. This would be my first time on horseback. My horse looked so big. He was friskier than the others and probably faster too. I just held on and hoped he would go along the trail slowly without needing too much direction from me.

Writing Dialogue ☑

Conversation in a story is called **dialogue**. When you write dialogue, you quote a person's exact words. Dialogue or conversation can make a story more interesting. You can use dialogue to tell how a character thinks or feels, or to show what a character is like.

I slowed my bike to let the others catch up with me.

"Come on," I yelled impatiently. "We'll never make it to the lake by noon."

"My bike isn't as good as yours," gasped Andy as he pulled up alongside me.

"Yeah," echoed Sol. "What's the big hurry, anyway?"

- How is Sol's question *"What's the big hurry, anyway?"* different from this sentence? *Sol wanted to know why we had to hurry.*
- Does the dialogue show you what the characters are like?
- Is the dialogue realistic?

Notice that you begin a new paragraph each time a new person begins speaking.

Dialogue can also show a person's thoughts. How does Donn's dialogue make this paragraph more interesting?

"Maybe," I thought, "I ought to sit down and wait for Henry and the man. They'd be along now any moment." But when I stood still, the cold, wet cloud seemed to wrap me in an icy blanket. I started an Indian war dance to warm up. "Christmas!" I finally said to myself. "No use in this. Might as well go on. I'll be sure to find Dad a little farther down!" But I didn't find him, and the going grew rougher and rougher.

from "Lost on a Mountain in Maine" by Donn Fendler

- To whom is Donn talking?
- What does the dialogue replace?
- How does the dialogue help you know how Donn feels?

Prewriting Practice

A. Change these sentences to dialogue. Try to make the speaker's feelings show.

Example: Rudy complained that his feet hurt from hiking.
"My feet are killing me from all this hiking," grumbled Rudy.

1. Darren said that his feet were sore too and suggested that he and Rudy rest for a while.
2. Rudy thought that that was a really good idea.
3. Darren wanted to know where they should set up camp.
4. Rudy told Darren about a campsite with a stream nearby.
5. Darren said they could soak their feet in the cool water.

B. Select one of the topics below. Write a conversation that might take place. Make your dialogue sound natural, the way that people actually talk. Then read your conversation aloud to a partner. Change your dialogue if necessary to make it more realistic or more interesting.

1. You, the customer, have just found a fly in your soup and are complaining to the waiter.
2. You need to borrow your brother's backpack.
3. Your sister has said that surely you aren't going to leave the house with your hair looking like that.
4. You have accidentally broken your neighbor's window, and you have to apologize.

The Grammar Connection

Stringy Sentences

Some run-on sentences go on and on without a break. Break up long, stringy sentences into shorter sentences that are easier to read and to understand. Read the following paragraph.

> I joined the Bike Club at school and we go biking every month, we learn about safety and the proper equipment and I always wear a helmet and if we bike in the evening, we wear reflectors so that we can be seen by traffic.

Practice Decide where to break the run-on sentence in the above paragraph. Rewrite the paragraph, using at least four sentences. Remember to use a comma before the conjunction in a compound sentence.

The Writing Process
How to Write a Personal Narrative

Step 1: Prewriting—Choose a Topic

Jeffrey made a list of some interesting events from his life. Then he thought about which one would make the best story topic.

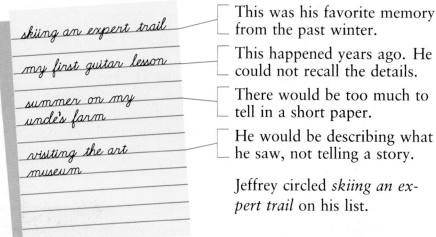

skiing an expert trail — This was his favorite memory from the past winter.

my first guitar lesson — This happened years ago. He could not recall the details.

summer on my uncle's farm — There would be too much to tell in a short paper.

visiting the art museum — He would be describing what he saw, not telling a story.

Jeffrey circled *skiing an expert trail* on his list.

On Your Own

1. **Think and discuss** List some story ideas from your own life. Use the Ideas page for suggestions. Discuss your ideas with a classmate.
2. **Choose** Ask yourself these questions about each topic on your list.
   Can I remember what happened in detail?
   Would it make an interesting story?
   Would *part* of this experience make an even better story?
3. **Explore** How will you capture this event in words? Do one of the activities under "Exploring Your Topic" on the Ideas page.

Ideas for Getting Started

Choosing Your Topic

Topic Ideas

The day I got lost
How I overcame my
    fear
My biggest mistake
How I got my cat
My brother's wedding
My first time on skates
The day we moved
How I saved the game
The surprise of my life
How I met my best
    friend

Time Traveling

Close your eyes and imagine yourself at a certain time and place in
your own past. Ask yourself,
"Where am I?" "How old am I?"
"What am I doing here?" "Who am
I with?" Use your mind like a
movie camera, and picture everything that is going on. Now open
your eyes. Did your memories trig-
ger any story ideas? If not, try taking another time trip.

Exploring Your Topic

A Memory Tree

On a large sheet of paper, draw a
tree with a trunk that states your
topic and three main branches that
ask *Who? Where?* and *What happened?* Add branches that answer
the three questions.
To each of *these*
branches, add two or
three more branches
that give details
about your answers.

Talk About It

Team up with a class-
mate and tell each
other your topics.
Then interview each
other to draw out the
details. Focus on the
five senses: How did
____ look? taste? feel?
smell? sound?

Step 2: Write a First Draft

Jeffrey decided to write his story for his friend David, who lived in another state. They had met on a ski trip.

Jeffrey wrote his first draft. He did not worry about spelling and grammar for now. Later he would correct his mistakes.

Jeffrey's first draft

- Did the opening catch your interest? Why?
- Which words and details help you picture the story clearly?
- Which part might Jeffrey replace with dialogue?

> The first time I took the expert ski slope the man running the ski lift warned me that it was dangerous. I said I could do it, but I was really scared a moment later, I was heading. Straight for a ~~big~~ patch of ice. I lost controle and wished I had never taken that trail. Just then I caught my balance and everything went smoothly for the rest of the trail. I ~~looked~~ felt like a real pro.

On Your Own

1. **Think about purpose and audience** Ask yourself these questions.

    Do I want my story to be funny? sad? exciting?

    Will my reader be about my age? older? younger? Will this make a difference in the words and details I use?

2. **Write** Write your first draft. Picture the story clearly in your mind and write it all down. Do not worry about making mistakes. Write on every other line so that you can correct mistakes and make other changes later.

Step 3: Revise

Jeffrey read his first draft. Somehow it did not sound exciting enough. He wrote a new beginning. Then he read his story to Paul.

Reading and responding

Jeffrey decided that the story would seem more complete if he told about the rest of the trail. He also added details that showed that he was not an expert skier.

Jeffrey's revised story became quite a bit longer than his first draft. This is how the beginning of it looked.

Part of Jeffrey's revised draft

> "Are you sure you're ready for the expert
> ∧The first time I took the expert ski
>   asked
> slope?" ∧the man running the ski lift at the
> bottom of the mountain. "Sure," I said∧
> warned me that it was dangerous. I said I
>   when I got off
> could do it, but I was really scared a∧
> the chair. The trail was really steep.
> moment later, I was heading. Straight for
> shining   skidded out of control over
> a∧big patch of ice. I lost controle and
> the slick surface. "Why did I take this trail!"
> wished I had never taken that trail. Just

Think and Discuss ✓

- Which parts did Jeffrey replace with dialogue? Why?
- Why did he add details about the ski lift?
- What new details did he add about the trail?

On Your Own

Revising Checklist

- ☑ Will the opening sentence catch my reader's interest?
- ☑ Did I use enough details? Have I chosen the best words?
- ☑ Did I use dialogue to show what people said or thought?

1. **Revise** Make changes in your first draft. Cross out any dull parts. Add interesting details. Use the thesaurus below or the one at the back of this book if you need a better word. Look for places to add dialogue.

2. **Have a conference** Read your description to someone in your class or to your teacher.

Ask your listener:	As you listen:
"Were you interested right from the start?" "Which parts really came to life?" "Was any part dull or hard to picture?"	I must listen carefully. Is everything clear? Can I share the writer's feelings? What would I like to know more about?

3. **Revise** How did your listener respond? Did you agree? If you found any new ways to improve your story, make those changes.

Thesaurus

brave valiant, courageous
do accomplish, fulfill, perform
fall plunge, sprawl, tumble
honest direct, frank
important major, significant, meaningful
leave abandon, quit
lively chipper, energetic, spirited
look gaze, contemplate

nervous anxious, edgy
pull haul, tug
quiet still, silent
run dash, race
slide coast, drift, glide
surprised amazed, astonished, astounded
talk chatter, gossip
throw fling, toss, heave
try attempt, test
use apply, utilize

Step 4: Proofread

Jeffrey proofread his story for mistakes in grammar, punctuation, and spelling. He checked his spellings in a dictionary. He used proofreading marks to make his changes.

Here is the way Jeffrey's proofread story looked.

Part of Jeffrey's proofread story

"Are you sure you're ready for the expert
^ ~~The first time I took the expert ski~~
asked
slope?" ^ the man running the ski lift *at the*
bottom of the mountain. ¶ *"Sure," I said*
~~warned me that it was dangerous. I said~~ ^ ~~I~~
when I got off
~~could do it,~~ but I was really scared ~~a~~ ^
the chair. The trail was really steep.
~~moment later~~, I was heading ~~s~~ Straight for
shining *skidded out of control over*
a ^ ~~big~~ patch of ice. I ^ ~~lost controle and~~
the slick surface. "Why did I take this trail!"
~~wished I had never taken that trail~~. Just

Think and Discuss

- Which word did Jeffrey correct for spelling?
- Why did he add a paragraph indent?
- How did he correct a sentence fragment?

On Your Own

1. **Proofreading Practice** Proofread this paragraph for mistakes in grammar and spelling. There is one spelling mistake, one run-on sentence, one sentence fragment, one incorrect possessive, and two other missing punctuation marks.

   As we trudged bearfoot up the steep hill of sand, Jody suddenly ran ahead. There it is!" she yelled. Then I saw it. The Atlantic Ocean glittering below. I grabbed Jodys hand, and we bounded down the dune to the shore and blue-green waves rushed toward us

Proofreading Marks

- ¶ Indent
- ∧ Add
- ∧ (with comma) Add a comma
- ∨ ∨ (with “ ”) Add quotation marks
- ⊙ Add a period
- ℓ Take out
- ≡ Capitalize
- / Make a small letter
- ∽ Reverse order

2. Proofreading Application Now proofread your story. Use the Proofreading Checklist and the Grammar and Spelling Hints below. If you wish, use a colored pencil to make your corrections. Check your spellings in a dictionary.

Proofreading Checklist

Did I

☑ **1.** indent the first line of each paragraph?

☑ **2.** correct any run-on sentences or sentence fragments?

☑ **3.** capitalize and punctuate properly?

☑ **4.** use the correct end marks for each sentence?

☑ **5.** spell all words correctly?

The Grammar/Spelling Connection

Grammar Hints

Remember these rules of punctuation from Unit 1.

- Use a period after a declarative sentence. *(I'm ready.)*
- Use a question mark after an interrogative sentence. *(Who?)*
- In a compound sentence, use a comma before the connecting word. *(I left the trail, but Henry stayed.)*

Spelling Hint

Homophones are words that sound alike but have different spellings and meanings. Because homophones sound alike, their meanings and spellings must be remembered. *(hair–hare; fir–fur; vane–vein)*

Step 5: Publish

Jeffrey found a photograph of himself and David skiing. He made a card and glued the photo to the front of it. He folded his story, put it inside the card, and mailed it to David.

On Your Own

1. **Copy** Write or type your story as neatly as possible.
2. **Add a title** Think of a title to catch your reader's interest. Remember to capitalize the first, last, and all important words.
3. **Check** Read over your story again to make sure you have not left out anything or made any mistakes in copying.
4. **Share** Think of a special way to share your story.

Ideas for Sharing

- Tape your story and pantomime it for your class.
- Draw a picture of the high point of your story.
- Join with others who wrote the same type of story you did—humor, family, adventure, and so on. Think of a song that you could use as a theme song for your stories.

Applying Personal Narrative

Literature and Creative Writing

"Lost on a Mountain in Maine" tells the exciting story of a young boy who becomes lost on Mt. Katahdin. In the midst of swirling clouds and mist, Donn Fendler attempts to make his way down the trail toward his father and brothers. He does not yet realize that he is beginning one of the longest journeys of his life.

Have fun using what you have learned about writing personal stories to complete one or more of these activities.

Remember these things ☑

Write an interesting beginning.

Add details to help the reader experience the story.

Use dialogue to add interest and to make the characters come to life.

1. **Where am I?** Have you ever thought you were lost? Where were you? How did you feel? Write your story.

2. **Watch over Donn.** Pretend that you are a squirrel that followed along watching Donn search his way down the mountain. What kind of story would you tell?

3. **Rain, rain go away.** Have you ever been on a camping trip? Pretend you have taken your first trip to the mountains. Everything is going well. You get unpacked. Your gear is all set. Your tent is up. Then, a terrible thunderstorm rolls in. Write your story.

Writing Across the Curriculum
Science

We often take the splendors and delights of the world around for granted. Writing about the wonders of the environment helps us focus our attention on them and increase our appreciation.

1. **Choose your solution.** Community, state, and national leaders make decisions that affect the quality of our environment. You too can affect the quality of your environment. Write a story about what you have done to improve your environment. The environment could be as large as a park you helped clean up or as small as your back yard.

Writing Steps
1. Choose a topic
2. Write a first draft
3. Revise
4. Proofread
5. Publish

2. **Think small.** Think of one of your favorite small electronic items that you use frequently, such as a computer, a calculator, an electronic gadget, or even a household appliance. Write a humorous story about the time you first learned to use it or a time you may have used it incorrectly.

Word Bank
miniature
portable
computerized
digital
functions

3. **Choose a favorite.** Clean water is one of our most precious resources. Write a story about a time you spent out of doors by a lake, a stream, an ocean, or some other body of water.

Extending Literature
Writing a Book Report

After Lisa read "Lost on a Mountain in Maine," she decided to read another story about survival. Lisa chose *Two on an Island* by Bianca Bradbury for her book report.

Two on an Island
Bianca Bradbury

INTRODUCTION

If you were stranded on an island, would you choose your little brother or sister for company? That is what happens to Jeff in the novel <u>Two on an Island</u>.

BODY

Jeff, his nine-year-old sister, Trudy, and their dog, Sarge, arrive at their grandmother's house in Bridgeton Harbor three days before she expects them. Since she isn't home, they take the rowboat to Middle Hump Island for a swim. In their hurry to get in the water, they forget to pull the boat up and it drifts away. Suddenly they are stranded on a little island. All they have with them are some oatmeal cookies, bananas, and milk. There isn't even any water. They realize that Gram won't expect them until Friday. No one will know they are lost.

CONCLUSION

If you want to find out how long Jeff and Trudy are marooned, read this book. The story may be fiction, but this brother and sister behave like real brothers and sisters you know.

Think and Discuss
- What did you learn about the characters?
- What did you learn about the setting?
- What do you know about the plot? What do you want to find out?

Share Your Book

Write a Book Report

1. **Write the title and the author.**
2. **Write an introduction.** Your introduction should include
   - whether the book is fiction or nonfiction
   - something that will catch your reader's interest
3. **Write the body of the report.** You should include
   - something about the plot, the characters, and the setting
   - important information. Which event will show your readers the problems the book characters face without giving away the story?
4. **Write a conclusion.** Your conclusion should
   - tell your readers why you liked the book or why they should or should not read it
   - give a hint about the ending

Other Activities

- Make a map that shows where the action in your book takes place. If it is a true story, use an atlas as a guide. Add details from the story. If it is fiction, reread the author's descriptions of places in the book. Then draw a careful map.
- Pretend you are in the situation your book characters faced. How would you react? What might you do differently?

The Book Nook

The Summer of the Swans *by Betsy Byars* Sarah leaves her own problems behind when her mentally retarded little brother becomes lost.	**Snowshoe Trek to Otter River** *by David Budbill* Even though he is going on a hike for just one day, Daniel packs survival gear.

Language and Usage

I never saw a moor—
I never saw the sea—
Yet know I how the heather looks
And what a wave must be. . . .

Emily Dickinson

Nouns

Getting Ready Remember when you first started school? Your teacher probably labeled things in the room with their names. There was a neatly printed name card for each child in the class too. Many of these names were the first words you learned to read. Everything you can name is a noun! Nouns are extremely important words. In this unit, you will learn more about different kinds of nouns.

ACTIVITIES

Listening
Listen as the verse on page 82 is read. What four things does the poet name that she has never seen? How can she know what each one is?

Speaking
Look at the picture. How many of the things the poet names are shown in this picture? What are other nouns that name these things? What nouns name other things in the picture?

Writing
Suppose you are writing a poem like the one on the opposite page. In your journal, list at least four familiar things that you know but have never seen.

83

1 | Recognizing Nouns

A **noun** is a word that names a person, a place, a thing, or an idea. When a noun names an idea, it names something that cannot be touched, such as *time, friendship, anger,* or *summer.*

person · idea · thing · place

Gina read about the history of farming tools in America.

A noun can be made up of more than one word.

PERSON: baby sitter, Jan Smith, Dr. Jones, President Adams
PLACE: dining room, Hill School, Pacific Ocean, New Mexico
THING: fire engine, credit card, drive-in, frying pan

Guided Practice

A. Does each noun name a person, a place, a thing, or an idea?

Example: freedom *idea*

1. America
2. excitement
3. fire station
4. microscope
5. scientist
6. Thomas Edison
7. fun
8. Indian Ocean
9. radio

B. Which words are nouns in each sentence?

Example: Inventors have special talents. *Inventors   talents*

10. A clever invention can save time for a person.
11. Our society has been changed by such creativity.
12. Many years ago, people hunted for food.
13. Then a hunter invented a bow and an arrow.
14. Farmers began growing plants to eat.
15. Families moved to villages and traded goods.
16. Now a store sells a meal in a can or a box.
17. Inventors are always creating new machines or engines.
18. Eli Whitney helped farmers in America.
19. His machine removed seeds from cotton.
20. The curiosity of the inventor has improved life.

▶ A noun names a person, a place, a thing, or an idea.

Independent Practice

A. Write each noun in these sentences.

Example: Rubber trees grow in South America.
trees   South America

21. Drops ooze from the bark like tears.
22. Indians once made waterproof shoes from the juice.
23. A chemist in England made an eraser from the liquid.
24. What a convenience that invention was!
25. Scientists began creating products from their dreams.
26. Factories in Europe made hoses and raincoats.
27. The first goods made of rubber weren't very strong.
28. An inventor in America solved this important problem.
29. Charles Goodyear discovered a way to make rubber better.
30. Eventually different countries grew this unusual tree.
31. The invention of the automobile created a new need.
32. John Dunlop developed a tire filled with air.
33. The popularity of rubber grows more every day.
34. Doctors use gloves and tape made of this material.
35. Swimmers wear stretchy suits and caps.
36. Children have fun with their flexible toys.
37. Rubber was certainly a great discovery.

B. **(38–52)** List the nouns in this paragraph.

Example: Kites have been used for centuries. *kites   centuries*

Benjamin Franklin flew a kite in a thunderstorm. Franklin found that lightning and electricity are the same thing. Kites can be used in many other ways. Scientists use kites to record temperature, humidity, and the speed of the wind.

Writing Application: Personal Narrative

Write a paragraph about a place away from home that you visit often. Describe what you do there. Circle every noun.

For Extra Practice, see p. 106.

2 | Common and Proper Nouns

Some nouns name a particular person, place, thing, or idea. These are called **proper nouns**. A proper noun begins with a capital letter. Nouns that do not name a particular person, place, thing, or idea are called **common nouns**.

COMMON: city   girl   ocean   state   month
PROPER: Boston   Amy   Indian Ocean   New York   July

If a proper noun is made up of more than one word, capitalize only the important words.

New Jersey   Gulf of Mexico   Statue of Liberty

Guided Practice

A. What are the nouns in these sentences? Is each noun a common noun or a proper noun?

Example: Edward White was the first American to walk in space.
*Edward White—**proper**   American—**proper**
space—**common***

1. The astronaut practiced daily in an airtight room for several hours.
2. Astronaut White walked in space above California.
3. Could White see the Gulf of Santa Catalina?
4. The astronaut did not want to return to the spacecraft immediately.
5. His pilot convinced White to come back.
6. The spacecraft orbited Earth before the flight ended.
7. A crew and a ship waited in the Atlantic Ocean.
8. Doctors gave the astronauts medical tests.
9. Their journey in space was a success.

B. How would you capitalize these proper nouns?

Example: edward white   *Edward White*

10. cape of good hope
11. atlantic ocean
12. baltimore
13. karen gerber
14. new hampshire
15. fourth of july

▶ A **common noun** names any person, place, thing, or idea.
▶ A **proper noun** names a particular person, place, thing, or idea.
▶ A proper noun always begins with a capital letter.

Independent Practice

A. Write each common noun in the sentence below.

    Example: Karl and Francie decided to start a newspaper.
              newspaper

16. Their friend Ellen wanted to be a reporter.
17. Francie wrote a story about a boy and his boat.
18. Karl took a picture of a new baby at Memorial Hospital.
19. Businesses bought advertisements in the newspaper.
20. Copies were sold at the school, the drugstore, and the market.
21. The manager of the Eliot Hotel ordered one hundred papers.
22. The last page was full of jokes, riddles, and cartoons.
23. Uncle Ted liked the editorial about honesty and truth.
24. Francie and Karl were filled with pride.

B. Each pair of nouns has a common noun and a proper noun. Capitalize the proper nouns.

    Example: egypt – country *Egypt*

25. thursday – day
26. ohio river – river
27. island – isle of wight
28. president – john f. kennedy
29. mars – planet
30. columbus day – holiday
31. state – wyoming
32. white house – building

Writing Application: A Description

Write a paragraph about life on your street. Circle the proper nouns. Underline the common nouns.

For Extra Practice, see p. 107.

3 | Singular and Plural Nouns

A noun that names one person, place, thing, or idea is a **singular noun**. A noun that names more than one person, place, thing, or idea is a **plural noun**. In most cases, you can change a singular noun to plural by adding *s*.

SINGULAR: truck   plant   letter   noise
PLURAL: trucks   plants   letters   noises

Many nouns, however, have irregular plural forms. The chart below shows you the different patterns for forming the plurals of these nouns.

Forming Plurals

Singular ending	Plural form	Example
s *ss* *ch* *sh* *x* *z*	add *es*	Thomas—Thomas**es** boss—boss**es** porch—porch**es** bush—bush**es** fox—fox**es** waltz—waltz**es**
o	add *es* (some add only *s*)	potato—potato**es** veto—veto**es** echo—echo**es** (Eskimo—Eskimo**s**) (solo—solo**s**)
consonant + *y*	change *y* to *i* and add *es*	baby—bab**ies** party—part**ies** country—countr**ies**
vowel + *y*	add *s*	day—day**s** turkey—turkey**s**
f or *fe*	change *f* to *v* and add *s* or *es*	life—li**ves** scarf—scar**ves** wolf—wol**ves**

Some nouns have the same spelling in the singular and the plural.

moose—moose   salmon—salmon   deer—deer

Other nouns are spelled differently in the plural.

child—children   woman—women   tooth—teeth
man—men   goose—geese   mouse—mice

Use your dictionary to check for correct plurals.

Guided Practice

A. For each pair of words in parentheses, choose the correct plural form.

Example: Put the (boxs, boxes) on those two (shelfs, shelves).
boxes   shelves

1. The new (puppies, puppys) have sharp (tooths, teeth).
2. The gardener weeded the berry (patchs, patches) and planted (tomatos, tomatoes).
3. Loggers use (axes, axs) to cut (treeses, trees).
4. The (moose, mooses) heard (echos, echoes) from the distant canyon.
5. There are four (Besss, Besses) in the (classs, classes).

B. What is the plural form of each noun?

Example: scarf   *scarves*

6. apple
7. policy
8. hero
9. watch
10. wife

11. dress
12. lake
13. donkey
14. Ross
15. waltz

Summing up
▶ Add *s* or *es* to most singular nouns to form the plural. Use the spelling of the singular noun to decide how to form the plural.
▶ Some nouns have the same singular and plural forms.
▶ Some nouns are spelled differently in the plural.

Independent Practice

A. For each of the following nouns, write *singular*, *plural*, or *singular and plural*.

Example: goose   *singular*

16. piano	**18.** women	**20.** Lewises	**22.** lilies
17. moose	**19.** dresses	**21.** deer	**23.** alleys

B. Write the plural form of each noun. Use your dictionary if you need it.

Example: knife   *knives*

24. brush	**28.** monkey	**32.** mouse	**36.** calf
25. opera	**29.** soprano	**33.** nursery	**37.** stereo
26. couch	**30.** cross	**34.** envelope	**38.** mix
27. county	**31.** style	**35.** studio	**39.** trolley

C. Write the sentences, using the plural form of each noun in parentheses.

Example: Today, ____ have ____ of ____.   (plastic, thousand, use)
Today, plastics have thousands of uses.

40. Most ____ and ____ use plastic ____.   (family, business, product)

41. ____, ____, and even ____ can be made of plastic.   (Box, shelf, scarf)

42. ____ make plastic by combining carbon with other ____. (Chemist, element)

43. Now most ____ have ____ that make plastic ____.   (country, factory, item)

44. Almost all _toys_ for _children_ contain some plastic _parts_.   (toy, child, part)

45. Many clothes for ____ and ____ are made with plastic. (man, woman)

Writing Application: Persuasion

Imagine that you are an inventor. You have just created a new invention. Write a paragraph to persuade people to buy it. Use at least five plural nouns, and underline them.

For Extra Practice, see p. 108.

4 | Possessive Nouns

You can change the form of a noun to show ownership, or possession. A **possessive noun** names *who* or *what* owns something.

Pat's coat = the coat owned by Pat
the babies' blocks = the blocks belonging to the babies

The chart below shows how to change nouns into their possessive forms.

Rules for Forming Possessive Nouns	
1. Singular nouns: Add 's.	a woman's gloves Mr. Ross's hat the teacher's question
2. Plural nouns that end in *s*: Add only an apostrophe (').	the students' papers the Williamses' house the girls' pens
3. Plural nouns that do not end in *s*: Add 's.	the men's umbrellas the geese's nest the women's uniforms

Guided Practice

A. What is the possessive form of each noun? Is the noun singular or plural?

Example: doctor
    doctor's singular

1. Janice
2. patients
3. horses
4. children
5. the Cronins
6. visitor

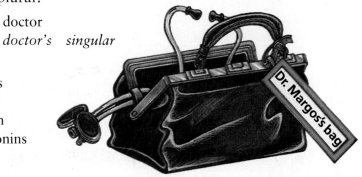

Dr. Margos's bag

B. How would you complete each sentence? Use the possessive form of the noun in parentheses. Does the possessive end in *'s* or *s'*?

Example: During her childhood, ___ dream was to become a doctor. (Elizabeth Blackwell)
Elizabeth Blackwell's   ends in 's

7. ___ applications to medical schools were not welcome. (Women)
8. After many months, one of ___ hospitals accepted her. (New York)
9. Her hard work and persistence gained her ___ respect. (professors)
10. Elizabeth Blackwell was this ___ first woman doctor. (country)

C. What is the possessive form of each noun in parentheses? Does the possessive end in *'s* or *s'*?

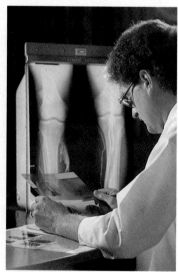

Example: ___ work   (Dr. Douglas)
Dr. Douglas's   ends in 's

11. ___ toys   (children)
12. the ___ apartment   (Perkinses)
13. the ___ webbed feet   (goose)
14. a ___ meeting   (parents)
15. ___ office   (Dr. Lewis)
16. the ___ photocopies   (library)
17. the ___ badges   (officers)
18. the ___ theme   (story)
19. ___ coat   (Mrs. Jones)
20. ___ decision   (Linn)

Summing up

▶ To form the possessive of most singular nouns, add *'s*.
▶ To form the possessive of a plural noun that ends in *s*, add only an apostrophe (*'*).
▶ To form the possessive of a plural noun that does not end in *s*, add *'s*.

Independent Practice

A. Rewrite each group of words, using a possessive noun.

Example: club of bowlers   *bowlers' club*

21. dish belonging to the cat
22. croaking of frogs
23. tail of the skunk
24. wings of the birds
25. meeting of fruit growers
26. tools of the plumber
27. pencil belonging to Mr. Lane
28. desk of Nicholas
29. the health of the Harrises
30. speeches of the president

B. Write the possessive form of each noun in parentheses.

Example: We ate Sunday dinner at my cousin _____ house.
(Chris) *Chris's*

31. Alan liked _____ chili.   (Gus)
32. The young children dressed in both their _____ old clothes. (grandparents)
33. Grandmother set up a special _____ table.   (children)
34. Everyone listened with great interest to Aunt _____ stories about her trip.   (Bess)
35. We all ate _____ strawberries for dessert.   (Helen)
36. After dinner Chris filled the _____ dish with leftover scraps. (dog)
37. Three of the _____ friends washed and dried the dishes. (boys)
38. We watched our three _____ slides of their fishing trip. (cousins)
39. Next week we will eat a holiday dinner at the _____ house. (Davises)
40. _____ specialty is Swedish meatballs.   (Mrs. Davis)

Writing Application: Writing About Yourself

Write a paragraph about a time you visited a friend's home.
Use at least five possessive nouns, and underline them.

For Extra Practice, see p. 109.

5 | Plural and Possessive Nouns

You have learned how to form plural nouns and possessive nouns. Do not confuse possessive nouns with ordinary plural nouns. Most plural nouns end in *s (two pilots)*. If the noun is possessive, you will find an apostrophe (') before or after the *s (one pilot's uniform, four pilots' opinions)*.

Forming Plural and Possessive Nouns		
Kind of noun	**Ending**	**Example**
Plural (more than one)	s or es	six boys the Lewises
Singular possessive (belongs to one)	's	a boy's shoe Betty Lewis's drum
Plural possessive (belongs to more than one)	' or 's	the boys' team the Lewises' drums the men's team

Guided Practice Is the underlined word plural, singular possessive, or plural possessive?

Example: <u>wolves'</u> den
plural possessive

1. six <u>wolves</u>
2. <u>wolf's</u> tail
3. three <u>boys</u>
4. two <u>boys'</u> shoes
5. one <u>boy's</u> socks
6. <u>Gus's</u> pencil
7. three <u>Guses</u>
8. the <u>Joneses'</u> dog
9. the <u>girl's</u> shirts
10. the <u>girls'</u> sneakers

This way to the wolves' den

> ▶ Do not confuse possessive nouns with plural nouns.
> ▶ Most plural nouns end in *s*.
> ▶ Possessive nouns have an apostrophe before or after the *s*.

Independent Practice

A. Which noun in parentheses is correct in each sentence?

> **Example:** In 1903 two _____ dreams became real.   (brothers, brothers')   *brothers'*

11. The Wright _____ invented the first plane.   (brothers, brother's)

12. Orville _____ flight lasted twelve seconds.   (Wright's, Wrights')

13. His brother _____ flight was longer.   (Wilburs, Wilbur's)

14. During the next few years, _____ improved.   (airplanes', airplanes)

15. The _____ invention was successful.   (brother's, brothers')

B. Write the correct form of the noun in parentheses.

> **Example:** Twenty hot-air _____ will race.   (balloon)   *balloons*

16. Two _____ are over there.   (owner)

17. Other _____ supported this balloon race.   (airport)

18. Give lunch to the _____ before they leave.   (driver)

19. One _____ son is in the race.   (driver)

20. Last year all the _____ reported the race.   (newspaper)

21. The festivities are a _____ delight.   (photographer)

22. Will all the _____ please climb aboard?   (passenger)

23. Many _____ cameras click.   (photographer)

24. The _____ friends wave goodbye to them.   (passenger)

25. Soon they do not hear their _____ voices.   (friend)

26. The balloons soar over one _____ house.   (passenger)

Writing Application: A Description

Imagine that you and some friends are taking a ride in a hot-air balloon. Describe what you see and how you feel. Use plural and possessive nouns correctly in your description.

For Extra Practice, see p. 110.   **Plural and Possessive Nouns**

6 | Combining Sentences: Appositives

An **appositive** is a word or group of words that immediately follows a noun. Appositives identify the nouns they follow.

Robin, our class president , planned the party.

Appositives can help you improve your writing. You can use an appositive to combine two choppy sentences into one.

Our summer party was a barbecue. It was great fun.

Our summer party, a barbecue , was great fun.

Notice that an appositive is usually set off from the rest of the sentence by commas.

Mr. McLean, Robin's father, furnished the chicken.
The party had a theme, careers.

Guided Practice

A. Use each noun and appositive in a sentence. Where would you place the commas?

Example: Paulette—the fastest runner
Paulette, the fastest runner, lost the race.

1. My barber—a talkative person
2. Last Thursday—my birthday
3. Cal's terrier—Ruffles
4. The volleyball game—an exciting event

B. Combine each pair of sentences into a single sentence with an appositive.

Example: Annie is my partner. She is building a new barn.
Annie, my partner, is building a new barn.

5. Mrs. Scott is Ken's mother. She is also my teacher.
6. My picture is in the local paper. The paper is the *Tribune*.
7. Harry is a disc jockey. Harry played my favorite record.
8. We're having tomato soup. It is my favorite.

▸ An **appositive** is a word or group of words that immediately follows a noun and identifies or explains it.
▸ An appositive is usually set off from the rest of the sentence by commas.

Independent Practice

A. Write each sentence. Use a word or group of words from the Word Box as an appositive to complete each sentence.

orange juice	Mrs. Adams	Will's Market
this gray one	a music teacher	Monday

Example: Our bus driver, ——, won a safety award.
Our bus driver, Mrs. Adams, won a safety award.

9. A cat, ——, was on our porch.
10. I take lessons from Mr. Cord, ——.
11. On my lucky day, ——, I won a radio.
12. Lyn brought along her favorite juice, ——.
13. Another store, ——, opened today.

B. Combine each pair of sentences into a single sentence with an appositive. Use commas to set off the appositives.

Example: Primo is my Italian pen pal. Primo sings in the opera.
Primo, my Italian pen pal, sings in the opera.

14. Primo's father is a singer. Primo's father drives a taxi.
15. An opera is a play with special music. An opera is being performed this week.
16. Arias are my favorite part of an opera. Arias are solos.
17. Primo's brother is a teen-ager. Primo's brother wants to sing in the opera.
18. I have a record of Caruso. Caruso was an opera star.

Writing Application: A Description

Write a paragraph about your favorite kind of music. Describe the music, tell who performs it, and mention specific songs or pieces. Use at least two appositives.

For Extra Practice, see p. 111.   **Combining Sentences: Appositives   97**

Grammar-Writing Connection

Combining Sentences with Possessive Nouns

You have already learned that possessive nouns show ownership or possession. A possessive noun can replace a phrase.

the names <u>of the characters</u>   the characters' names

Possessive nouns can also take the place of whole sentences. This means that you can combine sentences by using possessive nouns.

Louisa May Alcott wrote a book called *Little Women*. The book was very popular.

→ Louisa May Alcott's book called *Little Women* was very popular.

Revising Sentences

Rewrite the sentences, using possessive nouns to combine the sentences in each item.

1. Louisa May Alcott spent years in Concord, Massachusetts. The years were happy.
2. Louisa had a father. The father was not very clever in managing business matters.
3. The Alcotts had generous friends. The friends helped out during hard times.
4. The Alcotts had neighbors in Concord. The neighbors included many famous writers and thinkers.
5. Louisa wrote letters about the Civil War. The letters were made into a book.
6. Louisa had three sisters. The sisters were characters in some of her books.
7. May Alcott drew pictures. The pictures were used to illustrate *Little Women*.
8. Louisa had great success as a writer. The success ended the money problems of her family.

Creative Writing

If memories have no size or shape, is it possible to paint them? Marc Chagall thought so. This colorful patchwork represents Chagall's childhood in a Russian farming village. Among the images in this scene is a self-portrait of Chagall. He painted himself as a grown man, holding a spray of flowers and gazing into the friendly face of a barnyard cow.

- Why do you think Chagall painted this scene as a jumble of images?
- How does Chagall draw your attention to the two large faces?

I and the Village (1911)
Marc Chagall
Museum of Modern Art, Guggenheim Fund

Activities

1. **Write the story.** What is the meaning of this painting? What do these images represent? By painting such a mysterious scene, Chagall has invited us to answer these questions for ourselves. Write the story you think this picture tells.
2. **Describe a memory painting.** Suppose you decided to make a painting of your most important memories. What memories would you include in your painting? What images would you use to represent your memories? Write a description of your painting.

Check-up: Unit 3

Recognizing Nouns *(p. 84)* Write the nouns in the sentences below.

1. This drive-in belongs to Sid Newman and his family.
2. Sid works behind the counter in the summer and on holidays.
3. At night his brothers and sisters sweep the floor and clean tables.
4. His mother and father greet the guests and handle the money.
5. Dr. Jones often eats tuna fish or cottage cheese for lunch.
6. Many friendships have sprung up over meals in the restaurant.
7. Soon Sid will open a diner near Spring Lake in New Jersey.

Common and Proper Nouns *(p. 86)* Write each noun. Underline the common nouns once and the proper nouns twice.

8. Linda Chu and her family live in Fort Wayne, Indiana.
9. On weekends Linda and her mother catch fish in Lake Michigan.
10. Mrs. Chu ties the hook to the line.
11. Many people catch trout, catfish, and bass in the lake.
12. In July and August, Jim Dobbs sells tackle from his van.
13. Jim is known throughout the area for his honesty and his knowledge about fish and their habits.

Singular and Plural Nouns *(p. 88)* Write the plural forms of the nouns in parentheses.

14. Our city ___ have many ___. (park, bench)
15. Sometimes ___ hide in the ___. (fox, bush)
16. You can hear ___ of ___ from the bandstand. (echo, waltz)
17. Sometimes we have ___ on our ___. (party, porch)
18. Are ___ good places to grow ___? (city, potato)
19. The ___ honked on the ___ of the lake. (goose, shore)
20. The ___ hung next to the small green ___. (berry, leaf)

Possessive Nouns *(p. 91)* Write the possessive form of each noun in parentheses.

21. A ___ career can sometimes change. (person)
22. Good salespeople know all their ___ names. (customers)
23. An aircraft ___ job is very detailed. (mechanic)
24. Several ___ groups have held a number of different career work-shops. (women)
25. All of the ___ children became farmers. (Curtises)
26. The ___ shelves were built to last. (carpenter)

Plural and Possessive Nouns (p. 94)

Write the correct plural or posses-sive form of each noun in paren-theses.

27. One of ___ hobbies is folk dancing. (Alex)
28. He knows dances from many ___. (country)
29. Each ___ dances are different. (country)
30. Alex went to a folk dance at a ___ house. (friend)
31. Many of his ___ enjoy folk danc-ing. (friend)
32. Some of his ___ parents know dances from other lands. (friends)
33. ___ Polish grandmother remembers dances from her childhood. (Phyllis)
34. Her ___ favorite dance is a Polish Polka. (grandmother)
35. The ___ favorite dance is the Salty Dog Rag. (grandchildren)
36. ___ played ragtime and danced rags in the 1920s. (American)
37. ___ favorite rags included the Twelfth Street Rag. (Americans)
38. Folk dance ___ are held all over the world. (festival)
39. This ___ New England Folk Festi-val will attract thousands. (year)
40. For many ___, the festival has fea-tured music, dance, crafts, and other folk arts. (year)
41. My ___ best moments are when he tastes foods from his native land. (grandfather)

Combining Sentences: Appositives

(p. 96) Rewrite each pair of sen-tences as a single sentence contain-ing an appositive. Punctuate each sentence correctly.

42. The Simpsons are our neighbors. They walk their dog each morning.
43. Pepper barks every morning at nine. Their dog is Pepper.
44. Pepper is a small dog. He has a very loud bark.
45. Teresa is my oldest sister. Some-times she walks with Pepper.
46. Pepper's favorite toy is worn and faded. It is an old baby blanket.
47. Pepper's bed is next to the sofa. His bed is a little blanket.
48. Pepper is a very friendly dog. He always jumps on the sofa to play.
49. Mrs. Simpson tries to keep Pepper off her chair. The chair was a gift from her mother.
50. Pepper's favorite place is a mile away. That place is a lake.
51. Pepper's friend runs around the lake with us. His friend is a poodle.
52. The poodle lives down the street. The poodle is Timmy.
53. Both Pepper and Timmy hate the same thing. They hate baths.
54. One object makes them both disap-pear. That object is a plastic tub.
55. They think their hiding place will save them. The place is a tiny cave.
56. Their favorite treat usually brings them out. The treat is dog biscuits.

Cumulative Review

Unit 1: The Sentence

Kinds of Sentences *(p. 14)* Write the sentences with correct end punctuation. Write *declarative, interrogative, imperative,* or *exclamatory.*

1. Where did I put my glasses
2. I took them off to swim
3. How cold that water is
4. Swim with me, please
5. Can you do a butterfly kick

Subjects and Predicates *(pp. 16, 18)* Copy each sentence. Draw a line between the complete subject and the complete predicate. Underline the simple subject once and the simple predicate twice.

6. The roses blossomed first.
7. Susan watered them every day.
8. Her whole family loves flowers.
9. Susan's flowers grow every spring.
10. She will study plants in school.

Subjects in Imperative and Interrogative Sentences *(p. 20)* Write the simple subject of each sentence. Then write *imperative* or *interrogative* to label the sentence.

11. Hold on to the railing.
12. Where does this bridge go?
13. Shall we walk across it?
14. Turn left here.
15. Does John know the way?

Compound Subjects and Predicates *(pp. 22, 24)* Write the compound subjects and predicates in each sentence. Write the connecting word.

16. Terry and Fran went to the park.
17. They walked their bikes and talked.
18. Terry saw Kim and ran to her.
19. Sue and Joe have ridden horses.
20. John and Lee dismounted and fed carrots to their ponies.

Compound Sentences, Conjunctions *(pp. 26, 28)* Combine the simple sentences into a compound sentence. Use a comma and *and, or,* or *but.*

21. My sister lives at college. She comes home every other weekend.
22. She needed shelves. Cal built them.
23. Should I paint them white? Does this stain look better?
24. Cal will put biographies on the top shelf. Sue will put mysteries here.
25. Does Sue read novels? Does she prefer nonfiction?

Fragments and Run-ons *(p. 33)* Write a sentence from each fragment. Rewrite each run-on sentence.

26. Three brushes and a can of paint.
27. May I help may I hold the ladder?
28. Early tomorrow afternoon.
29. Mom will paint the door I'll paint this wall Dad will do that one.
30. By this time next week.

Unit 3: Nouns

Common and Proper Nouns
(pp. 84, 86) Write each noun. Label it *common* or *proper*.

31. Norman Rockwell was an artist.
32. He lived in Massachusetts.
33. He painted scenes of life in America.
34. His paintings appeared on the cover of the *Saturday Evening Post*.
35. Rockwell studied at the Art Students League.

Singular and Plural Nouns (p. 88)
Write the plural form of each noun.

36. crutch
37. piano
38. worry
39. wax
40. alley

41. glass
42. rose
43. buzz
44. potato
45. child

Possessive Nouns (p. 91) Write the possessive form of each noun in parentheses.

46. ___ careers are now open to women. (Men)
47. A ___ job is very dangerous. (firefighter)
48. Tugboat ___ training takes seven years. (pilots)
49. ___ programs take one year. (Nurses)
50. ___ dream is to be an astronaut. (Dolores)
51. Customers appreciate ___ good service. (waitresses)

Plural and Possessive Nouns (p. 94)
Write the correct form of the noun in parentheses.

52. Charles ___ solo flight across the Atlantic Ocean took place in May 1927. (Lindbergh)
53. Everyone waited for ___ of his plane. (report)
54. His ___ name was the *Spirit of St. Louis*. (plane)
55. His flight captured ___ imaginations all over the world. (people)
56. ___ coast was lit with bonfires to guide his way. (France)
57. The ___ of many cars lined the runway in Paris. (headlight)
58. ___ waited at the airport for his arrival. (Thousand)

Appositives (p. 96) Combine each pair of sentences into a single sentence with an appositive. Use commas to set off the appositives.

59. Karen runs her own business. Karen is a house painter.
60. Karen's partner helps. Karen's partner is her brother.
61. People like her business. Her business is called Star Painters.
62. The painters came last week. The painters were Karen and Rudy.
63. They painted our house red. Red is a very popular color.
64. Another building was painted red. The other building was the barn.
65. Our house is in the country. Our house is an old farmhouse.

Enrichment

Using Nouns

▦ Proper Places

Players—2 or more. **You need**—timer, index cards, and an atlas to check correct spelling. Each player chooses two common nouns from geography such as *river* or *mountain.* The players then write each noun on a separate index card. **How to play**—Mix the cards and place them face down in a pile. Someone draws the first card and sets the timer to three minutes. In secret, players write as many proper nouns as possible that are specific examples of the common noun. At the end of three minutes, players exchange papers and check each other's answers. Another player draws a card, and the process is repeated. **Scoring**—5 points for each correct proper noun; 2 extra points if the noun is spelled correctly. The player with the most points wins.

Treasure Hunt

You are having a party and decide to hold a treasure hunt. Your plan is to divide the guests into three teams. You will then give each team a different list of items to find. Think up ten items for each team. Make these items singular and plural nouns. Design special cards and copy your lists onto them. Decorate them if you wish.

Appositive Interview

Have an interview with a classmate. Write ten questions that will have names of people, places, or things as the answers.

Use facts from your interview in an informative paragraph about your friend. Use three or more different appositives in your paragraph. Be sure that you use possessive nouns correctly.

My classmate, *Angela Perkins*, lives on Maple Street. She has many hobbies. Angela's favorite hobby is walking her cat, *Midnight*, on a leash.

Extra! Collect the interviews and turn them into a class newspaper.

Add the Ending

Players—2–3. **You need**—index cards. Each player copies these endings on separate cards:

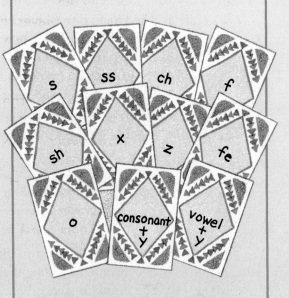

s
ss
ch
f
sh
x
z
fe
o
consonant + y
vowel + y

How to play—Mix the cards. Place them face down. The first player draws a card and writes a singular noun with that ending. That player also writes the plural of the noun. The next player then has a turn. Play until cards are gone. **Scoring**—1 point for each correct singular noun; 2 points for each correct plural. The player with the most points wins the game.

Extra Practice: Unit 3

1 | Recognizing Nouns (p. 84)

● Write the noun that names the word in parentheses.

Example: Benjamin Franklin was born in Massachusetts. (person)
Benjamin Franklin

1. The young boy worked in his father's shop. (place)
2. Later he published a newspaper for his half-brother. (thing)
3. Ben Franklin left Boston at the age of seventeen. (place)
4. He went to Philadelphia to try his luck. (idea)
5. Later he went to London to buy printing equipment. (thing)
6. He returned to Philadelphia in 1726. (place)
7. Ben Franklin was interested in politics. (idea)

▲ Write all the nouns in the sentences below.

Example: Benjamin Franklin became an ambassador representing the
American colonies in Great Britain.
Benjamin Franklin   ambassador   colonies   Great Britain

8. During the Revolution, Ben Franklin became a leader.
9. Few people had hope that the two countries could be friends.
10. Ben Franklin gave advice to George Washington.
11. Mr. Franklin also was a member of the committee that wrote the
Declaration of Independence.
12. A printer, a writer, a thinker, and a leader, Benjamin Franklin
was mostly a great citizen and patriot.

■ Write your own nouns to complete the following sentences.
Write the type of noun shown in parentheses.

Example: I visited the birthplace of ____. (person) *John Adams*

13. ____ and ____ were great Americans. (persons)
14. They worked hard for ____ and ____. (ideas)
15. My favorite American was born in ____. (place)
16. I read about this person in a ____. (thing)
17. One of the presidents of the United States was ____. (person)
18. Many ____ have been written about him. (thing)

2 | Common and Proper Nouns (p. 86)

● Write the proper noun in each sentence.

Example: My cousin Jay is a pilot. *Jay*

1. This man lives in the city of New York.
2. He made many trips in April.
3. One trip began at Kennedy Airport.
4. His plane flew to Rome that day.
5. He returned home on a Tuesday.
6. Once my cousin flew to England.
7. My sister Mary went on that trip.

▲ Write the nouns in these sentences. Underline the common nouns once. Underline the proper nouns twice.

Example: Willa Brown was a young pilot who lived in Chicago.
Willa Brown   pilot   Chicago

8. One day this woman visited an editor named Enoch Waters.
9. This man worked for a newspaper called the *Chicago Defender*.
10. Willa wanted to let people know about black flyers.
11. Students from the Coffey School held shows at the Harlem Airport in Chicago.
12. The shows were held on Sundays.
13. The reporter wrote about them, and crowds of people came.
14. The planes did exercises like flip-overs.
15. After a flight in the air, Enoch wrote that the experience was thrilling but gave him a fright.

■ Rewrite each sentence by supplying a proper noun to replace each underlined word or group of words.

Example: The pilot had a mission. *Al Grant had a mission.*

16. The mission was to cross the ocean.
17. The hard part would be to cross it by tomorrow.
18. The trip had to be taken during this month.
19. The pilot wanted to start from a certain city.
20. Officials from a state wanted the trip to start there.
21. They promised to put stories in their newspaper.
22. Their paper even sent reporters to another country.

3 ‖ Singular and Plural Nouns (p. 88)

● One of the underlined words in each sentence is a plural noun. Write the plural noun.

Example: The <u>students</u> in Adam's <u>class</u> took a trip.   *students*

1. They visited a <u>farm</u> where <u>potatoes</u> grew.
2. <u>Boxes</u> of potatoes were piled on the <u>porch</u>.
3. Two <u>women</u> were reading a <u>list</u>.
4. One <u>woman</u> spoke to the other <u>workers</u>.
5. She told the other <u>people</u> where each <u>box</u> went.
6. Some were going to <u>stores</u> in the <u>city</u>.
7. Some went across the <u>country</u> in big <u>trucks</u>.
8. Many <u>cartons</u> were loaded on a <u>train</u>.
9. A <u>man</u> wrote <u>codes</u> on them.

▲ Write the plural form of each noun in parentheses.

Example: Dawn's school has two music ____.   (studio)   *studios*

10. One room has two ____.   (piano)
11. One wall is covered with ____.   (shelf)
12. The two ____ are used often.   (room)
13. Last week several ____ gave a jazz concert.   (class)
14. ____ were tapping for an hour.   (Foot)
15. Two students played ____.   (solo)
16. People never looked at their ____.   (watch)
17. Some concerts are like ____.   (party)
18. ____ of the music remained in the air.   (Echo)

■ Write one sentence for each pair of nouns, using the plural form of both nouns. Underline the plurals.

Example: record, stereo
   We bought five new <u>records</u>, but neither of our <u>stereos</u> was working.

19. brush, tooth
20. boot, foot
21. man, sheep
22. knife, tomato
23. mouse, cage

24. zoo, monkey
25. train, whistle
26. worker, factory
27. glass, dish
28. bus, ticket

4 | Possessive Nouns (p. 91)

● Write the correct form to complete each sentence.

Example: One of the (nations, nation's) space heroes was a chimpanzee. *nation's*

1. The (animals, animal's) name was Ham.
2. (Hams', Ham's) trip made him famous.
3. The (rocket's, rockets') speed was almost six thousand miles per hour.
4. The (chimps, chimp's) fame lasted for years.
5. (Peoples, People's) understanding about space travel grew.
6. Other (chimp's, chimps') flights have been useful too.
7. (Scientist's, Scientists') photographs show (animal's, animals') behavior during space flights.

▲ Rewrite each phrase. Use possessive nouns.

Example: quiz for the student   *the student's quiz*

8. job of my sister
9. hoof of the horse
10. antler of the moose
11. book belonging to Chris
12. dog of the Harrises
13. tails of the mice
14. smile of Louis
15. bike belonging to two brothers

■ Rewrite each sentence by using a possessive noun instead of the underlined phrase.

Example: The field trip of my class was interesting.
My class's field trip was interesting.

16. The faces of the monkeys made Kim laugh.
17. The children of the Joneses wanted to rest.
18. The friends of Jess took her picture.
19. The den of the fox was a deep hole.
20. All the voices of the children sounded excited.
21. The students of Mrs. Brown wrote reports.
22. The reports were about the homes of the animals.

5 | Plural and Possessive Nouns (p. 94)

● One noun in each sentence matches the description in parentheses. Write the noun described in parentheses.

Example: Dan is very interested in airplanes.   (plural)
airplanes

1. Look at these pictures.   (plural)
2. That plane's design is very old.   (singular possessive)
3. Hang gliders first appeared in 1804.   (plural)
4. Is there a hang gliders' club?   (plural possessive)
5. He flies silently below the clouds.   (plural)
6. There is no engine's roar.   (singular possessive)
7. The pilots' friends watch.   (plural possessive)

▲ Write the correct form of the noun in parentheses. Then write whether it is plural, singular possessive, or plural possessive.

Example: Did you hear the (teachers, teacher's) instructions?
teacher's **singular possessive**

8. The museum (guides, guides') spoke to us.
9. This (week's, weeks') topic was helicopters.
10. (Helicopters', Helicopters) hover noisily.
11. (Pilots, Pilots') voices cannot be heard over the noise.
12. Other (museums', museums) show movies.
13. There is the (visitors', visitors) lobby.
14. (Pams, Pam's) mother bought T-shirts for us.

■ Write a sentence for each noun, using the form shown in parentheses.

Example: pilot   (plural possessive)
The pilots' flight paths were the same as they approached the airport.

15. cloud   (plural)
16. pilot   (singular possessive)
17. propeller   (plural)
18. astronaut   (singular possessive)
19. rocket   (plural)
20. crew   (plural possessive)

6 | Combining Sentences: Appositives (p. 96)

● Write the appositive in each sentence.

Example: Lulu, a large ape, lived in a zoo.   *a large ape*

1. The ape, a new mother, would not let anyone near her baby.
2. The baby's name, a boy's name, had to be changed.
3. The female baby got a new name, Patty Cake.
4. The zoo, Patty Cake's home, has a birthday party every year.
5. Children bring presents for this famous ape, Patty Cake.

▲ Combine each pair of sentences into a single sentence with an appositive.

Example: New York is a huge city. It has many buildings.
New York, a huge city, has many buildings.

6. One building is a lighthouse. It is called "Li'l Red."
7. A woman wrote a book about it. The woman's name was Hildegarde Smith.
8. The lighthouse was built on a long river. The river is the Hudson River.
9. A huge bridge was built over the lighthouse. The bridge is the George Washington Bridge.
10. "Li'l Red" is New York City's only lighthouse. It is now a playground.

■ (11–22)   Rewrite the paragraph below, using appositives where you can.

Example: Peter Cooper was an American businessman. He had many talents.
Peter Cooper, an American businessman, had many talents.

He built Cooper Union. Cooper Union is a school in New York. Cooper also invented one of the first locomotives. He called it the *Tom Thumb*. The *Tom Thumb* was a steam engine. It became famous when it raced a horse and lost. However, the race saved a new railroad. This was the Baltimore and Ohio Railroad. Peter Cooper was a great public servant. He worked for free education. With another man, he helped plan the first Atlantic Cable. The other man was Cyrus Field.

Literature and Writing

In comparing Earth with its neighbors within the planetary system, it is safe to say . . . that our planet is unique. In fact, it is the only one with a world-wide ocean. All the others . . . are covered either by absolutely dry desert or by vast layers of ice and frozen methane and ammonia.

Heinz Haber
from *Our Blue Planet*

Comparison and Contrast

Getting Ready You are in a department store, trying to decide which of two jackets to buy. First you think of ways in which the jackets are alike: They cost the same. They are both blue. Then you think of ways in which they are different. Jacket A has a hood. It must be dry-cleaned. Jacket B does not have a hood. It can be washed. You decide on Jacket B because you seldom wear a hood, but you always get your jackets dirty. By comparing and contrasting the two jackets, you made a decision. In this unit, you will write paragraphs of comparison and contrast.

ACTIVITIES

Listening   Listen to the paragraph on the opposite page. With what is Earth compared? What makes Earth unique?

Speaking   Look at the photograph. Compare and contrast Earth in this picture with the moon. List all the similarities you can think of. Then list all the differences.

Writing   In your journal, compare life on Earth with your imagined life on the moon.

LITERATURE

What might happen if the sun suddenly left its course?
What happens in the story of Phaethon?

PHAETHON

Retold by Ingri and Edgar Parin D'Aulaire

Helios, the sun, mounted his glowing chariot and drove out in great splendor as soon as Eos threw open the gates of his golden palace in the east. His radiance lit up the wide expanse of sky. So bright was he that only the gods could look straight at him without being blinded. Brilliant rays encircled his head, and his chariot glowed like fire.

With a strong hand, Helios guided his four fiery steeds up the vault of the heavens. The path was steep and narrow and the horses were wild, but Helios held them well on their course. At high noon, he stopped at the top of the sky and looked around, and nothing

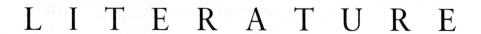

could escape his piercing gaze. Again he drove on and now he gave free rein to his steeds. Far to the west they could see his glittering evening palace, and, eager to reach their stables, they raced on the downhill course, faster and faster. They passed a great herd of white cows hurrying homeward to Helios' palace and met a large flock of sheep going out to pasture in the sky. For Helios owned a snow-white cow for each day of the year and a woolly sheep for each night.

The shadows grew long and dusk settled over the world when Helios and his foaming team arrived. His five daughters, the Heliades, awaited them. They unharnessed the tired horses and let them plunge into the ocean for a cooling bath. Then the horses rested in their stables and Helios talked with his daughters and told them all he had seen that day.

In the dark of the night, he boarded a vessel of gold with his team and sailed around the world, back to his palace in the east. The way was far shorter by sea than by air, so he had time to stay for a while in his morning palace too before he set out on another day's journey.

Helios had a son named Phaethon. He was a mortal and very proud of his radiant father. One morning as Helios was about to set off on his daily journey across the sky, Phaethon came to him and begged him to grant his dearest wish. Helios,

who was very fond of his handsome son, rashly promised to give him any wish he might have, but when he heard Phaethon's wish, he sorely regretted his decision. He tried in vain to make his son change his mind, for what Phaethon wanted was to drive the sun chariot for one day, and Helios knew that no one but he himself could handle the spirited steeds.

Phaethon was determined to have his wish, and Helios had to give in. Sadly, he put his golden rays on his son's head and rubbed divine ointment on his skin so he could withstand the searing heat of the chariot. He barely had time to warn him to stay well in the middle of the heavenly path when the gates of the palace were thrown open, and the rearing horses were brought forth. Phaethon leaped into the chariot, grasped the reins, and the horses rushed out.

At first, all went well and Phaethon stood proudly in the glowing chariot. But the fiery steeds soon felt that unskilled hands were holding the reins. They veered off the heavenly path and brushed by the dangerous constellations that lurked on both sides of it. The animals of the zodiac were enraged: the bull charged, the lion growled, the scorpion lashed out with its poisonous tail. The horses shied and Phaethon was thrown halfway out of the chariot. Far down below he saw the earth and he grew so dizzy that he dropped the reins. Without a firm hand to guide them, the horses bolted. They raced so close to the earth that the ground cracked from the heat of the chariot and rivers and lakes dried up. Then upward they sped so high that the earth froze and turned to ice.

Zeus stood on Olympus and shook his head. He had to stop the careening chariot to save the earth from destruction, and he threw a thunderbolt at it. In a shower of sparks, the chariot flew apart and Phaethon plunged into the river Po. On the riverbanks his sisters mourned so long that Zeus took pity on them and changed them into poplar trees and their tears into drops of golden amber.

Hephaestus had to work the whole night through to mend the broken chariot so Helios could drive it again the next day. Helios grieved over his lost son, and he never again allowed anyone to drive his chariot except for Apollo, the god of light.

Think and Discuss

1. What is the effect on the earth when Phaethon cannot keep the horses of the sun on course?

2. The story of Phaethon is a **myth**—a special kind of story that comes to us from ancient times. Myths were the attempts of early people to explain the world they lived in. Many myths explain natural events, such as why volcanoes erupt, or what causes thunder. What natural event does the myth of Phaethon explain?

3. Helios knew that Phaethon would not be able to handle his horses. Why did he allow Phaethon to drive the chariot? Do you think he did the right thing?

Why should we care what the other planets in our solar system are like?

Earth and Its Nearest Neighbors

By Sue Becklake

Many of the Greek and Roman myths were attempts to explain the ancient world and the mysteries of the skies above it. Today we have a greater understanding of Earth and its place in the solar system. The following selection compares and contrasts Earth with two of its neighbors in space. These neighbor planets are named for ancient Roman gods.

O ur home, Earth, is part of a family of planets and other bodies, called the solar system. The sun is the center of the solar system and the other bodies circle around it. The sun is really a star and is much larger than all the other members of the family. It provides nearly all the heat and light in the solar system. The planets shine by reflecting the sun's light.

There are nine major planets. In order of distance from the sun, they are Mercury, Venus, Earth, Mars, Jupiter, Saturn, Uranus, Neptune and Pluto. Sometimes Pluto's orbit brings it closer to the sun than Neptune. Some scientists think there may be other planets farther away that we do not know about. Four of the planets are smaller than Earth and four are much larger.

Astronomers think that Earth and its two nearest neighbors, Mars and Venus, were originally formed from the cloud of gas which also produced the sun. The planets are very different from each other today. Venus has a thick, poisonous atmosphere and is very hot. Mars is a cold, dry, desert planet with only a thin atmosphere.

No life has been discovered on Venus and Mars. Earth, however, which lies between these planets, has an enormous variety of life on its surface. Life depends on water. Water remains in our seas and atmosphere because Earth is just the right distance from the sun to stop all the water evaporating.

Venus is the nearest planet to Earth and the brightest object, apart from the moon, in our night sky. But its surface is hidden under a veil of cloud. Radar measurements show that it spins very slowly, in the opposite direction to most of the other planets.

Venus has proved a very difficult planet to explore, partly because it has very high atmospheric pressure. The atmospheric pressure at the surface of Venus is ninety-two times greater than that on Earth. This pressure crushed the early Russian Venera probes which were sent to explore the planet. However, in 1975 Veneras 9 and 10 survived to send pictures of the rocky surface back to Earth.

Although Mars is farther from us than Venus, it has captured our imagination because its surface can be seen through a telescope.

Mars is half the size of Earth but it is similar to our planet in several ways. Its day is almost the same length as our day. White polar caps, looking like Earth's ice caps, can be seen, and astronomers have watched the surface markings change with the seasons.

We study the solar system to learn more about Earth. If we can discover how the sun and planets were formed, and why they are so different from each other, we will understand more about Earth and its atmosphere. This will help us to preserve our planet as the ideal place for us to live.

Think and Discuss

1. What reason does the author of "Earth and Its Nearest Neighbors" give for our study of the solar system? What other reasons might people have for wanting to explore other planets?
2. Which two planets are Earth's nearest neighbors? Has life been discovered on either planet?
3. The article about Earth is an example of **expository writing.** Expository writing gives readers facts. Use the information given in this article to fill in the table below. Use a separate sheet of paper. If the article does not give the facts you need for a category, write *not given* in the blank.

	Temperature compared to Earth	Size compared to Earth	Type of atmosphere
Venus			
Mars			

RESPONDING TO LITERATURE

The Reading and Writing Connection

Personal Response Have you ever made a promise without thinking and had to decide later whether to keep it? Write a paragraph or two, telling what the promise was and what you decided to do.

Creative Writing Make up a myth that explains something in nature. It might be about where the stars go during the day—anything that you think needs an explanation!

Creative Activities

Draw On a large sheet of paper, draw a diagram of the solar system. Label each planet. Try to make the planets the right size in relation to each other and to the sun. Use information from an encyclopedia or a science textbook.

Dramatize Instructions Pretend that you are Helios and that you *do* have the extra time to give your son Phaethon instructions on how to control the horses of the sun. Give him a speech on what to do to keep them under control, and tell him the results if he fails.

Vocabulary

Except for Earth, the names of all the planets in our solar system come from Greek and Roman mythology. Use a dictionary to find the mythological character for which each planet was named.

Looking Ahead

Comparing and Contrasting In this unit you will compare and contrast two things. To *compare* things is to show how they are alike. To *contrast* things is to show how they are different.

VOCABULARY CONNECTION

Using Context Clues

You can often figure out the meaning of an unfamiliar word by using **context,** the other words in the sentence and even the surrounding sentences.

> Sadly, he . . . rubbed divine **ointment** on his skin so he could withstand the **searing** heat of the chariot.
> *from "Phaethon" by Ingri and Edgar P. D'Aulaire*

If you read the sentence carefully, you should be able to figure out the meanings of these two words. You probably got your clues from the other words in the sentence. *Ointment* is a medicine to rub on the skin and *searing* means "burning."

Sometimes the context will not help you understand the meaning of a word. Use your dictionary for help.

Vocabulary Practice

A. Use the context to figure out the meaning of each under-lined word in these sentences from "Phaethon." Write each meaning.

1. His <u>radiance</u> lit up the wide expanse of sky.
2. Helios, who was very fond of his handsome son, <u>rashly</u> prom-ised to give him any wish he might have, but when he heard Phaethon's wish, he sorely regretted his decision.
3. They <u>veered</u> off the heavenly path and brushed by the danger-ous constellations that lurked on both sides of it.

B. Use the following words from "Phaethon" in sentences of your own. Give context clues to make the meaning of each word clear.

4. lurk   5. careening   6. steeds   7. amber

Prewriting
Comparison and Contrast

Listening: For Organization

How are the facts below organized?

Mars is half the size of Earth but it is similar to our planet in several ways. Its day is almost the same length as our day. White polar caps, looking like Earth's ice caps, can be seen. . . .
from "Earth and Its Nearest Neighbors" by Sue Becklake

The facts are arranged to show similarities between Earth and Mars. The words *is similar to, the same,* and *like* give you clues about the passage's organization. Now read this passage.

The planets are the nine largest objects that travel around the sun. However, many other objects also orbit the sun. These smaller bodies include the planets' moons, asteroids, meteoroids, comets, and drifting bits of dust.

These facts are given in order of importance, with the most important fact given first. The words *largest, smaller,* and *bits of* give you clues about the importance of the facts.

Guidelines for Listening for Organization

1. Listen for time sequence if the topic involves events that happened in a certain order.
2. Listen for words that show likenesses or differences.
3. Listen for words that signal the importance of facts.

Prewriting Practice

Listen as your teacher reads two passages. How are the facts in each passage organized?

Thinking: Classifying

There are billions of objects in our galaxy. To help us identify and understand so many objects, we divide them into groups, or **classifications.** Items that share certain features are classified together. Here are examples.

PLANETS: Mercury, Venus, Earth, Mars, Jupiter, Saturn,
Uranus, Neptune, Pluto

STARS: Sirius, Vega, Alpha Centauri, Castor . . .

CONSTELLATIONS: Aquarius, Ursa Major, Taurus, Andromeda . . .

As you read in "Earth and Its Nearest Neighbors," the planets are similar because they all rotate around the sun. The other objects noted above are grouped together because they are alike in some way. Stars give off light and heat, and constellations are groups of stars that form patterns.

Each group of objects can be further classified, based on shared features. These subgroups are **categories.** Here are some categories into which the planets can be grouped.

Planets	
Visible to the eye	Mercury, Venus, Mars, Jupiter, Saturn
Farther from the sun than Earth	Mars, Jupiter, Saturn, Uranus, Neptune, Pluto
Larger than Earth	Jupiter, Saturn, Uranus, Neptune

- Which planets fall into more than one category?
- What other ways can you think of to classify the planets?

The way you classify anything will depend on your purpose. If you are comparing the other planets to Earth, for example, the last two groups above will interest you most.

Suppose you want to classify the following celestial events, which will occur during a given time period.

eclipse of the moon visible in Australia   moonrise
new moon   meteor shower visible in the United States
sunrise   eclipse of the sun visible in Indonesia

First, think about *why* you are classifying. Are you giving a talk about the moon? about the sun? Are you writing a report about eclipses?

Next, ask yourself which events are alike and which are different. This step is especially valuable when you are preparing a comparison and contrast.

Finally, categorize the events based on their shared features. The celestial events can be categorized like this.

LUNAR EVENTS: moonrise, new moon, eclipse of
                       the moon
SOLAR EVENTS: sunrise, eclipse of the sun
EVENTS VISIBLE IN moonrise, new moon, sunrise,
THE UNITED STATES: meteor shower

Guidelines for Classifying

1. Determine your purpose for classifying.
2. Decide what features the objects or events share.
3. Select the shared features that suit your purpose.
4. Group the objects or events that share the selected features.

Prewriting Practice

A. With a partner, see how many different ways you can classify the following holidays:

New Year's Day, Flag Day, Lincoln's Birthday, Thanksgiving, Veterans Day, Independence Day, Memorial Day, Martin Luther King Jr.'s Birthday, Washington's Birthday

B. In this unit you read about the vehicle known as a chariot. With a partner, list all the vehicles you can think of. Classify them in one way. Then classify them in another way.

Composition Skills
Comparison and Contrast

Topics and Main Ideas ☑

A paragraph is made up of sentences that discuss one **topic.** Each sentence in the paragraph should be about that topic. The sentences present one **main idea** about the topic. What is the topic of this paragraph? Can you state the main idea?

> Venus has proved a very difficult planet to explore, partly because it has very high atmospheric pressure. The atmospheric pressure at the surface of Venus is ninety-two times greater than that on Earth. This pressure crushed the early Russian Venera probes which were sent to explore the planet. However, in 1975 Veneras 9 and 10 survived to send pictures of the rocky surface back to Earth.
> *from "Earth and Its Nearest Neighbors" by Sue Becklake*

The topic of the paragraph is the atmospheric pressure on Venus. Which of the following statements best describes the main idea of the paragraph?

1. The atmospheric pressure on Venus has made it difficult for scientists to get information about Venus.
2. The Russian space program has had many setbacks, including its explorations of Venus.
3. Venus is a mysterious planet.

Prewriting Practice

What is the topic of the following paragraph? What is the main idea? Discuss your answers with a partner.

July 20, 1969, was a thrilling day. A billion people gathered around televisions all over the world to watch the great event. A man was going to walk on the moon! As Neil Armstrong stepped out of the spaceship, he said these words. "That's one small step for a man, one giant leap for mankind."

Topic Sentences and Supporting Details ☑

Many paragraphs contain one sentence that clearly states the main idea. It is called the **topic sentence.** Often it is the first sentence in the paragraph. The rest of the sentences in the paragraph give **supporting details** about the main idea. Read this paragraph.

> Our home, Earth, is part of a family of planets and other bodies, called the solar system. The sun is the center of the solar system and the other bodies circle around it. The sun is really a star and is much larger than all the other members of the family. It provides nearly all the heat and light in the solar system.
> *from "Earth and Its Nearest Neighbors" by Sue Becklake*

The first sentence is the topic sentence. It states the main idea. The other sentences give supporting details about the main idea.

The topic sentence can come anywhere in a paragraph. Where is the topic sentence in the following paragraph?

> Mars has white polar caps that look like Earth's ice caps. Water may be frozen in these large polar caps. Mars also has bright areas and dark areas. These surface markings change with the seasons. Many scientists now believe that some form of life may exist on Mars.

The topic sentence is about the possibility of life on Mars. Each sentence gives supporting details.

What is the topic sentence in the next paragraph? What sentence does not support the topic sentence?

> The solar system is a tiny part of a galaxy called the Milky Way. The sun is the center of the solar system. The Milky Way is made up of planets and billions of stars. The solar system is thirty thousand light-years from the center of the Milky Way.

Prewriting Practice

A. For each of these topic sentences, write three sentences that give supporting details.

1. You can learn a lot from watching television.
2. Owning a pet is a big responsibility.
3. People have different opinions about what makes an ideal vacation.

B. This paragraph does not have a topic sentence. Read the paragraph. Then write a topic sentence that tells the main idea.

The ancient Greeks believed that the sun, the moon, and the stars revolved around Earth. This view of the universe was accepted for almost two thousand years. Not until the 1500s did scientists begin to realize that Earth is one of a family of planets that revolve around the sun.

The Grammar Connection

Exact Nouns

Using exact nouns will make your writing clearer and easier to understand. A good writer chooses words that carry the exact meanings. Which word in parentheses best completes the following sentence?

Phaethon could not control the fiery _____.   (horses, steeds)

A **steed** is a spirited horse. What image does *steed* bring to mind? Why would *steeds* be a better word choice than *horses*?

Practice Write each sentence, using the noun in parentheses that best fits the meaning of the sentence.

1. Helios lived in a beautiful _____.   (house, palace, dwelling)
2. Phaethon could not control the sun chariot because he was a _____.   (man, mortal)
3. The _____ resulted in the destruction of Earth.   (mishap, mistake, disaster)

Comparing and Contrasting ☑

> Mars is half the size of Earth but it is similar to our planet in several ways. Its day is almost the same length as our day. White polar caps, looking like Earth's ice caps, can be seen, and astronomers have watched the surface markings change with the seasons.
>
> *from "Earth and Its Nearest Neighbors" by Sue Becklake*

This paragraph tells how Mars and Earth are alike. It is called a **paragraph of comparison.** The topic sentence states the main idea of the paragraph: Mars is similar to Earth in several ways. The supporting details tell *how* Mars is similar to Earth.

A paragraph that tells about the differences between two subjects is called a **paragraph of contrast.** Here is a list of supporting details that might be put into a paragraph of contrast about Earth and Mars.

1. There is no life on Mars.
2. Mars is much smaller than Earth.
3. Mars is a cold, desert planet.

Can you think of a good topic sentence for this paragraph?

Prewriting Practice

Choose one of the following pairs of subjects. First, list ways in which the two items are similar. Then list ways in which they are different. Include at least three similarities and three differences in each list.

1. an elephant and a giraffe
2. a banana and a bowl of lima beans
3. Thanksgiving and the Fourth of July
4. basketball and soccer
5. a glass of milk and a glass of water
6. summer and winter

Step 1: Prewriting—Choose a Topic

Mandy listed several pairs of things that were alike in some ways and different in others. Then she thought about her list.

Texas and Georgia

— She had lived in both states, but this topic was too large.

magazines and books

— There are too many different kinds.

a balloon and a cloud

— She thought that she would rather use this idea for a poem.

a typewriter and a computer

— She had just learned to use a computer in school.

an ocean and a lake

— She was not very interested in this topic.

Mandy circled *a typewriter and a computer* on her list.

On Your Own

1. **Think and discuss** List some pairs of things that you can compare or contrast. Use the Ideas page. Discuss your ideas with a classmate.
2. **Choose** Ask yourself these questions about each pair.
   Do I know enough about both things to write about them?
   Are they alike or different in at least three ways?
   Would I enjoy writing about them?
3. **Explore** What interesting points will you make about your topic? Do an "Exploring Your Topic" activity on the Ideas page.

Ideas for Getting Started

Choosing Your Topic

Topic Ideas

Morning and evening
The sun and the moon
Soccer and ice hockey
Country music and
    rock music
A painting and a
    photograph
Winter and summer
A stereo and a radio
A canoe and a kayak
A dog and a cat
A movie and a play

An Idea Grab Bag

Form a small group. Choose a general category like sports. Everyone in the group writes the name of a sport on a scrap of paper. Put all the scraps of paper into a paper bag and pick two of them. Discuss whether these two would make a good topic to compare or contrast. Pick two more pairs to discuss. Then start over with a new category.

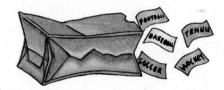

Exploring Your Topic

Opposite Sides

Fold a sheet of paper in half the long way. On one side, list all the ways the two parts of your topic are alike. On the other side, list the differences. Decide which items you will use in your paragraph. Then number them to show the order you will use.

Talk About It

Have a partner guess both parts of your topic by playing Twenty Questions. You may have to give two answers to a question to cover both things that you are comparing and contrasting.

Step 2: Write a First Draft

Mandy decided to write her paragraph for her mother. Her mother would soon be using a computer at work.

Mandy wrote her first draft. She did not worry about making mistakes. She would correct them later. First she wanted to get her ideas on paper.

Mandy's first draft

A typewriter can only type, a computer can do other things. Many stores ~~have~~ sell computers. With a typewriter you can't see your misteaks untill they're already on paper. With a computer you see everything first before you print it out.

On Your Own

1. **Think about purpose and audience** Ask yourself these questions.

   What reader will I have in mind as I write?

   Do I want my reader to learn something? to look at something in a new way?

   How can I make this interesting to my reader?

   Do I want to compare or contrast?

2. **Write** Write your first draft. Remember to have one clear main idea. Write on every other line to leave room for changes. If you make mistakes, you can correct them in the next draft. Right now your ideas are more important.

Step 3: Revise

Mandy read her first draft. She noticed that her paragraph needed a topic sentence. She also noticed that the second sentence did not help show how computers are different. Mandy corrected these problems.

Mandy wanted to see whether her paragraph would make sense to someone who had never used a computer. She read it to Amy.

Reading and responding

Mandy added a few lines to explain how a computer displays type. She also added another thing a computer can do.

Mandy's revised draft

*A computer looks like a typewriter,
but it's really very different.*

∧A typewriter can only type, a computer
       For example, it can do
can do other things.∧Many stores ~~have~~
math problems.
~~sell computers.~~ With a typewriter you

can't see your misteaks untill they're

already on paper. With a computer you see
                    on a screen
everything ∧~~first~~ before you print it out.

Think and Discuss ✓

- Why did she cross out a sentence?
- What is the topic sentence that Mandy added? How does it help?
- What details did Mandy add? Why?

On Your Own

☑ Is my main idea clear?

☑ Did I include a topic sentence?

☑ Are my details interesting? Do I need more of them?

☑ Do my details support my comparison or contrast?

1. **Revise** Make changes in your first draft. Cross out parts that do not belong. Use a caret (∧) to show where new details go. If you need to find exact words, use the thesaurus below or the one in the back of this book.

2. **Have a conference** Read your paragraph to someone in your class or to your teacher.

WRITING CONFERENCE

Ask your listener:	As you listen:
"Can you tell what my main idea is?" "Does anything seem unclear or out of place?" "Which parts are the most interesting?"	I must listen closely. What is the main idea? Can I picture everything clearly? What else would I like to know?

3. **Revise** Did your listener make any helpful suggestions? Do you have other ideas? Make these changes on your paper.

Thesaurus

ask question, examine
big great, important, large
calm quiet, still, serene
cold chill, nippy, icy
fat chunky, heavy, thick
happy cheerful, glad, merry
health fit, sound, well
hot boiling, scorching, sizzling, sweltering
little small, unimportant

nice agreeable, pleasant
sharp keen, clear, distinct
smart intelligent, clever, bright
teach instruct, tutor, train
thin lean, feeble, slender, skinny
think believe, consider
unclear fuzzy, confusing, cloudy, faint
wish desire, crave

Step 4: Proofread

Mandy proofread her paragraph for mistakes in grammar, capitalization, and punctuation. She checked her spellings in a dictionary. She used proofreading marks to make her changes. Here is the way Mandy's proofread paragraph looked.

Mandy's proofread paragraph

¶ A computer looks like a typewriter,
but it's really very different. but
∧ A typewriter can only type,∧ a computer
For example, it can do
can do other things. ∧ Many stores ~~have~~
math problems.
~~sell computers.~~ With a typewriter you
mistakes
can't see your ~~misteaks~~ until̷ they're

already on paper. With a computer you see
on a screen
everything ∧ ~~first~~ before you print it out.

Think and Discuss

- What mark did Mandy use at the beginning? Why?
- What run-on sentence did she correct? How?
- What spelling mistakes did she correct?

On Your Own

1. **Proofreading Practice** Proofread this paragraph for mistakes in grammar and spelling. There are six spelling mistakes, one incorrect proper noun, two run-on sentences, and one incorrect end mark. Write the paragraph correctly.

        I have two dogs, Ben and jerry.
    Ben is no bigger than a cat he's black
    and curley and has eyebrows that
    stick out like wiskers. Jerry is a
    big, tan-colored dog with short,
    smooth hair. Ben sleeps most of the
    time, Jerry spends evry day roming the
    neighberhood. Would you beleive they
    are brothers.

Proofreading Marks

¶	Indent
∧	Add
⩔	Add a comma
⌄⌄	Add quotation marks
⊙	Add a period
ℓ	Take out
≡	Capitalize
/	Make a small letter
∩	Reverse order

2. Proofreading Application Now proofread your paragraph. Use the Proofreading Checklist and the Grammar and Spelling Hints below. A colored pencil can help make your corrections easy to read. Check your spellings.

Proofreading Checklist

Did I

☑ **1.** indent the first line of my paragraph?

☑ **2.** begin each sentence with a capital letter?

☑ **3.** use the correct end marks for each sentence?

☑ **4.** capitalize all proper nouns?

☑ **5.** spell all words correctly?

The Grammar/Spelling Connection

Grammar Hint

Remember this rule from Unit 3 when you use nouns.

- Capitalize the names of specific persons, places, or things. When a proper noun is made up of more than one word, capitalize only the important words.

    Jenna Stone   Whitman School   Tower of London

Spelling Hint

- To spell many words with the vowel combination *ie* or *ei*, remember this rule: "Use *i* before *e* except after *c* or in words with (ā), as in *neighbor* and *weigh*."

    thief   receive   freight   (EXCEPTIONS: either   seize)

Step 5: Publish

Here is the way Mandy presented her paragraph to her mother. She drew a large picture of a computer keyboard and a screen. On the screen she pasted a computer print-out of her paragraph.

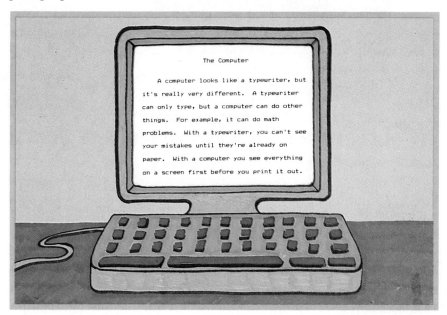

The Computer

A computer looks like a typewriter, but it's really very different. A typewriter can only type, but a computer can do other things. For example, it can do math problems. With a typewriter, you can't see your mistakes until they're already on paper. With a computer you see everything on a screen first before you print it out.

On Your Own

1. **Copy** Write or type your paragraph as neatly as you can.
2. **Add a title** Think of a title to catch your reader's interest. Remember to capitalize the first, last, and all important words.
3. **Check** Read over your paragraph again to make sure you have not left out anything or made any mistakes in copying.
4. **Share** Think of a special way to share your work.

Ideas for Sharing

- Make a poster showing the two things you compared or contrasted. Display them as you read your paragraph aloud.
- Make two class booklets with your paragraphs. Title one *Comparing* and the other *Contrasting*.

Applying Comparison and Contrast

Literature and Creative Writing

The myth of Phaethon was the story of a boy whose dearest wish—to drive the sun chariot—was granted. When he was unable to keep the chariot on its course, he was struck down by Zeus. Use what you have learned in this unit about comparison and contrast to complete one of the following activities.

> **Remember these things** ☑
> Write a topic sentence that states the main idea.
> Give details that support the main idea.
> Compare two things by telling how they are alike.
> Contrast two things by telling how they are different.

1. **Compare the palaces of Helios.** In the myth "Phaethon," the author tells us that Helios has two palaces. One is described as his "golden palace in the east" and his "morning palace." The other is described as his "glittering evening palace." Use your imagination to write a paragraph about the differences between the morning palace and the evening palace.

2. **Who's in charge?** Helios and Phaethon were very different in their ability to drive the sun chariot. Write a paragraph, contrasting the skills of each driver. Think about how the horses knew whether a skilled driver was holding the reins.

3. **What happened to Earth?** When Phaethon brought the sun chariot too close to Earth, the ground cracked from the heat. When he took it too far away, Earth froze. Write a paragraph contrasting these two disasters.

Writing Across the Curriculum
Speech Class

Have you ever given a speech to your classmates? Perhaps you have a speech class in school where you have practiced preparing and giving speeches.

Choose one or more of the following activities and write a speech. Follow the five steps you learned in this unit.

1. **Compare the activities.** All sports, dance, and gymnastics take strength, flexibility, and practice. However, they all require different skills. Choose two sports, types of dance, or types of gymnastics. Prepare a speech, telling how they are alike and different. What skills are required? Which is more difficult? Can you demonstrate some of the movements as you give your speech?

Writing Steps
1. Choose a topic
2. Write a first draft
3. Revise
4. Proofread
5. Publish

Word Bank
strength
practice
concentration
balance
attention
flexibility

2. **Compare the medium.** Has one of your favorite books been made into a film or weekly TV program? How is the original like the film or program? How is it different? Compare and contrast the two versions.

3. **Compare the pets.** Having pets can be a very rewarding experience and lots of fun! Each pet, or kind of pet, is different from another one. Tell your classmates about the likenesses and differences you have noticed about two different pets. Tell the good points and the bad points about caring for them. You may want to bring in pictures of the pets.

Extending Literature
Book Report: Comic Strip

When Carl finished reading Phaethon, he wanted more myths to read. At the library he found *Myths and Legends of the Greeks* by Nicola Ann Sissons. He decided to share his favorite story with his classmates by making a comic strip about it. This is how part of the comic strip looked.

Think and Discuss

- Why do you think Carl chose this part of the story?
- What do you find out about the characters?
- What do you learn about the plot?

Share Your Book

Make a Comic Strip

1. Decide which part of the book you will share. Choose a part that you think is interesting and that you can illustrate.
2. Decide how many frames or sections you will need. Divide a large sheet of drawing paper into that many frames.
3. Draw the picture of each frame, leaving enough room for the dialogue bubbles. Write in the bubbles what each character says. You do not have to use the exact words from your story.
4. Include the title and author of the book in which you found your myth.

Other Activities

- Draw pictures of two important characters from your book. Show each character in action that illustrates how the two characters are alike or how they are different. Include each character's name, the name of the myth, and the title and the author of your book.
- Make a mobile of the important characters in one myth. Draw the characters on heavy paper and cut them out. Write their names on the drawings. Attach the cutouts to a wire coat hanger, and label them with the title and the author of the book.

The Book Nook

Norse Gods and Heroes *by Edgar and Ingri D'Aulaire* An introduction to myths of the Scandinavian countries.	Stories of the Gods and Heroes *by Sally Benson* A selection of Greek and Roman myths and stories.

Language and Usage

An eagle wings gracefully
  through the sky.
On the earth I stand
  and watch.
My heart flies with it.

Alonzo Lopez
"Eagle Flight"

Verbs

Getting Ready Without thinking much about it, we all use verbs to express action or being. If we stop to think about the way we use verbs and which verbs we use, we can make our language more exciting, colorful, and precise. Take *go*, for example. A sentence like "He *goes* to school" can become "He *races* to school" or "He *plods* to school." You could say, "He *had walked* to school in the morning, but he *ran* home in the afternoon." In this unit, you will learn more about verbs and how to use them.

ACTIVITIES

Listening   Listen to the poem. List the four verbs in it. Replace each verb with another and then read the poem. How does it sound now? What difference did changing the verbs make?

Speaking   Look at the picture of the eagle. How well do the first two lines of the poem describe this picture? Think of other verbs to describe the eagle's flight.

Writing   Think of your favorite animal and list verbs in your journal to describe its actions.

1 | Action Verbs

You know that a verb is the main word in the predicate of a sentence. An action verb tells what the subject *does*.

We walked on the beach.   We ran toward the ocean.

Sometimes an action verb tells about an action that you cannot see.

We wanted seashells.   I wondered about the tides.

Guided Practice Find the action verbs.

Example: I found a sand dollar on the beach. *found*

1. It confused me at first.
2. I took it into the house.
3. I held it in my hand.
4. I studied the sand dollar carefully.
5. I placed it on the windowsill in the sunlight.

Summing up

▶ An **action verb** tells what the subject of the sentence does.

Independent Practice Write the action verb in each sentence.

Example: Sand dollars live on the ocean floor. *live*

6. Sometimes they float onto the beach.
7. Tiny spines and feet cover their bodies.
8. Sand dollars eat tiny plants.
9. They crawl through the sand.
10. I think about their lives.

Writing Application: A Description

Write a paragraph about an animal that you like. Tell what the animal does. Use action verbs and underline them.

2 | Main Verbs and Auxiliaries

Some verbs are only one word. Sometimes several words together make up the verb.

Kenneth walked home.

I will be going home soon too.

A verb that is made up of more than one word is called a **verb phrase.** The last word in a verb phrase is the **main verb.** The other verbs are called **auxiliary verbs** or **helping verbs.**

Bill Moore has arrived home.

The door had been locked .

Common Auxiliary Verbs

am	were	do	has	must	might
is	be	does	had	will	would
are	being	did	can	shall	should
was	been	have	may	could	

Sometimes the auxiliary verb in one sentence is the main verb in another. Be sure to read the whole sentence before you identify a main verb and its auxiliaries.

Verb	Main verb	Auxiliary verb
did	I did my homework.	I did wait for you.
has	Bob has it.	Bob has taken it.

Questions are often formed with auxiliary verbs. In questions, the main verb and its auxiliaries may be separated by the subject of the sentence.

Should we leave now?

Will the show start early?

Who would like a ticket?

Guided Practice Find the verb phrase in each sentence. Which words are main verbs? Which are auxiliaries?

Example: Before 1803 the land between the Missouri River and the Rocky Mountains was owned by France.
verb phrase: *was owned*   **main verb**: *owned*
auxiliary verb: *was*

1. By 1803 this land had been bought by the United States.
2. The purchase was called the Louisiana Purchase.
3. The United States had paid fifteen million dollars for this land.
4. No one had explored this area.
5. Who would explore the land?
6. The explorers would be selected carefully.
7. A dangerous journey would begin soon.
8. Many men would take this trip.
9. The journey would last more than two years.
10. Meriwether Lewis and William Clark were chosen by President Thomas Jefferson.
11. They had lived in the wilderness.
12. A route to the Pacific Ocean would open fur trading.
13. President Jefferson had wanted information about the Northwest.
14. Did the explorers leave from St. Louis?
15. Did the travelers have a map of the land?
16. By 1805 Lewis and Clark had become the first explorers in Idaho.
17. The Oregon region was claimed by the United States.
18. The exploration had opened a new area for pioneers.
19. It was considered a great success.
20. Should I write a report about their expedition?

Summing up

▶ **Auxiliary verbs** are helping verbs.
▶ A **verb phrase** is made up of one or more auxiliary verbs and a main verb.
▶ The **main verb** is the last word in a verb phrase.

Independent Practice Write each verb phrase.
Underline the auxiliary verbs once and the main verbs twice.

Example: A Native American princess may have saved the Lewis and
Clark expedition. *may have saved*

21. Sacajawea was born in Idaho in 1787.
22. She had been kidnapped from her tribe.
23. In 1805 her French husband was hired
    as a guide for Lewis and Clark.
24. Would the princess stay behind?
25. Could they cross the Rocky Mountains on foot?
26. Horses were needed for that part of the trip.
27. They had met a Native American tribe.
28. The princess had belonged to the tribe at birth.
29. Her brother had been made a chief of the tribe.
30. Her tribe, however, has distrusted strangers.
31. The princess must have helped the explorers.
32. The tribe was given gifts in exchange for horses.
33. The explorers had hoped for information.
34. The tribe did tell them about paths in the mountains.
35. The Rocky Mountains were crossed at last.
36. The trip through the mountains had taken one month.
37. Did the explorers return to St. Louis by 1806?
38. They had traveled almost eight thousand miles.
39. People had lost hope for their return.
40. The explorers were welcomed with cheers from the people.
41. Lewis was made the governor of Louisiana.
42. Clark was promoted to a higher rank in the army.
43. Lewis and Clark had written about their journey.
44. Their writing was read by many people.
45. People can read this material today.

Writing Application: Creative Writing
Pretend that you have a machine that takes you backward in
time. Write about a historical event that you went back in time
to witness. Use verb phrases in at least three of your sentences.

For Extra Practice, see p. 176.   **Main Verbs and Auxiliaries**

3 | Direct Objects

An action verb is often followed by a word that tells who or what receives the action.

Fran made the basket.

Lou finished the book.

She returned it to the library.

The word that tells who or what receives the action is called the **direct object**. To find the direct object, first find the verb. Then ask who or what receives the action.

Ann programmed the computer . (Ann programmed *what?*)

Jerry has made a model plane . (Jerry has made *what?*)

The music annoys Mr. Nelson . (The music annoys *whom?*)

In some sentences, the direct object is compound.

I need oil paints and a brush for my hobby.
(I need *what?*)

Jane received a guitar and a songbook for her birthday.
(Jane received *what?*)

Guided Practice Find the direct object in each sentence. The direct object may be compound.

Example: Last weekend we took a trip to the science museum. *trip*

1. We attended a show on electricity.
2. A huge generator produced light and energy.
3. Then we saw a model of the Apollo spacecraft.
4. We examined the large control board.
5. Lauren and Rodrigo watched a film about rockets.
6. Later we visited the exhibit on natural history.
7. I like the stuffed giraffes and elephants best.
8. My friends preferred the dinosaurs and other prehistoric animals.

> ▸ A **direct object** receives the action of a verb.
> ▸ Some direct objects are compound.
> ▸ To find the direct object, find the action verb, and ask who or what receives the action.

Independent Practice Write the action verb and the direct object in each sentence. The direct object may be compound.

Example: Sir Francis Drake planned a voyage around the world.
　　　　　　action verb:　*planned*　　*direct object*:　*voyage*

9. The Queen of England encouraged Sir Francis.
10. Drake treated the members of his crew well.
11. He won their respect and loyalty.
12. Drake commanded three ships at once.
13. Two smaller ships carried supplies.
14. They visited many ports in South America.
15. Drake's skill and courage helped England.
16. The British people greeted the weary sailors.
17. The Queen knighted Sir Francis Drake.
18. She praised him and the entire crew.
19. She also encouraged authors and artists.
20. The Queen enjoyed their talent and energy.
21. She rewarded many talented people.
22. She made many speeches.
23. She spoke several languages.
24. She also loved music.
25. She could play a musical instrument.
26. The Queen won the love of the people.
27. Musicians received her support.
28. Actors performed plays for the Queen.
29. Audiences enjoyed dramas and comedies.
30. Writers told stories of love and adventure.

Writing Application: Writing About Yourself
Write a personal narrative about what you do each morning before school. Describe your activities. Use direct objects in some of your sentences.

For Extra Practice, see p. 177.

4 | Transitive and Intransitive Verbs

A **transitive verb** is an action verb that has a receiver of the action. Usually the receiver of the action is a direct object. An **intransitive verb** has no direct object. The same verb can be transitive in one sentence and intransitive in another.

Verb	Transitive	Intransitive
spoke	The students spoke <u>French</u>.	They spoke well.
studied	Tom studied <u>grammar</u>.	He studied hard.

Some action verbs are always intransitive. They never have direct objects.

INTRANSITIVE VERBS: Her eyes twinkled .

Carla will listen to her carefully.

Guided Practice Find the verb or verb phrase in each sentence. Which ones are transitive, and which ones are intransitive?

Example: We will celebrate Ann's birthday tomorrow.
will celebrate **transitive**

1. Ann's family bought a present for her.
2. They chose a watch with a yellow band.
3. Ann wore her new watch to school.
4. Now she will know the correct time.
5. She talks about her present all the time.
6. The second hand sweeps around the numbers.
7. Ann keeps the watch in its case at night.
8. The small jewels in the watch gleam brightly.
9. The numbers glow in the dark.
10. Ann can tell the time without a light.

> ▶ A **transitive verb** is an action verb that has a receiver of the action, which is usually a direct object.
> ▶ An **intransitive verb** has no direct object.
> ▶ Some action verbs are always intransitive.

Independent Practice Write the verb or verb phrase in each sentence. Label it *transitive* or *intransitive*.

Example: We have new neighbors. *have* **transitive**

11. They moved into the house across the street.
12. Maria brought flowers to them.
13. Berto introduced his twin sisters to us.
14. His sisters will enter my school.
15. Mrs. Garcia spoke very softly.
16. She smiled at us.
17. We invited the Garcias for Sunday dinner.
18. Maria played the guitar after dinner.
19. Everyone listened to the beautiful music.
20. The applause delighted Maria.
21. Mr. Garcia also played.
22. Everyone danced around the room.
23. Berto sang the words to the music.
24. We clapped our hands to the music.
25. I collapsed onto the sofa.
26. Ana and Rita slept peacefully next to the cat.
27. The Garcias carried the girls home in their arms.
28. We like our new friends.
29. I will see Ana and Rita soon.
30. We will talk about many things.

Writing Application: A Description
Think about someone you know who has a special talent.
Write a paragraph about what that person does so well.
Underline the transitive verbs once and the intransitive verbs twice.

For Extra Practice, see p. 178.

5 | Being Verbs and Linking Verbs

Some verbs do not show action. They show what the subject is or is like. Verbs called **being verbs** show a state of being.

Mr. Wong is the principal.   He seems kind.   He is here.

A being verb is often a **linking verb**. It links the subject of the sentence with a word in the predicate that tells more about it.

This newspaper *feels* damp.   It *became* wet in the rain.

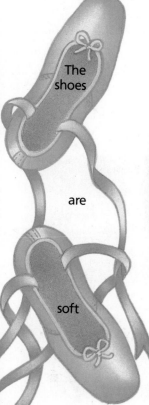

The
shoes

are

soft

Common Being and Linking Verbs				
am	was	be	become	feel
is	were	being	look	taste
are	seem	been	appear	smell

Linking verbs link the subject with a word in the predicate. The word can be a **predicate noun** or a **predicate adjective**. A predicate noun renames the subject. A predicate adjective describes the subject. Linking verbs never have direct objects.

PREDICATE NOUNS: Don is our leader . (Don = leader)

He has become my friend . (He = friend)

PREDICATE ADJECTIVES: Ms. Hill was friendly .

She appeared shy to strangers.

Guided Practice
What is the linking verb in each sentence? What is the predicate noun or predicate adjective?

Example: The Black Hills are really mountains. *are   mountains*

1. Thunderhead Mountain is part of the Black Hills.
2. Someday the mountain top will become a huge statue.
3. The statue will be a profile of Chief Crazy Horse.
4. Chief Crazy Horse was a Sioux Indian chief.
5. The statue is rough now.

▶ A **being verb** is a **linking verb** when it links the subject of a sentence with a predicate noun or a predicate adjective.
▶ A **predicate noun** renames or identifies the subject.
▶ A **predicate adjective** describes the subject.

Independent Practice

A. Write each sentence. Underline the linking verb. Draw an arrow from the simple subject to the predicate noun.

Example: The Iroquois were Native American tribes in New York.

The Iroquois <u>were</u> Native American tribes in New York.

6. Five tribes were part of the Iroquois nation.
7. One tribe was the Mohawks.
8. The Mohawks were enemies of another Iroquois tribe.
9. Hiawatha was a powerful chief of the Mohawks.
10. Hiawatha became a peacemaker.
11. Hiawatha was the hero of a poem by Longfellow.
12. This poem is *The Song of Hiawatha*.

B. Write each sentence. Underline the linking verb. Draw an arrow from the simple subject to the predicate adjective.

Example: The chances for peace looked hopeless.

The chances for peace <u>looked</u> hopeless.

13. Hiawatha felt unhappy because of the wars.
14. Peace was important to him.
15. Soon the Iroquois became famous for their friendship.
16. Their constitution was useful to other governments.
17. The Iroquois tribes were powerful around 1570.
18. Their power was great for more than one hundred years.

Writing Application: A Persuasive Letter

Imagine that you and a friend had a disagreement. Write a letter to convince your friend to agree with you. Use being verbs and linking verbs in your sentences.

For Extra Practice, see p. 179.

6 | Verb Tenses

The **tense** of a verb tells when the action or the state of being takes place. "Tense" comes from the Latin word for *time*. The words *present, past,* and *future* all refer to time.

The **present tense** tells that something is happening now.

PRESENT TENSE: The band arrives .

The dancers perform outdoors.

The gardens are beautiful.

The **past tense** tells that something has already happened. Usually the past tense of a verb is formed by adding *-ed*. The past tense of the verb *be* is *was* or *were*.

PAST TENSE: The audience applauded .

We stayed until the end.

The play was wonderful.

The **future tense** tells that something is going to happen. It is usually formed with the auxiliary verb *shall* or *will*.

FUTURE TENSE: Gail and Tim will be late.

We shall wait for them.

Our friends will save the seats for us.

Guided Practice Is the tense of each underlined verb present, past, or future?

Example: The Olympic Games <u>started</u> in ancient Greece. *past*

1. Today's Olympics <u>developed</u> from Greek festivals.
2. Until the seventy-seventh festival, the Games <u>lasted</u> only one day.
3. Now they <u>last</u> for two weeks.
4. Olympic athletes <u>are</u> heroes to the public.
5. Thousands of people <u>will attend</u> the next Olympic Games.
6. The International Olympic Committee <u>will decide</u> the location of the next games.

► The **tense** of a verb tells when the action or the state of being takes place.
► The **present tense** tells that something is happening now.
► The **past tense** tells that something has already happened.
► The **future tense** tells that something is going to happen.

Independent Practice

A. Write each verb. Then write the past tense and the future tense of the verb.

Example: push   *pushed   will (shall) push*

7. plant
8. subtract
9. rent
10. move
11. call

B. Write the form of the verb in parentheses that correctly completes each sentence.

Example: Last year my family ____ an old house.   (purchase)
purchased

12. At first we ____ on it a little at a time.   (work)
13. My parents ____ our attic last week.   (clean)
14. A few months from now, we ____ a back porch to the house.   (add)
15. Yesterday we ____ friends to an all-day painting party. (invite)
16. In six hours, we ____ seven rooms.   (paint)
17. Today we ____ a freshly painted house.   (own)
18. Tomorrow afternoon everyone ____ the windows and the screens.   (wash)

Writing Application: A Paragraph
Write a paragraph, describing a project that you once worked on or a chore that you do at home. Use verbs in the present, past, and future tenses correctly.

For Extra Practice, see p. 180.   **Verb Tenses   155**

7 | Principal Parts of Verbs

You have already learned about the present tense *(ask)*, the past tense *(asked)*, and the future tense *(will ask)*. Verbs have other tenses too. All the tenses of a verb come from four basic forms. These basic forms are the **principal parts** of the verb.

Principal Parts of Verbs			
Verb	Present participle	Past	Past participle
work	(is) working	worked	(has) worked
share	(is) sharing	shared	(has) shared
ride	(is) riding	rode	(has) ridden
know	(is) knowing	knew	(has) known

The present participle and the past participle are always used with an auxiliary verb.

Most verbs have past and past participle forms that are formed by adding *-d* or *-ed*. These verbs are called **regular verbs** because they follow this pattern. Notice in the chart that *work* and *share* are regular verbs.

The past and the past participle of some verbs are not formed by adding *-d* or *-ed*. These verbs are **irregular verbs**. In the chart, the verbs *ride* and *know* are irregular verbs.

Remember, when a regular verb ends with a consonant and *y,* change the *y* to *i* before adding *-ed*. When a regular one-syllable verb ends with a vowel and a consonant, double the consonant before adding *-ed*.

cry—cried   hurry—hurried   hop—hopped   fan—fanned

Guided Practice What are the present participle, the past, and the past participle of the following verbs?

Example: walk *(is) walking walked (has) walked*

1. hike   **2.** wait   **3.** drop   **4.** ride   **5.** know

▶ The **principal parts**, or basic forms, of a verb include the verb, the present participle, the past, and the past participle.
▶ When the past and the past participle of a verb are formed by adding *-d* or *-ed*, the verb is **regular**. When the past and the past participle are formed in some other way, the verb is **irregular**.

Independent Practice   Write the main verb in each sentence. Label it *regular* or *irregular*.

Example: People have watched birds for thousands of years.
  watched   **regular**

6. Many scientists studied the secret of flight.
7. No one had found the answer until 1903.
8. Orville and Wilbur Wright changed the world.
9. They built a flying machine.
10. In 1905 Wilbur kept his plane in the air for thirty-three minutes.
11. Five days later Wilbur flew in a complete circle.
12. In 1927 one man surprised the entire world.
13. He did something entirely new.
14. Charles A. Lindbergh completed the first solo airplane flight across the Atlantic Ocean.
15. He flew nonstop from New York City to Paris, France.
16. During the flight, Lindbergh met many challenges.
17. Severe storms lashed his small plane.
18. Again and again, he fought drowsiness.
19. Finally, after thirty-three hours and thirty minutes in the air, Lindbergh saw the Paris airfield.
20. He told his story in the book *The Spirit of St. Louis*.

Writing Application: Paragraphs

Write two or more paragraphs describing your first real or imaginary flight in an airplane. Reread your paragraphs. Underline each regular main verb once and each irregular main verb twice.

8 | More Irregular Verbs

You probably know the principal parts of most irregular verbs just from hearing them used. The best way to learn the principal parts that you do not know is to memorize them.

Principal Parts of Some Irregular Verbs

Verb	Present participle	Past	Past participle
be	(is) being	was	(has) been
blow	(is) blowing	blew	(has) blown
do	(is) doing	did	(has) done
drive	(is) driving	drove	(has) driven
fly	(is) flying	flew	(has) flown
freeze	(is) freezing	froze	(has) frozen
have	(is) having	had	(has) had
lend	(is) lending	lent	(has) lent
make	(is) making	made	(has) made
ring	(is) ringing	rang	(has) rung
see	(is) seeing	saw	(has) seen
speak	(is) speaking	spoke	(has) spoken
steal	(is) stealing	stole	(has) stolen
swim	(is) swimming	swam	(has) swum
take	(is) taking	took	(has) taken
tear	(is) tearing	tore	(has) torn
throw	(is) throwing	threw	(has) thrown
write	(is) writing	wrote	(has) written

Guided Practice Without looking back at the chart, give the principal parts of the following verbs.

Example: speak *speak (is) speaking spoke (has) spoken*

1. blow
2. ring
3. throw
4. tear
5. drive
6. write
7. take
8. steal
9. do
10. swim
11. lend
12. fly

▶ Many commonly used verbs are irregular. You need to memorize their principal parts.

Independent Practice

A. Write the present participle, the past, and the past participle of the following irregular verbs. Include the auxiliary verbs. Use your dictionary if you need help.

Example: eat   *(is) eating   ate   (has) eaten*

13. go   **15.** shrink   **17.** come   **19.** buy
14. know   **16.** ride   **18.** bring   **20.** think

B. Write the correct verb in parentheses for each sentence.

Example: Our art class had (did, done) a sculpture.   *done*

21. We (spoke, spoken) to another class about it.
22. Have you (took, taken) art classes?
23. A bus (drove, driven) us to a museum.
24. I had (wrote, written) about the paintings.

C. Complete each pair of sentences, using the past or the past participle form of the verb in parentheses.

Example: You may have ____ paintings by Grandma Moses.
              We ____ some at a museum.   (see)   *seen   saw*

25. Grandma Moses ____ her first oil painting at age sixty-seven. She had ____ her life as a farmer.   (begin)
26. Grandma Moses ____ pictures with charcoal as a child. She has ____ scenes from her childhood on a farm.   (draw)
27. She has ____ the art world by surprise. Grandma Moses never ____ an art lesson.   (take)
28. Grandma Moses ____ about her life and her painting. Scholars have ____ about her primitive art.   (write)

Writing Application: Comparison and Contrast
Write a paragraph about what you were like three years ago and what you are like now. Use the present participle, the past, and the past participle forms of verbs.

For Extra Practice, see p. 182.   **More Irregular Verbs   159**

9 | Subject-Verb Agreement

A verb and its subject must agree in number. Use a singular verb with a singular subject and a plural verb with a plural subject. A compound subject joined by *and* takes a plural verb.

SINGULAR: The boy calls .   PLURAL: The boys call .

The girl plays .   The boy and the girl play .

Singular verbs in the present tense usually end in *s* or *es*. However, when the singular subject is *I* or *you*, the singular verb does not end in *s* or *es*. Plural verbs in the present tense do not usually end in *s*.

SINGULAR: I laugh .   PLURAL: The girls run .

The verb *be* does not follow the usual rules.

Agreement with the Verb *be*

Subject	Verb	Sentence
I	am (present) was (past)	I am well today. I was sick yesterday.
he, she, it, and all singular nouns	is (present) was (past)	It is raining now. The cat is playful. She was hungry.
we, you, they, and all plural nouns	are (present) were (past)	We are cousins. You are friendly. They were teammates.

Guided Practice Choose the correct verb in parentheses.

Example: Horses and ponies (is, are) important to people. *are*

1. Many people (ride, rides) horses for pleasure.
2. Often a horse and a rider (become, becomes) good friends.
3. In many different jobs, a horse (work, works) hard.
4. Some farmers (plow, plows) their fields with horses.
5. Horses (is, are) helpful to ranchers.

- A subject and its verb must agree in number.
- Singular subjects take singular verbs, and plural subjects take plural verbs.
- If the parts of a compound subject are joined by *and*, use a plural verb.

Independent Practice Write the correct present tense form of the verb in parentheses to complete each sentence.

Example: Many types of horses ____ in the world. (live) *live*

6. Horses ____ different in size, color, strength, and speed. (be)
7. The largest horses ____ six feet tall. (stand)
8. A very large one ____ up to two thousand pounds. (weigh)
9. A pony ____ a horse under fifty-eight inches tall. (be)
10. The workhorse and the racehorse ____ special abilities. (have)
11. A pair of workhorses ____ thousands of pounds. (pull)
12. A racehorse ____ faster than thirty miles an hour. (run)
13. The coats of pintos ____ splashed with color. (be)
14. For this reason, people ____ them "paints." (call)
15. Often police officers ____ horses in their work. (ride)
16. Some popular performers ____ horses. (be)
17. Horses and ponies even ____ in movies. (act)
18. A worker on a ranch ____ a horse for ranch work. (need)
19. Ranchers ____ great distances on horseback. (cover)
20. Horses ____ the commands of the trainer. (follow)
21. A trained horse ____ every command. (obey)
22. Riders ____ commands through the reins. (give)
23. Horses ____ well to rewards. (respond)
24. A horse ____ good and bad treatment. (remember)
25. A good rider ____ a horse with patience. (treat)
26. These animals ____ people in many ways. (help)

Writing Application: Comparison and Contrast
Write a paragraph comparing and contrasting two of your favorite animals. Use some compound subjects joined by *and*. In your sentences, be sure that subjects and verbs agree.

For Extra Practice, see p. 183.   Subject-Verb Agreement   161

10 | More About Subject-Verb Agreement

You know that the verb in a sentence must agree with the subject. You have also learned that when the parts of a compound subject are joined by *and,* the verb is plural.

When *or, either . . . or,* or *neither . . . nor* is used to join the parts of a compound subject, the verb may be singular or plural. Use a plural verb if both parts of the subject are plural.

Books or magazines were always on the table.

Use a singular verb if both parts of the compound subject are singular. If one part is singular and one part is plural, make the verb agree with the subject that is closer to it.

Neither Jim nor Sally is ever without a good book.

Neither Ted nor his friends like mystery books.

Neither his friends nor Ted likes mystery books.

The verb in a sentence beginning with *here* or *there* must also agree with the subject. *Here* or *there* is never the subject of a sentence. To find the subject, ask, Who or what is here? or Who or what is there?

Here is the index . (What is here?)

There is Ms. Ryan . (Who is there?)

There are the card catalogs . (What is there?)

Guided Practice Which verb in parentheses is correct?

Example: Here (is, are) the school office and the library. *are*

1. Either this library or the city library (is, are) open.
2. There (is, are) the dictionaries.
3. Either books or magazines (is, are) excellent references.
4. Neither the atlas nor the dictionary (is, are) on the shelf.
5. Here (is, are) an atlas and a map.

Summing up

▶ If a compound subject is joined by *or*, *either . . . or*, or *neither . . . nor*, make the verb agree with the subject that is closer to it.
▶ In sentences beginning with *here* or *there*, first find the subject, and then make the verb agree with it.

Independent Practice Write the verb in parentheses that correctly completes each sentence.

Example: Here (is, are) many old cars.   *are*

6. There (was, were) no cars before the 1800s.
7. Either trains or horses (was, were) the means of transportation.
8. There (is, are) a model of the first car.
9. There (is, are) an old Model T and a Maxwell.
10. There (was, were) many Hudsons on the road in the early twentieth century.
11. Either the Model T or the Oakland (was, were) purchased by many people in 1908.
12. Either steam or electricity (was, were) used to power the early cars.
13. Neither steam cars nor electric cars (was, were) fast.
14. There (was, were) no trucks or buses at first.
15. Neither tolls nor a speed limit (was, were) in use.
16. Neither cars nor roads now (looks, look) like early ones.
17. Either my great-grandmother or my great-grandfather (remembers, remember) the Stanley Steamer.
18. Either horse-drawn carriages or buggies (was, were) popular before the invention of the car.
19. Now cars or buses (is, are) used for travel.
20. American cars or foreign cars (is, are) popular today.

Writing Application: A Description

Write a description of your favorite way of traveling. Begin some of your sentences with *here* and *there*. Include examples of *either . . . or* and *neither . . . nor* as conjunctions in compound subjects. Be sure to use verbs that agree in number with their subjects.

For Extra Practice, see p. 184.   **Subject-Verb Agreement   163**

11 | Contractions

A **contraction** is a word formed by combining two words and shortening one of them. An apostrophe takes the place of the letter or letters left out.

Sometimes the verb is shortened.

we're = we are   they've = they have   I'll = I will

Often a verb and *not* are combined. The word *not* is shortened. Most contractions with *not* are formed by using an apostrophe to replace the *o* in *not*.

Contractions Formed with *not*	
isn't (is not)	can't (cannot)
aren't (are not)	couldn't (could not)
wasn't (was not)	doesn't (does not)
weren't (were not)	hasn't (has not)
won't (will not)	haven't (have not)

Only the part of the contraction that is a verb is part of the verb phrase. The word *not* and the contracted form *n't* are never part of a verb phrase.

He's mixed the chemicals carefully. (verb phrase = has mixed)
Kenneth shouldn't add too much acid. (verb phrase = should add)

Guided Practice What words make up the contraction in each sentence? What words make up each verb phrase?

Example: I'm working with a group of scientists.
        I am   am working

1. They're studying the history of the earth.
2. They don't really know about the earth a million years ago.
3. They've already looked at the earth of the present.
4. Now they'll imagine the earth of the past.
5. We're thinking about the beginning of the earth.

▶ A **contraction** is the shortened form of two words. Dropped letters are replaced by an apostrophe.

▶ Make contractions with verbs or with the word *not*. The *n't* part of the contraction is not part of the verb phrase.

Independent Practice Write each contraction and verb phrase.

Example: They've often worked as a team. *they've   have worked*

6. The scientists haven't completed their project.
7. They're studying a damaged forest in Washington.
8. I've seen the nearby volcano.
9. It's thrown ash onto the trees of the forest.
10. Now the trees aren't looking very healthy.
11. One scientist hasn't taken samples of the soil.
12. Another one can't finish his research.
13. They're solving new problems as fast as possible.
14. Finally, they'll write a report about the project.
15. They shouldn't need too much more time.
16. They're making new discoveries every day.
17. They haven't solved every problem.
18. They don't really know enough yet.
19. They've already looked at samples of the ash.
20. They're studying the effect of ash on the trees.
21. I've read about their task in the newspaper.
22. We're all concerned about the forest.
23. It's been important for animals and other wildlife.
24. They've needed the forest to live.
25. We've needed the forest for lumber.
26. I'm waiting for the scientists' report.
27. They'll find a way to save the forest.
28. We'll need their help.

Writing Application: Creative Writing

Imagine that you are conducting scientific research. Write a story about your work. Use contractions in some of your sentences.

For Extra Practice, see p. 185.

12 | *sit, set; lie, lay; rise, raise*

Some verbs have related but different meanings. Three confusing pairs are *sit, set; lie, lay;* and *rise, raise.*

Verb	Definition	Sentence
sit	to rest in an upright position	I sit in the chair.
set	to put or place an object	I set down the cup.
lie	to rest or recline	I lie on the blanket.
lay	to put or place an object	I lay the book down.
rise	to get up or go up	We rise early.
raise	to move something up, to grow something, or to increase	They raise their hands. Farmers raise corn. Ed will raise his fee.

To decide which verb to use, ask yourself what the subject is doing. If the subject is placing an object somewhere, use *set* or *lay.* If the subject is resting, use *sit* or *lie.* To decide whether to use *rise* or *raise,* ask yourself, Raise what? If your answer names something, use *raise.* If the question has no answer, you should use *rise.*

Guided Practice Which word in parentheses correctly completes each sentence?

Example: (Set, Sit) the ball here.   *Set*

1. You may (set, sit) next to me.
2. He will (lie, lay) that board down here.
3. You can't (lie, lay) on that.
4. I (set, sit) the chairs here so that people can (set, sit).
5. Sarah (rises, raises) hens on a farm in Virginia.
6. She (rises, raises) early to feed the chickens.
7. The chickens come when Sarah (rises, raises) her hand.
8. Next year her family will (rise, raise) their prices.

▶ Use the verbs *sit* and *lie* to refer to a resting position.
▶ Use the verbs *set* and *lay* to mean "put an object somewhere."
▶ Use the verb *rise* to mean "get or go up."
▶ Use the verb *raise* to mean "move something up, grow something, or increase something."

Independent Practice

A. Write the correct word in parentheses for each sentence.

Example: I often (sit, set) by the kitchen window.   *sit*

9. A squirrel (lies, lays) on a mound of leaves.
10. Dad will help me (sit, set) its broken leg in a splint.
11. Now the squirrel (lies, lays) on a soft cushion.
12. I will (lie, lay) the cushion next to my bed tonight.
13. The squirrel will (lie, lay) beside my bed.
14. Soon we can (sit, set) the squirrel by the window.
15. Then I will (sit, set) next to the squirrel.
16. I will (lie, lay) fresh newspaper on the cushion.

B. Write the correct word in parentheses for each sentence.

Example: Tomorrow I will (rise, raise) at six o'clock.   *rise*

17. The sun will (rise, raise) before six.
18. I will (rise, raise) the window shade.
19. Do you think that the squirrel will (rise, raise) early too?
20. If you (rise, raise) your voice, you might scare it.
21. We can (rise, raise) the window to let the squirrel go.
22. The smells of breakfast (rise, raise) to greet me.
23. My brother (rises, raises) early to make breakfast.
24. Steam (rises, raises) from my bowl of hot oatmeal.
25. Local farmers (rise, raise) the oats for cereal.

Writing Application: Instructions

Pretend that you are directing a school play. Write a paragraph that tells the actors what to do. Use the verbs *sit, set, lie, lay, rise,* and *raise.* Use each verb at least once.

13 | *lend, borrow; let, leave; teach, learn*

May I borrow that?

I will lend it to you.

Here are three more verb pairs that are sometimes confused. *Lend* means "to give." *Borrow* means "to take."

Will you lend me your boots? (Will you give them?)

May I borrow them for a hike? (May I take them?)

Let and *leave* have different meanings too. The verb *let* means "to permit." The verb *leave* means "to go away" or "to allow to remain in one place."

My brothers let me play with them. (They permit.)

Tomorrow we leave for a camping trip. (We go away.)

I will leave my camera in the tent. (It will remain.)

The third confusing pair is *teach* and *learn*. *Teach* means "to give instruction." *Learn* means "to get instruction."

Alice will teach tennis. (She will instruct.)

Babies learn very fast. (They receive instruction.)

Guided Practice Which word in parentheses correctly completes each sentence?

Example: Did I (let, leave) my umbrella at your house? *leave*

1. Please (leave, let) me go outside.
2. We (let, leave) for the supermarket this afternoon.
3. (Let, Leave) the rain stop first.
4. Please (lend, borrow) me your umbrella.
5. Please return it if you (lend, borrow) it.
6. Shari can (teach, learn) how to grass ski this weekend.
7. Her uncle will (teach, learn) her in his back yard.
8. Next summer she will (teach, learn) her brother.
9. He will (teach, learn) to snow ski at a resort.
10. Shari will (teach, learn) to snow ski next winter.

> ▸ *Borrow* means "to take." *Lend* means "to give."
> ▸ *Let* means "to permit." *Leave* means "to go away."
> ▸ *Teach* means "to give instruction." *Learn* means "to receive instruction."

Independent Practice

A. Write the verb *borrow, lend, let,* or *leave* to complete each sentence.

Example: Do you remember the flashlight you wanted to _____ from me? *borrow*

11. Yes, you were going to _____ it to me, and I was going to _____ your hedge clipper too.
12. Could you _____ me use it for a few days?
13. I promise not to _____ it out in the rain.
14. My sister-in-law and brother _____ my snowblower every week in the winter.
15. Should they _____ it so often?
16. Why shouldn't I _____ it to them?
17. They might not _____ you have it back for a long time.
18. Will you _____ me guess who else does the same thing?
19. I will _____ the flashlight on this table for you.

B. Write the verb *teach* or *learn* to complete each sentence.

Example: I will _____ you about plants. *teach*

20. Will you _____ me about poison ivy?
21. First, you must _____ to notice plants with three leaves.
22. I will _____ you which ones are dangerous.
23. Then you can _____ other people what you know.
24. Did you _____ about the shiny stem too?
25. If you catch poison ivy, you will _____ the hard way.

Writing Application: A Description

Write a paragraph about your classroom activities. Use the verbs *lend, borrow, let, leave, teach,* and *learn.* Use each verb at least once.

For Extra Practice, see p. 187.
   Easily-Confused Verb Pairs   169

Grammar-Writing Connection

Using Compound Subjects in Writing

One way to make your sentences more interesting and easier to understand is to eliminate unnecessary words. You can often do this by combining two simple sentences into one sentence with a compound subject. It is important, however, to make the verb agree with the new subject.

Water **is** used by plants.
Air **is** used by plants.
> Water and air **are** used by plants.

You have learned that the conjunctions *either . . . or* and *neither . . . nor* can join two nouns to form a compound subject. One part of the compound subject can be singular and one part can be plural. In these cases the verb agrees with the subject that is closer to it.

Soil **is** not used by plants to make food.
Roots **are** not used by plants to make food.
Neither roots nor soil **is** used by plants to make food.
Neither soil nor roots **are** used by plants to make food.

Revising Sentences

Combine each pair of sentences into one sentence with a compound subject. Write the new sentence, using the conjunction in parentheses. Be sure that the subject and the verb agree.

1. The leaves contain chlorophyll. The stem contains chlorophyll.   (and)
2. Chlorophyll helps green plants make food. Sunlight helps green plants make food.   (and)
3. Yeast is not able to make food. Mushrooms are not able to make food. (neither . . . nor)
4. Human beings rely on plants for food. Many animals rely on plants for food.   (and)

Creative Writing

Is this what you see when you gaze at a starlit summer sky? Vincent van Gogh painted what he felt, not just what he saw.

- How does van Gogh create a sense of energy in this painting?
- Do you think van Gogh was more interested in painting the buildings, or the landscape and the sky? Explain.

The Starry Night (1889), Vincent van Gogh
Museum of Modern Art, Lillie P. Bliss Bequest

Activities

1. **Write a poem.** Imagine that you have slipped outside on a warm, clear summer night long after everyone else has gone to bed. What thoughts and feelings do you have as you look up at the stars? Write a poem that describes your experience.
2. **Describe the painting.** Suppose that you wanted to describe *The Starry Night* to a friend who has never seen it. Write a description, explaining what it looks like and how it makes you feel.

Check-up: Unit 5

Action Verbs *(p. 144)* Write the action verb in each sentence.

1. I visited a computer science center.
2. We saw a room full of terminals.
3. We heard computer voices.
4. A computer asked us questions.
5. We wrote computer programs.

Main Verbs and Auxiliaries *(p. 145)* Write the verb phrase in each sentence. Underline the auxiliary verbs once and the main verbs twice.

6. Don Quixote had read many tales.
7. He could ignore warnings.
8. He did consider himself brave.
9. His old horse had been given a special name.
10. The knight and his horse would conquer giants.

Direct Objects *(p. 148)* Write the action verb and the direct object in each sentence.

11. Carla requested information from the National Park Service.
12. She received maps and booklets.
13. Carlsbad Caverns covers many miles.
14. They have three underground levels.
15. Mammoth Cave has many visitors.
16. Luray Caverns in Virginia contains many colorful columns.
17. You also see colors in Wind Cave.
18. Carla read the details with interest.

Transitive and Intransitive Verbs *(p. 150)* Write each verb. Then label it *transitive* or *intransitive*.

19. Jazz began in New Orleans.
20. Jazz musicians played by ear.
21. They played blues and spirituals.
22. Many musicians put their hearts into their music.
23. They had swing rhythm.
24. They invented new sounds.
25. People danced to great jazz bands.
26. The great Louis Armstrong was the king of jazz.

Being Verbs and Linking Verbs *(p. 152)* Write each linking verb and the predicate noun or the predicate adjective.

27. Ann is a newspaper carrier.
28. She feels proud of her job.
29. Her route is Main Street.
30. The blocks are hilly.
31. The papers become heavy.

Verb Tenses *(p. 154)* Write the correct form of the verb in parentheses.

32. Last week Maggie ___ her first trophy in the rodeo. (earn)
33. Tomorrow her brother ___ in bull riding. (compete)
34. Next weekend her family ___ to another rodeo. (travel)
35. Both Maggie and her brother ___ hard all last year. (practice)
36. Winning ___ practice. (take)

Principal Parts of Verbs *(p. 156)*
Write the verb in each sentence.
Then label it *regular* or *irregular*.

37. Aaron did many things.
38. He flew in an airplane.
39. He rode in a helicopter.
40. He built many toy cars.
41. His friends teased him.
42. He laughed with them.
43. Aaron became famous.

More Irregular Verbs *(p. 158)*
(44–50) Write the past participle of each irregular verb in Exercises 37–43 above.

Subject-Verb Agreement *(p. 160)*
Write the verb in parentheses that agrees with the subject in each sentence.

51. Charlotte and her brother (take, takes) swimming lessons.
52. Two lifeguards (watch, watches) every class.
53. Charlotte (was, were) in a swimming meet last week.
54. The competition (was, were) very strong.
55. Charlotte (is, are) a good swimmer.
56. She and her brother (compete, competes) in swimming meets.
57. They (enjoy, enjoys) team races.
58. Usually four swimmers (race, races) on each team.
59. Often Charlotte's team (win, wins) the meet.
60. Both Charlotte and her brother (swim, swims) for fun too.

Subject-Verb Agreement *(p. 162)*
Write the verb in parentheses that correctly completes each sentence.

61. Neither Ida nor they (rides, ride).
62. Here (is, are) the horses.
63. Either Al or Jo (ski, skis).
64. There (is, are) Al's other pole.
65. Either they or she (skate, skates).

Contractions *(p. 164)* Write each contraction. Then write the verb phrase.

66. They've removed the bottles.
67. We're mixing the chemicals.
68. Shouldn't we fill this test tube?
69. I'd added too much acid.
70. Haven't you finished yet?

sit, set; lie, lay; rise, raise *(p. 166)*
Write the word in parentheses that is correct in each sentence.

71. I (set, sit) in the middle row.
72. Suddenly a man (raises, rises).
73. (Lay, Lie) your package here.
74. He (sits, sets) the box down.
75. Let's (rise, raise) the window.
76. Let your dog (lie, lay) there.

lend, borrow; let, leave; teach, learn *(p. 168)* Write the word in parentheses that completes each sentence correctly.

77. He will (teach, learn) the class.
78. Please (let, leave) me sit here.
79. Libraries (lend, borrow) books.
80. May I (lend, borrow) your globe?
81. Shall we (let, leave) for home now?
82. How did you (teach, learn) to sew?

Enrichment

Using Verbs

Campaign Speech

You are running for president of your class. You were vice president before and did a good job. Write a campaign speech, telling what you have done and what you will do if elected. Use auxiliary verbs in your speech.

Extra! Think up a slogan, using an auxiliary verb, and design a campaign poster.

Health Acrostic

In an **acrostic,** the first letters of each line spell out a name or a message. Write your name *down* one side of your paper. Beside each letter, write an action verb beginning with that letter. Use verbs telling what you can do to keep healthy. Add words to complete each phrase. Underline each verb.

To stay healthy, I should

<u>B</u>rush my teeth.
<u>R</u>est when I feel tired.
<u>A</u>dd less salt to my food.
<u>D</u>o some exercise daily.

Math in Action

Chart your math success. Make three columns on your paper: *Present, Past,* and *Future.* Under *Present,* list action verbs for math skills you use now. Under *Past,* write past tense verbs for skills you mastered earlier. Then write future tense verbs for skills you will continue to use. Using verbs from the chart,

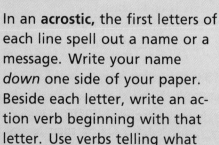

PRESENT	PAST	FUTURE
add	added	will add
measure		will measure
count	counted	
		will prove

write a paragraph about your present, past, and future success in math.

Extra Practice: Unit 5

1 | Action Verbs (p. 144)

● Write an action verb from the Word Box to complete each sentence. Use each verb only once.

Example: My father _____ as a scientist. *works*

1. He _____ starfish and other sea animals.
2. Dad _____ me a lot about starfish.
3. Scientists _____ about many different kinds.
4. They have _____ starfish of many colors.
5. Starfish _____ in oceans.
6. They _____ many arms covered with tiny feet.
7. They _____ on their feet along the ocean floor.
8. Starfish _____ clams, oysters, and other animals.

know
move
have
works
taught
studies
eat
found
live

▲ Write the action verb in each sentence.

Example: My family took a vacation. *took*

9. We traveled down the coast of Oregon.
10. We stopped at windy beaches.
11. Big waves crashed onto the shore.
12. Huge rocks stood in the surf.
13. We explored the shore.
14. I found a big orange starfish.
15. We also discovered unusual plants.

■ Complete each sentence, adding an action verb that makes sense.

Example: A few kinds of jellyfish _____ people. *sting*

16. The people _____ the jellyfish by accident.
17. You can _____ jellyfish in every ocean in the world.
18. They _____ along with the ocean currents.
19. They _____ tiny plants.
20. Most jellyfish _____ no color.
21. I _____ a jellyfish at a museum.
22. Have you ever _____ a jellyfish?

● ▲ ■ **Three levels of practice**   175

2 | Main Verbs and Auxiliaries (p. 145)

● Write the verb phrase in each sentence. Underline the main verb in each phrase.

Example: Had Lewis and Clark explored all the new land?
Had explored

1. They had taken one trip.
2. Did they see it all?
3. Another man, Pike, was planning a trip.
4. Was he looking for fame?
5. He did find a new mountain.
6. It was named Pikes Peak in his honor.
7. Pike and his men were taken prisoner.
8. They did return home later with new information.

▲ Write the verb phrase in each sentence. Underline the auxiliary verbs once and the main verbs twice.

Example: The new lands were being filled with settlers.
were being filled

9. Pioneers were traveling in wagons.
10. They had formed wagon trains for safety.
11. Did the travelers face many hardships?
12. A scout would ride ahead of the wagon train.
13. A scout was always looking for possible dangers.
14. Many families were going to California.
15. Did some people search for gold?
16. Many miners had found gold in the mountains.

■ Use each verb phrase in a sentence. Include at least one question. You do not need to keep the parts of the phrase together.

Example: could have explored
Could we have explored the woods behind your home?

17. might have wanted	21. had traveled
18. would call	22. would have carried
19. did build	23. may have felt
20. must have scared	24. might have seen

3 | Direct Objects (p. 148)

● Write a direct object from the Word Box to complete each sentence. Make sure your choice makes sense.

Example: This morning I made my ____.
    breakfast

Word Box
dishes
milk
breakfast
bread
cereal
sandwich
lunch
oranges

1. First, I put dry ____ into a bowl.
2. Then I poured ____ over it.
3. Later I toasted some ____.
4. I also squeezed ____ for juice.
5. I washed the ____ after breakfast.
6. Finally, I packed my ____.
7. I always take a ____ to eat.

▲ Write the direct object in each sentence. If the direct object is compound, write *compound*. Do not include the conjunction.

Example: The Polos showed jewels and riches from Asia.
    *jewels   riches   **compound***

8. In 1295 Marco Polo gave a large party.
9. He and his father and his uncle invited many friends.
10. A man wrote a book about Marco Polo's travels.
11. In the book, he described China, Persia, and Java.
12. Few people had seen these places.
13. Marco Polo brought stories and maps back from his travels to these distant lands.
14. Many other explorers admired Marco Polo.
15. Christopher Columbus carried a book about Marco Polo with him on his travels.

■ For each verb listed below, write a sentence that includes the verb and a direct object. Write at least two sentences that have compound direct objects.

Example: discovered *I discovered a torn map in my backpack.*

16. dug	**19.** drew	**22.** followed
17. bought	**20.** opened	**23.** whispered
18. hid	**21.** counted	**24.** waited

4 | Transitive and Intransitive Verbs (p. 150)

● Copy the underlined verb. Label it *transitive* or *intransitive*.

Example: Tom <u>plays</u>   *plays*   **intransitive**

1. Tom <u>plays</u> basketball.
2. He <u>dribbles</u> skillfully.
3. He <u>dribbles</u> the ball.
4. He <u>shoots</u> the ball from both sides.
5. Sometimes he <u>misses</u> the basket.
6. Sometimes he <u>misses</u>.
7. He <u>waves</u> to the crowd.
8. He <u>waves</u> his arms.

▲ Write the verbs. Label them *transitive* or *intransitive*.

Example: June finished the race. *finished* **transitive**

9. She was proud.
10. She drank thirstily.
11. She drank water.
12. Her mother's eyes sparkled.
13. The coach pinned a ribbon on her.
14. June hugged her mother.
15. Her mother smiled.
16. Everyone cheered.
17. Everyone cheered loudly for her.

■ Write an ending to complete each sentence. Use a transitive or intransitive verb as shown in parentheses. Write the sentences.

Example: Before the game, the crowd _____.   (transitive)
        Before the game, the crowd bought tickets.

18. Soon the teams _____.   (intransitive)
19. The referee _____.   (transitive) called a foul
20. The cheerleaders _____.   (intransitive)
21. Mrs. Lewis _____.   (transitive)
22. At half time, the band _____.   (intransitive)
23. Outside the stadium, cars _____.   (transitive)
24. No one inside the stadium _____.   (intransitive)

5 | Being Verbs and Linking Verbs (p. 152)

● Write the linking verb in each sentence.

Example: A checkerboard is black and red.   *is*

1. The game of checkers is very old.
2. Checkers was a favorite game in England in the 1700s.
3. Two good players were William Payne and Andrew Anderson.
4. Their advice is still practical today.
5. The game of checkers appears easy.
6. Strategies are important, however.
7. Even children feel excited about this game.

▲ Copy each sentence. Underline the linking verb. Draw an arrow from the simple subject to the predicate noun or the predicate adjective.

Example: The kite exhibit at the science museum is wonderful.

The kite exhibit at the science museum is wonderful.

8. Kites became popular hundreds of years ago.
9. The Chinese were responsible for the first kites.
10. Those kites looked different from today's kites.
11. They were large leaves with twisted vines.
12. In contrast, modern kites seem fantastic.
13. Kites also have been helpful to weather forecasters.

■ Write the linking verb. Then write the predicate noun or the predicate adjective, and label it.

Example: In 1932 a man named Charles Darrow was unemployed.
    was   unemployed—predicate adjective

14. He became an inventor.
15. Mr. Darrow felt very good about one of his inventions.
16. It was a game about the streets in Atlantic City.
17. Mr. Darrow's friends were eager for the game.
18. It was hard for him to meet the demand.
19. Several toy companies were unwilling to make it.
20. Would Darrow's game be a failure forever?

6 | Verb Tenses (p. 154)

● Label each underlined verb *present*, *past*, or *future*.

Example: Rosa <u>entered</u> a four-mile race. *past*

1. She <u>will race</u> on Saturday.
2. First, Rosa <u>breathed</u> deeply.
3. She <u>stretches</u> her legs.
4. Rosa <u>chooses</u> her lightest running shoes.
5. Heavy shoes <u>will slow</u> her down.
6. The runners all <u>start</u> together.
7. Rosa <u>ran</u> quickly.

▲ Change the tense of each underlined verb to the tense named in parentheses.

Example: The house <u>will need</u> a foundation. (past) *needed*

8. Someone <u>arrived</u> to dig the basement. (future)
9. Then large trucks <u>carried</u> the wet concrete. (present)
10. Wet concrete <u>will fill</u> the empty forms. (present)
11. Workers <u>smooth</u> the top of the concrete. (future)
12. The concrete <u>dries</u> for days. (future)
13. Finally, the workers <u>remove</u> the wooden forms. (past)
14. The carpenter <u>will build</u> the first floor. (past)
15. The carpenters <u>will complete</u> the house in four months. (past)
16. The Goldberg family <u>lived</u> in the house. (present)

■ Write verbs to complete the following sentences. Write each verb in the tense named in parentheses.

Example: Ken ____ a secret message. (past) *discovered*

17. Ken ____ the message in a hollow tree. (past)
18. Later Ken ____ to the library. (future)
19. He ____ books on codes and symbols. (future)
20. Ken and Alice ____ their own message in code. (present)
21. They ____ a map too. (future)
22. Alice ____ a plan that Ken ____. (present, present)
23. They ____ clues where people ____ them. (present, future)
24. They ____ the message and map, but they ____. (past, past)

7 | Principal Parts of Verbs (p. 156)

● Write the present participle, the past, and the past participle forms of the following regular verbs. Be sure to include the auxiliary verbs.

Example: try *(is) trying tried (has) tried*

1. open
2. taste
3. dance
4. ask
5. answer
6. cry
7. skip
8. bury
9. hope
10. hop
11. laugh
12. worry
13. want
14. like

▲ Write the verb in each sentence. Label each verb *regular* or *irregular*.

Example: Last summer my family drove to Washington, D.C.
          *drove **irregular***

15. We visited the National Air and Space Museum.
16. We saw both old and new aircraft.
17. The Wright brothers' plane surprised me.
18. It looked like a large model plane.
19. In school I had written about a trip to the moon.
20. Here I crawled inside an Apollo lunar module.
21. The huge Saturn rocket engines amazed me.
22. I felt so tiny beside them.

■ Write the correct form of the verb in parentheses to complete each sentence.

Example: Many scientists have ____ to study birds. (choose)
          chosen

23. Years ago a group ____ to study the Arctic tern. (choose)
24. These birds can ____ thousands of miles a year. (fly)
25. Last fall one bird's trip ____ in Canada. (begin)
26. In a few weeks, the bird had ____ thousands of miles. (fly)
27. A trip that had ____ in Canada ended in Antarctica. (begin)
28. The bird ____ twenty thousand miles in one year. (fly)

8 | More Irregular Verbs (p. 158)

● Write the basic verb form of each underlined verb. Use your dictionary if you need help.

Example: Luis <u>had chosen</u> a science project.   *choose*

1. He <u>drew</u> a poster about polar bears.
2. The polar bears <u>swam</u> in the Arctic Ocean.
3. Luis <u>took</u> two hours to draw the poster.
4. He <u>had written</u> many facts about polar bears.
5. Mr. Kraft, his teacher, <u>spoke</u> to Luis later.
6. He <u>had lent</u> Luis a book about bears.
7. Luis <u>had done</u> an interesting project.
8. He <u>had written</u> a thorough report.
9. Luis <u>made</u> a cover for his report.

▲ Write the correct verb form in parentheses to complete each sentence.

Example: The library (lend, lent) Beth an art book.   *lent*

10. Beth (brought, bringed) the book home.
11. She (know, knew) the picture of the smiling woman.
12. Beth had (saw, seen) many pictures of the Mona Lisa.
13. An artist named Leonardo da Vinci had (did, done) it.
14. The book (gave, given) Beth other details about him.
15. She had (knew, known) about his handwriting.
16. Leonardo had (wrote, written) from right to left.
17. The letters and words all (went, gone) backwards.
18. Leonardo had (make, made) many drawings of plants and animals.
19. He had (drew, drawn) a flying machine.

■ Write a sentence using the present participle, the past, or the past participle form of each verb below. Label the verb form.

Example: go *Jim had gone yesterday.*   **past participle**

20. begin	23. throw	26. come
21. drink	24. stand	27. read
22. bite	25. build	28. swim

9 | Subject-Verb Agreement (p. 160)

● Write the verb that is correct in each sentence.

Example: The first Morgan (were, was) named for its owner. *was*

1. Trail riders (enjoy, enjoys) Morgans as pleasure horses.
2. A Morgan's sleek coat (look, looks) dark in color.
3. Most Morgans (have, has) few white marks.
4. Their thick manes and tails (flows, flow) in the wind.
5. This rather small horse (have, has) special abilities.
6. It (are, is) known for both strength and speed.
7. It (pull, pulls) a plow or buggy with its strong legs.

▲ Write the correct form of the verb for each sentence.

Example: Today, quarter horses ____ popular. (be) *are*

8. This gentle horse still ____ a good family pet. (make)
9. Quarter horses ____ used in races at rodeos. (be)
10. Each race ____ a quarter of a mile long. (be)
11. Workers and ranchers ____ quarter horses on the range. (ride)
12. This strong, sturdy horse ____ cattle well. (herd)
13. It ____ fast over short distances. (run)
14. The horse also ____ very quickly. (turn)
15. Quarter horses ____ these skills in rodeos. (display)

■ Choose a present tense verb to complete each sentence. Write the sentences.

Example: The students ____ horses around the ring.
The students ride horses around the ring.

16. Each rider ____ the speed and the direction of the horse.
17. The students ____ the reins in the correct way.
18. Each rider's voice ____ signals to the horse.
19. The person's legs and hands ____ the horse too.
20. The horse and the rider ____ together.
21. First, the horse ____ at a slow pace.
22. Then it ____ a bit faster.
23. All the riders ____ their new skills.
24. Each horse ____ the commands of the rider.

10 | More About Subject-Verb Agreement (p. 162)

● Write the verb in parentheses that is correct in each sentence.

Example: Neither Julio nor Dale (like, likes) mystery books.   *likes*

1. Julio or Dale (is, are) fond of *The Wizard of Oz*.
2. Here (is, are) a little girl and her dog.
3. There (is, are) strange people and animals.
4. A tin man or a lion (meet, meets) Dorothy.
5. Neither the lion nor the straw man (is, are) very happy.
6. Either her friends or Dorothy (talk, talks) to the wizard.
7. There (go, goes) the wizard in a balloon.
8. Dorothy or her friends (get, gets) what they want.

▲ Write a present tense verb to complete each sentence.

Example: Either Holly or Ted ____ golden hamsters.   *has*

9. There ____ the hamsters in the living room.
10. Either Holly or Ted ____ the hamsters.
11. There ____ the sticks for the hamsters to chew.
12. Either hamster ____ at night.
13. Holly or Ted ____ the hamsters out of their cages.
14. Neither Holly nor Ted ____ them.
15. Hamsters or gerbils ____ easily in a city.
16. Here ____ Holly's hamster.
17. Either Holly or her parents ____ the hamster's cage.

■ Write sentences using each group of words below. Be sure that the verb in each sentence agrees with the subject.

Example: Roller skates or bicycles ____.
    Roller skates or bicycles make wonderful gifts.

18. Either skates or a bike ____.
19. There are ____.
20. Here is ____.
21. Either one person or several people ____.
22. There is ____.
23. Neither my parents nor I ____.
24. Bikes, skates, or even skateboards ____.
25. Here are ____.

11 | Contractions (p. 164)

● Write the contraction in each sentence.

Example: Don't you know the story about Isaac Newton?   *Don't*

1. Didn't an apple fall on his head?
2. That's the way he discovered gravity.
3. He'd also studied sunlight.
4. It's made of the colors of the rainbow.
5. I'll prove it to you.
6. Haven't I shown you my prism?
7. It's hanging in a sunny window.
8. On the wall we'll see a beam of sunlight.
9. Like a rainbow, it's a pattern of colors.

▲ Write each contraction. Then write the verb or verb phrase.

Example: Before 1758, people didn't understand comets.
　　　　　didn't   did understand

10. They'd feared comets for centuries.
11. Explanations for comets weren't based on facts.
12. Edmund Halley wasn't satisfied with the explanations.
13. He'd asked questions about the comet of 1682.
14. Weren't there old records of a similar comet?
15. Didn't they appear every seventy-five years?
16. Couldn't one comet travel around the sun?
17. Hadn't he predicted the return of the comet in 1758?
18. In fact, it's returned about every seventy-five years.
19. It's named Halley's Comet in his honor.

■ Write a contraction for the underlined words. If the sentence contains a verb phrase, write the verb phrase.

Example: I <u>have not</u> finished my report.   *haven't   have finished*

20. <u>It is</u> about a recent discovery by some scientists.
21. <u>They had</u> dived eight thousand feet underwater.
22. That far below the surface, <u>there is</u> no sunlight.
23. On the ocean floor, <u>they have</u> found hot springs.
24. They <u>did not</u> expect plants or animals down there.
25. <u>I have</u> read about the unusual creatures.

● ▲ ■ **Three levels of practice   185**

12 | *sit, set; lie, lay; rise, raise* (p. 166)

● Write the correct present tense verb for each sentence.

Example: When we go hiking, we (rise, raise) early.   *rise*

1. We never (lie, lay) in bed beyond five o'clock.
2. The night before, we (sit, set) our packs by the door.
3. We (lie, lay) our boots and heavy socks there too.
4. We (sit, set) down to plan each hike.
5. We (rise, raise) our hands to ask questions.
6. We hike for two hours before we (sit, set) down for lunch.
7. Tired hikers (lie, lay) on the grass and rest.
8. Let's (rise, raise) the number of hikes we take.

▲ If the underlined word in each sentence is correct, write *correct*. If it is incorrect, write the word that should replace it. Use the words *sit, set; lie, lay;* and *rise, raise*.

Example: Your dog can <u>lay</u> on the blanket.   *lie*

9. Let's <u>set</u> on a blanket and watch the football game.
10. <u>Set</u> the picnic basket over here.
11. Before the game, a student will <u>rise</u> the flag.
12. Will Tom play, or will he <u>sit</u> on the bench?
13. The referee will <u>set</u> the ball on the field.
14. An injured player <u>lies</u> on the field.
15. He will <u>raise</u> from the field and play now.
16. I think he should <u>set</u> down and rest for a while.

■ Answer each question by writing a complete sentence containing one of the words in parentheses. You may change the tense of the word you choose.

Example: Where is your dog?   (sit, set)
    Butch is sitting on the couch.

17. I can't hear John. What should he do?   (rise, raise)
18. Where did you put the flashlight?   (sit, set)
19. What crops does that farmer grow?   (rise, raise)
20. I am very tired. What should I do?   (lie, lay)
21. What seats should we take in the theater?   (sit, set)
22. At what time will you get up tomorrow?   (rise, raise)

13 | *lend, borrow; let, leave; teach, learn* (p. 168)

● Write the correct word to complete each sentence.

Example: Anyone can (teach, learn) to type.   *learn*

1. (Let, Leave) me show you how.
2. (Lend, Borrow) me your chair a moment.
3. Do not allow your eyes to (let, leave) the page.
4. Do not (let, leave) one finger strike two keys.
5. You can (lend, borrow) Dion's typewriter.
6. This book can (teach, learn) you more than I can.
7. Please turn off the lights when you (let, leave).
8. The class will (teach, learn) how to fix mistakes.
9. The teacher will (lend, borrow) any student a dictionary.

▲ If the underlined word in each sentence is correct, write *correct*. If it is incorrect, write the word that should replace it.

Example: Mr. Lopez will <u>learn</u> us typing.   *teach*

10. The school will <u>borrow</u> typewriters from a store.
11. My father will <u>leave</u> me stay after school.
12. We will <u>learn</u> touch typing.
13. A local business will <u>lend</u> us typewriters.
14. The people might <u>leave</u> us try computer keyboards.
15. I wish someone would <u>borrow</u> me one.
16. All students can <u>learn</u> to use keyboards.
17. We must <u>leave</u> the keyboards here.

■ Use one phrase from each pair in a written sentence. You do not have to keep the phrase together.

Example: lend a red sweater; borrow a red sweater
  Please lend me a red sweater until tomorrow.

18. borrow a math book; lend a math book
19. let three people; leave three people
20. leave the players; let the players
21. teach me to; learn how to
22. learn a new skill; teach a new skill
23. let her shaggy dog; leave her shaggy dog
24. borrow your radio; lend your radio

Literature and Writing

There is a mighty mountain in the northlands. It rises from the placid waters of a beautiful lake and its summit catches the glint of the sun. On all sides but one are other towering peaks, but none rivals the mighty mountain, for here dwells the great white stag whom no hunter can kill.

Arthur C. Parker
from *The Ghost of the Great White Stag*

Story

Getting Ready Many stories have been created in the midst of danger. People trapped in caves and mines or adrift in lifeboats have often passed the long hours and maintained their courage by telling each other stories. If you were trapped with two friends, what story would you tell? Would your story be funny or frightening? Would it take place in the city or in the mountains? Start thinking of story ideas because in this unit you will write your own story.

ACTIVITIES

Listening　Listen as the story beginning on the opposite page is read. The writer described the setting of the story very carefully. Imagine yourself in that place. What is all around you?

Speaking　Look at the picture. As a class make a list of characters—animal or human—that might live here. Save the list for story ideas.

Writing 　What do you think will happen later in the story that begins on the opposite page? Write your ideas in your journal.

LITERATURE

The Wolf Cry

By Lew Sarett

The Arctic moon hangs overhead;
The wide, white silence lies below.
A starveling pine stands lone and gaunt,
Black-penciled on the snow.

Weird as the moan of sobbing winds,
A lone, long call floats up from the trail;
And the naked soul of the frozen North
Trembles in that wail.

Think and Discuss

1. Does the poem describe a daytime or a nighttime scene?

2. A poet uses **imagery** to appeal to our senses of sight, smell, sound, taste, or touch. Imagery creates mental pictures or images for the reader. What pictures do you imagine when you read the poem? What two colors would you use if you were to paint a picture of this poem? Explain your choice.

3. In the line "Weird as the moan of sobbing winds," the poet compares the sound of the wind to crying. Giving human traits to things or animals is called **personification**. What other words could you use to describe the wind in human terms?

What decision did Noni come to? Why couldn't he go through with it?

Two Were Left

By Hugh B. Cave

On the third night of hunger, Noni thought of the dog. Nothing of flesh and blood lived upon the floating ice island except those two.

In the breakup, Noni had lost his sled, his food, his furs, even his knife. He had saved only Nimuk, his great devoted husky. And now the two, marooned on the ice, eyed each other warily—each keeping his distance.

Noni's love for Nimuk was real—as real as hunger and cold nights and the gnawing pain of his injured leg. But the men of his village killed their dogs when food was scarce, didn't they? And without thinking twice about it.

And Nimuk, he told himself, when hungry enough would seek food. "One of us will soon be eating the other," Noni thought. "So . . ."

He could not kill the dog with his bare hands. Nimuk was powerful and much fresher than he. A weapon, then, was needed.

Removing his mittens, he unstrapped the braces from his leg. When he had hurt his leg a few weeks before, he had made the brace from bits of harness and two thin strips of iron.

Kneeling now, he wedged one of the iron strips into a crack in the ice and began to rub the other against it with firm, slow strokes.

Nimuk watched him, and it seemed to Noni that the dog's eyes glowed more brightly.

He worked on, trying not to remember why. The slab of iron had an edge now. It had begun to take shape. Daylight found his task completed.

Noni pulled the finished knife from the ice and thumbed its edge. The sun's glare, reflected from it, stabbed at his eyes and momentarily blinded him.

Noni steeled himself.

"Here, Nimuk!" he called softly.

The dog suspiciously watched him.

"Come here," Noni called.

Nimuk came closer. Noni read fear in the animal's gaze. He read hunger and suffering in the dog's labored breathing and awkward crouch. His heart wept. He hated himself and fought against it.

Closer Nimuk came, aware of his intentions. Now Noni felt a thickening in his throat. He saw the dog's eyes, and they were wells of suffering.

Now! Now was the time to strike!

A great sob shook Noni's kneeling body. He cursed the knife. He swayed blindly, flung the weapon far from him. With empty hands outstretched, he stumbled toward the dog and fell.

The dog growled as he circled the boy's body. And now Noni was sick with fear.

In flinging away the knife, he had left himself defenseless. He was too weak to crawl after it now. He was at Nimuk's mercy, and Nimuk was hungry.

The dog had circled him and was creeping up from behind. Noni heard the rattle in the savage throat.

He shut his eyes, praying that the attack might be swift. He felt the dog's feet against his leg, the hot rush of Nimuk's breath against his neck. A scream gathered in the boy's throat.

Then he felt the dog's hot tongue licking his face.

Noni's eyes opened. Crying softly, he thrust out an arm and drew the dog's head down against his own. . . .

The plane came out of the south an hour later. Its pilot, a young man of the coast patrol, looked down and saw the large floating iceberg. And he saw something flashing.

It was the sun gleaming on something shiny, which moved. His curiosity aroused, the pilot banked his ship and descended. Now he saw, in the shadow of the peak of ice, a dark, still shape that appeared to be human. Or were there two shapes?

He set his ship down in a water lane and investigated. There were two shapes, boy and dog. The boy was unconscious but alive. The dog whined feebly but was too weak to move. The gleaming object which had trapped the pilot's attention was a crude knife, stuck point first into the ice a little distance away, and quivering in the wind.

Think and Discuss

1. What decision would the men of Noni's village have made in his place?

2. Why did Noni fling the knife away?

3. **Irony** involves opposites. A situation that contrasts sharply with what might be expected is **ironic**. The ending of "Two Were Left" is ironic: when Noni flung the knife away, he was giving up. However, as it happened, this action saved his life! Why would the pilot not have seen the knife if Noni had not thrown it away?

4. What would you have done in Noni's place? Do you think Noni did the right thing?

Poem

By Langston Hughes

I loved my friend.
He went away from me.
There's nothing more to say.
The poem ends,
Soft as it began —
I loved my friend.

Think and Discuss

1. What happened to the friend in "Poem"?

2. The main idea of a story or poem is called the **theme**. Which of the following best states the theme of "Poem"?

   —Friends are people we love.
   —Sometimes friends we love leave us.
   —People leave us all the time.
   —Friends' leaving makes you speechless.

3. The emotional tone of a story or poem is called the **mood**. The mood creates feelings the author hopes the reader will experience. Is the mood of "Poem" happy? sad? quiet? excited? Why do you think the poet begins and ends the poem with the same line? How does this repetition help create the mood of the poem?

RESPONDING TO LITERATURE

The Reading and Writing Connection

Personal Response Follow the pattern in the first two lines of "Poem," and tell something about one of your friends. Write five two-line beginnings. Choose your favorite beginning and write a short poem.

Example: *I loved my friend.*
He made me laugh.

Creative Writing "Two Were Left" is told from Noni's point of view. Rewrite the story from Nimuk's point of view. Give Nimuk human traits and feelings. Let him communicate with speech.

Creative Activities

Partner Talk Pretend that you are the pilot who found Noni and Nimuk. Using your airplane radio, tell the news of their survival to your partner at the airport. What else besides the news of their discovery would you include in your report to your partner?

Draw In the last three paragraphs of "Two Were Left," the author describes what the rescue pilot saw. Read the paragraphs and draw a picture of the description.

Vocabulary

"Noni pulled the finished knife from the ice and thumbed its edge." What does the verb *to thumb* mean? Use these words as verbs in sentences:

nose   eye   elbow

Looking Ahead

Story Later in this unit, you will be writing a story. A good ending solves the problem in a story in a way that makes sense. Read the ending of "Two Were Left." Did the ending surprise you?

VOCABULARY CONNECTION

Synonyms

Words that have almost the same meanings are called **synonyms.** You can use synonyms to add variety to your writing. Notice how the author of "Two Were Left" used two different words for *looked at.*

> And now the two, marooned on the ice, **eyed** each other warily. . . .
>
> Nimuk **watched** him, and it seemed to Noni that the dog's eyes glowed more brightly.
>
> *from "Two Were Left" by Hugh B. Cave*

Here are some other synonyms for *looked at.*

observed   surveyed   gazed at   peered at

When you write, use a thesaurus to look up synonyms. They can keep you from using the same words over and over. They can also help you say exactly what you mean.

Vocabulary Practice

A. Write each sentence, replacing the underlined word with one of the following synonyms from "Two Were Left."

awkwardly   warily   quivering   rattle

1. An odd <u>clattering</u> woke me in the middle of the night.
2. <u>Shaking</u>, I went to my window.
3. I looked around <u>cautiously</u>.
4. A raccoon was <u>clumsily</u> dancing with our trash can.

B. Using your Thesaurus Plus, find two synonyms for each of the following words from "Two Were Left."

5. scarce   **6.** feeble   **7.** suspicious   **8.** labored   **9.** devoted

Listening: Predicting Outcomes

A speaker may provide hints about what will happen next rather than tell you everything. You use a story's details and descriptions as clues for **predicting outcomes.** Your own experience can also help you to make predictions.

Sometimes you must change a prediction when you get new information. Listen as your teacher reads this passage.

> The dog had circled him and was creeping up from behind. Noni heard the rattle in the savage throat.
>
> He shut his eyes, praying that the attack might be swift. He felt the dog's feet against his leg, the hot rush of Nimuk's breath against his neck. A scream gathered in the boy's throat.
>
> Then he felt the dog's hot tongue licking his face.
>
> *from "Two Were Left" by Hugh B. Cave*

- What is your first prediction?
- How did the last line make you change your prediction?

Guidelines for Predicting Outcomes

1. Listen actively and question what you are hearing.
2. Use the speaker's clues to predict what may happen.
3. Base your predictions on facts and on your experience.
4. Change your prediction as new information is provided.

Prewriting Practice

Listen as your teacher reads about Julie, an Eskimo girl in the Arctic. Listen for clues about what will happen. When your teacher stops reading, write a prediction. Then listen to the ending. Was your prediction right?

Thinking: Solving Problems

In "Two Were Left," Noni and Nimuk faced a terrible problem. Each had to decide whether to starve or to kill the other. With luck, you will never have to face a problem such as this. However, you must solve problems every day: What should you wear to school? How can you save money for a bike? No matter what your problems are, you can follow these steps to find solutions.

Guidelines for Solving Problems

1. **Define the problem.** Be sure to state your problem clearly.
2. **Consider possible solutions.** List some ways that the problem can be solved.
3. **Examine possible solutions.** Look at all the information you have for each solution in your list.
4. **Decide on a solution.** Choose the best solution.
5. **Carry out the solution.** Put your solution into action.

Suppose that a hungry, frightened puppy has been found in the bushes outside your classroom. The principal has said that the puppy cannot stay at school. The class must decide what happens to it. Here is how one sixth-grade class tackled this special problem.

1. **Define the problem.** The puppy needs to be returned to its home or be placed in a new home.
2. **Consider possible solutions.** Students brainstormed to list possible solutions:
   –Have the principal announce over the loudspeaker that a puppy has been found.
   –Call the Animal Rescue League to come and get the puppy.
   –Hold a drawing. The winner gets to keep the puppy.
   –Ask around the neighborhood to find out if anyone has lost a puppy.
   –Leave the puppy alone and maybe it will go home.

3. **Examine possible solutions.** Students discussed what would happen if they followed each suggested solution:
   - –The loudspeaker announcement might notify the owner.
   - –Calling the Animal Rescue League wouldn't give the owner a chance to claim the puppy.
   - –Holding a drawing might work if all other efforts did not turn up the owner.
   - –Asking neighbors would be a good way to find the owner.
   - –Letting the puppy go away would not mean that the puppy had found a home.

4. **Decide on a solution.** Students looked at the evidence and decided that making a loudspeaker announcement and asking neighbors would be the best solutions. These solutions would reach the most people.

5. **Carry out the solution.** The principal made a loudspeaker announcement. When no one claimed the puppy, the students asked people in the neighborhood. The puppy's owner was found in the neighborhood. The class had found a solution to the problem.

Prewriting Practice

A. Many stories present a problem and then work out a solution. Assume that you have a story idea in which you are marooned, alone, on a desert island. How can you get help? In a small group, apply the problem-solving steps to this problem. Share your solution with the class.

B. After school one day, you find a message from your mother, asking you to meet her at a certain restaurant for dinner at six o'clock. She left you money for public transportation, but you do not know where the restaurant is. What must you do to get to the restaurant on time? Follow the problem-solving steps.

C. You want to buy a friend a birthday gift but are not sure what to get. Follow the problem-solving steps to list your choices and decide on a gift.

Plot ☑

The **plot** of a story is the series of events that tells what happens. Usually, stories follow a three-part plan: the **problem,** the **climax,** and the **resolution.** Look at the way "Two Were Left" fits this framework.

PROBLEM: *the issue that the characters must deal with*
Noni and Nimuk are starving to death. If one is killed for food, the other may survive.

CLIMAX: *the moment of greatest excitement*
Noni and Nimuk each try to attack the other but cannot go through with it.

RESOLUTION: *the solution to the problem*
A pilot rescues Noni and Nimuk.

You know that the order in which the events in a plot happen is the sequence of events. The events that make up the plot may be told in **chronological order.** Chronological order follows the events as they happen, from first to last. For example, first Noni and Nimuk are marooned without food. Second, Noni makes a knife. Third, Noni throws the knife away. Fourth, the dog refuses to attack Noni. Fifth, the plane arrives.

Not all stories follow chronological order. Some stories begin in the present and go back to past events. Through the use of **flashback,** the author interrupts the action to show an earlier event or to give you background information. For example, suppose that "Two Were Left" began with Noni, a grown man, working on his fishing boat. First, one of Noni's helpers asks him about the crude knife he always has with him. Second, Noni picks up the knife, with a thoughtful look on his face. Third, Noni—as a child—is marooned on an ice island with his husky Nimuk. Fourth, Noni makes the knife. . . . The change of scenes to an earlier time is a flashback.

Prewriting Practice

1. Work with a partner. Choose a story that you and your partner know. Use it to make a plot plan like the one on page 200. Write the main problem or problems, the climax, and the resolution of the story.
2. With a partner, describe a character from a story that you both know. Plan a flashback that will help the reader better understand the character.

Setting

The backdrop against which a story unfolds is called the **setting**. The setting includes both the time and the place of the action. The setting can directly affect the plot and the atmosphere of the story. Does the action take place at night in an old castle? Are the characters hiking in the mountains on a warm, sunny day, or are they caught in a blizzard? How will these settings affect the characters and the action?

Read the two sentences below. How will the setting affect the plot? Notice the details the author uses to establish where and when the action takes place.

> On the third night of hunger, Noni thought of the dog. Nothing of flesh and blood lived upon the floating ice island except those two.
>
> *from "Two Were Left" by Hugh B. Cave*

*   Where does the story take place?
*   How long have the characters been there?
*   What else is on the island?

Prewriting Practice

Write two sentences that describe a setting for a science fiction story. Then write two sentences about a setting for a mystery story. Make your reader see and feel what you are describing.

Characters ☑

Sometimes the most important part of the story is the characters. Perhaps they learn something new about themselves or about other people. Perhaps they fall in love or lose someone close to them. Characters do not have to be human beings, of course. They can be any creature you make up. Whatever they are, there could be no story without them.

Details about a character's attitudes, thoughts, and personality make the character seem real to the reader. The details help the reader form conclusions about the character. Read these two passages.

> Nimuk came closer. Noni read fear in the animal's gaze. He read hunger and suffering in the dog's labored breathing and awkward crouch. His heart wept. He hated himself and fought against it.
>
> Closer Nimuk came, aware of his intentions. Now Noni felt a thickening in his throat. He saw the dog's eyes, and they were wells of suffering.
>
> Now! Now was the time to strike!
>
> A great sob shook Noni's kneeling body. He cursed the knife. He swayed blindly, flung the weapon far from him. With empty hands outstretched, he stumbled toward the dog and fell. . . .

> Noni's eyes opened. Crying softly, he thrust out an arm and drew the dog's head down against his own. . . .
>
> *from "Two Were Left" by Hugh B. Cave*

- What do the passages tell you about Noni? What kind of a person is he? Explain.
- What words and actions tell you his feelings for Nimuk?
- How is Nimuk described?

Before you write a story, you should know something about your characters. Who are they? Are they human beings, animals, or other creatures? What do they look like? What do they enjoy doing? What are their faults? What are their strengths? Knowing about your characters before you start writing will help you make them more real to your readers.

Prewriting Practice

1. Describe a character from a story that you have read. Include details of how the character looked and acted.
2. Make up a character you might want to use in a story. What is your character's

   favorite sport?
   physical description?
   age?
   favorite color?
   favorite expression?
   main strength?
   attitude toward other people?

The Grammar Connection

Vary Your Verbs

Have you ever told someone about a conversation you have had? When you repeat a conversation, do not use the verb *go* as a substitute for the verb *said*. To add variety and interest to your speech or writing, do not overuse the verb *said*. Read the following conversation.

Eve said, "We have to decide what to bring to the picnic."
Roger goes, "We need more than last year."
"I'll make some sandwiches," said Fran.
Stu goes, "Don't we have to decide where to have the picnic?"
Kim goes, "Right. Let's take a vote."
"Let's have it at Great Lakes Park!" said Joyce.
Stu said, "That's fine with me."

Practice Replace the verbs *goes* and *said* in the above conversation. You can use the verbs in parentheses. *(asked, declared, suggested, replied, stated)*

The Writing Process
How to Write a Story

Step 1: Prewriting—Choose a Topic

Shane made a list of story ideas. Then he thought about which one to use.

finding the lost island of Atlantis

Shane loved adventure stories, especially ones about imaginary places.

solving a mystery by computer

He was interested in computers, but he could not think of a good idea for the mystery.

winning a hot-air balloon race

He would need to find out how hot-air balloons worked.

growing up poor and becoming a famous movie star

This idea seemed much too big for a short story.

Shane circled *Atlantis*.

On Your Own

1. **Think and discuss** List several story ideas of your own. Use the Ideas page to help you. Discuss your ideas with a classmate or your teacher.
2. **Choose** Ask yourself these questions about each idea on your list.
   Can I think of a good plot? How will it begin and end? What will happen in the middle?
   Will I be able to tell the story in enough detail?
   Will I enjoy writing this story?
3. **Explore** Do one of the "Exploring Your Topic" activities on the Ideas page.

Ideas for Getting Started

Choosing Your Topic

Topic Ideas

Losing a friend
Surviving a storm
Traveling in time
A house cat's first
    time outdoors
A ride in space
Creating a robot
Taming a wild horse
Solving a crime
Finding a magic coin
Making friends with
    an enemy

Story Starters

Read these story starters for ideas.

No one in the whole school wanted
    to be friends with him.

"I can't do it," she thought, and
    turned back for the hundredth
    time.

The cabin was buried almost to the
    chimney, and the snow was still
    falling.

With a final yank, Laura reeled in
    her catch. The thing she had
    caught wasn't a fish.

Exploring Your Topic

Build an A-Frame

Plan the plot of your story by writing the answers to these questions.
Problem: What problem must the characters solve? What will happen in the beginning? middle?
Climax: What will be the turning point of the action?
Resolution: How will the problem be solved?

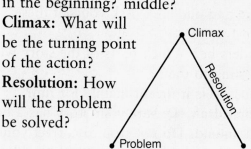

Talk About It

Develop your characters by deciding how they talk. Write how two of your characters would say *I'm cold*. Use words that reflect your characters' personalities. Then ask a classmate if the dialogue shows what the characters are like.

Step 2: Write a First Draft

Shane decided to write his story for his older brother, Robert. One of the characters would be a boy Robert's age.

Shane wrote his first draft. He did not worry about his mistakes. He wrote on every other line so that he could make changes later.

Part of Shane's first draft

Think and Discuss

- What is the plot? the resolution?
- What is the setting? Can you picture it clearly? Why or why not?
- Who are the people? How could Shane bring them to life?

My family had just moved to an old house in Salem, Massachusetts. ~~We~~ In the basement, my brother Eric and I found a map to the lost city of Atlantis. It ~~was~~ said the city was 40 miles offshore and 60 feet under. We borrowed my father's boat and scuba gear and went there. We found lots of gold and brought back all we could carry. ~~My~~ We had to take it to the police.

On Your Own

1. **Think about purpose and audience** Ask yourself these questions.

    Who will my readers be? Which parts of the story will be the most interesting to them?

    Is my story serious, or is it meant mainly for fun?

2. **Write** Write your first draft. Be sure your story has a beginning, a middle, and an end. Do not stop to correct your mistakes. Write on every other line so you will be able to make changes later.

Step 3: Revise

Shane read his first draft. He was surprised at how short it seemed. This was not the way he had pictured the story in his mind. He added some details and dialogue.

Then he read his story to Pablo.

Reading and responding

PABLO: It's a great idea, but I want to know more!

SHANE: Good! What?

PABLO: Well, what was Atlantis like? Where was the gold hidden?

SHANE: Right. Thanks. I have another new idea too.

Shane liked Pablo's suggestions. He also liked the idea of putting some danger into his story. He added the problem of sharks and more description about Atlantis.

Part of Shane's revised draft

feet under. We borrowed my father's boat and scuba gear and went there. ~~We found~~

When we reached the spot, we lowered ourselves into the gray water. I thought I saw something dark moving far below. "Just my nerves," I thought, but was it?

Then we saw Atlantis! The white city shimmered. It looked like

Think and Discuss ✓

- How did Shane make this part of his story clearer?
- How did he make it more exciting?
- What dialogue did he add?

On Your Own

Revising Checklist

☑ Does the story have a good plot? Is there a problem, a climax, and a resolution?

☑ Did I use details to bring the characters to life?

☑ Have I described the setting to make it easy to picture?

1. **Revise** Make changes in your first draft. If you need to add a large section, write it in a margin and draw an arrow to show where it goes. Do all of your words say just what you mean? To find the best word, use the thesaurus below or the one in the back of this book.

2. **Have a conference** Read your story to a classmate.

WRITING CONFERENCE

Ask your listener:	**As you listen:**
"Did the plot of the story make sense? Was it interesting?" "Did the characters seem real?" "Could you picture the setting?"	I must listen carefully. Is the story holding my interest? Do I understand what is happening? What would I like to know more about?

3. **Revise** Did your partner offer any good hints? Do you have any other ideas? Make those changes on your paper.

Thesaurus

argue quarrel, clash	**cruel** mean, ferocious
boring dull, dry, monotonous, tedious	**easy** simple, uncomplicated, effortless
break shatter, smash, crack	**hurry** scurry, dash, rush
bright shining, brilliant	**jump** hurdle, leap, spring
bring carry, fetch	**perfect** ideal, excellent, delightful
change transform, alter	**smile** grin, beam
clean spotless, unsoiled	**strange** peculiar, unusual
clear transparent, sunny, cloudless	**upset** cranky, crabby

Step 4: Proofread

Shane proofread his story for mistakes in spelling, grammar, capitalization, and punctuation. He used a dictionary to check his spellings. He used proofreading marks to make his changes.

Here is the way Shane's ending looked after he proofread it.

Shane's proofread story ending

A long time went by, and we forgot all about the gold. Then one day the phone rang. My father ansered it. "Yes," he said. "Yes, of coarse. Thank you." When he hung up, he was trying not to smile. "You kid's dont still want those saks of gold, do you?" he said to us.

Think and Discuss

- Where did Shane add a comma? Why?
- Why did he add an apostrophe? Why did he take one out?
- Which misspelled words did he correct?

On Your Own

1. **Proofreading Practice** Proofread this paragraph for mistakes in grammar, spelling, and punctuation. There are four words used incorrectly, one misspelled word, one error in subject-verb agreement, and one run-on sentence. There is one incorrect end mark.

"Your crazy if you go. Neither Robby nor Rich are going. What are you trying to prove." Paul set on the edge of Benjamin's bed.
Benjamin starred at the window and watched the curtains raising and lowering in the night breeze, he wished his brother would leave him sleep.

Proofreading Marks

- ⌿ Indent
- ∧ Add
- ⋏ Add a comma
- ⱽⱽ Add quotation marks
- ⊙ Add a period
- ℓ Take out
- ≡ Capitalize
- / Make a small letter
- ∿ Reverse order

2. **Proofreading Application** Now proofread your story. Use the Proofreading Checklist and the Grammar and Spelling Hints below. It may be helpful to make your corrections with a colored pencil. Use a dictionary to check spellings.

Proofreading Checklist

Did I

☑ **1.** indent the first line of every paragraph?

☑ **2.** use the correct form of every verb?

☑ **3.** use apostrophes and commas where they are needed?

☑ **4.** write complete sentences?

☑ **5.** spell all words correctly?

The Grammar/Spelling Connection

Grammar Hints

Remember these rules from Unit 5 when you use verbs.

- The verb *sit* means "to rest or recline." *(Sit down.)*
- The verb *set* means "to put or place an object." *(Set your bag down.)*

Spelling Hints

Remember these rules when adding *-ed*.

- When a word ends with *e*, drop the *e* before adding the ending. *(care, cared)*
- For one-syllable words ending in a vowel and a consonant, double the consonant and add *-ed*. *(sip, sipped)*

Step 5: Publish

Here is the way Shane shared his story with Robert. He drew the map from the story and glued it to a large sheet of colored paper. He stapled his story below it.

On Your Own

1. **Copy** Write or type your story as neatly as you can.
2. **Add a title** Think of a title to catch your reader's interest. Remember to capitalize the first, last, and all important words.
3. **Check** Read over your story again to make sure you have not left out anything or made any mistakes in copying.
4. **Share** Think of a special way to share your story.

Ideas for Sharing

- Turn your story into a comic strip.
- Write a play based on your story. Ask classmates to perform it.
- Make a class anthology. Think of a title for this collection of short stories.

Applying Story Writing

Literature and Creative Writing

In the story "Two Were Left," Noni and his dog, Nimuk, were marooned for three days without food on a piece of ice. Noni faced the decision of saving his life by killing Nimuk or sharing an uncertain future with his faithful husky. The story was happily resolved when a pilot rescued them.

Have fun using what you have learned about writing stories to complete one or more of these activities.

Remember these things ☑
- Determine the order of events in your story.
- Develop the action toward a climax.
- Use details to describe the setting.
- Know your characters.

1. **My best friend Nimuk.** Noni and Nimuk were devoted to each other. Write a story about how Noni raised Nimuk from a puppy.
2. **Investigate the light.** Imagine that you are a pilot in Alaska. You are flying over the coastline and see a light shining in a forest clearing. You decide to land your plane and investigate. Write a story about what you find.
3. **Go on a fishing trip.** Imagine that while you and a friend are on a fishing trip, your rowboat capsizes on the lake. You both swim to a deserted island. What happens? How long are you marooned? How are you rescued?

Writing Across the Curriculum
Physical Education

Many stories have been written about sports events and outdoor activities. The competition, the sudden twists of fate, and the daring and skill of the participants make for action-packed stories.

Choose one or more of the following activities.

1. **Go for the gold.** Imagine that you are an athlete with special needs. You might be a hearing-impaired swimmer, a blind skier, or a basketball player in a wheelchair. All your hopes are set on winning the championship. Write the story.

Writing Steps
1. Choose a topic
2. Write a first draft
3. Revise
4. Proofread
5. Publish

2. **Write a newspaper article.** Imagine that you are a reporter covering the biggest school game of the season. If your school team wins, the team will become the champions. Make this game come to life in an article. Use action-packed words and an attention-grabbing headline.

Word Bank
power
sprint
speed
falter
race
defeat

3. **Become a storyteller.** Imagine that you are leading a group of hikers up a mountain trail. All is peaceful, when suddenly. . . . Finish the story.

When she finished reading "Two Were Left," Elena wanted to read more adventure stories. At the library, she chose *Island of the Blue Dolphins* by Scott O'Dell. Elena wanted to share this book with her class. She decided to share her book by giving a talk. She had just three minutes to present her talk. Here are some note cards she used in giving her talk.

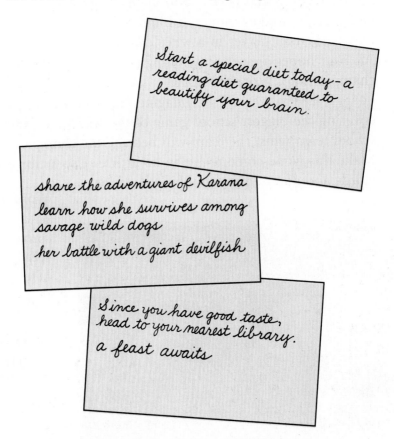

Start a special diet today—a reading diet guaranteed to beautify your brain.

share the adventures of Karana
learn how she survives among savage wild dogs
her battle with a giant devilfish

Since you have good taste, head to your nearest library.
a feast awaits

Think and Discuss

- How does Elena try to interest her class in this book?
- Why does she try to interest her listeners quickly?
- Why is this a good way to share a book?

Share Your Book

Give a Talk

1. Plan what you want to tell your audience.
   - Start with something to catch your listeners' attention.
   - Tell the name of the book, the author, who the main characters are, and something exciting that happens.
   - Prepare note cards. Write the main points you want to mention on these cards so that you can glance at them when you speak. Just include key words and phrases.
2. Practice giving your talk to some friends.
   - Become comfortable using your note cards.
   - Speak clearly and show enthusiasm for your subject. Vary your pitch so that you don't speak in a flat monotone.
   - Use gestures and movements whenever appropriate to illustrate the action or to hold your listeners' attention.
   - Look around at your listeners when you speak. Try to make eye contact with as many listeners as possible.
3. Give your talk. Try to relax and enjoy the experience!

Other Activities

- Make a large poster for your book to display when you speak. Draw a picture of an exciting part of the story. Put the title of the book and the author's name on your poster.

The Book Nook

Zia *by Scott O'Dell* Meeting her Aunt Karana, who lived alone on an island for many years, is a great experience for Zia.	Trapped on a Golden Flyer *by Susan Fleming* When an avalanche blocks the train, Paul is courageous and helpful to the other stranded passengers.

Language and Usage

M arbles picked up
Heavy by the handful
And held, weighed,
Hard, glossy
Glassy, cold
Then poured clicking,
Water-smooth, back
To their bag, seem
Treasure: round jewels,
Slithering gold.

Valery Worth
"Marbles"

Modifiers

Getting Ready Do you remember the first time you had a box of crayons? Did you smell the crayons or try to taste them? Did you learn that they break? Crayons seem such a simple thing, yet there was a lot of experimenting to be done before you began to draw or to color the outlines in a coloring book! We learn to use words much as we learn to use crayons. There are rules to learn about their use, but we experiment with them too. In this unit, you will learn more about adding modifiers to those plain outlines of nouns and verbs.

ACTIVITIES

Listening   Listen as the poem on page 216 is read. Which words tell you how marbles look? how they feel? how they sound? How does the writer feel about marbles?

Speaking   Look at the picture. Suppose you are there. How does one marble feel in your hand? What is it like to scoop up a handful? What can you see if you look at the world through a clear marble?

Writing   Suppose that you found a small, mysterious bag that you immediately opened. Write a short poem in your journal about what you find in the bag.

1 | Adjectives

An **adjective** describes, or modifies, a noun or a pronoun. One adjective can change the meaning of a whole sentence.

We take exciting trips.   We take boring trips.

Adjectives can tell what kind, which one, or how many.

WHAT KIND: We climbed steep , rocky trails.

WHICH ONE(S): Those hikers met at this stream.

HOW MANY: Several boys carried two canteens.

Sometimes adjectives come before the noun they describe. At other times, adjectives follow the noun they describe.

Three hungry and tired campers stumbled home.

Children, cheerful and noisy, called to us.

You know that a predicate adjective can follow a linking verb. A predicate adjective describes the subject of a sentence.

Mary felt sleepy. I was anxious to get home.

An adjective may be more than one word. When such an adjective comes before a noun, it is usually hyphenated.

Part-time jobs helped us buy equipment.

We bought three-sided tents.

Guided Practice Which words are adjectives?

Example: Gene builds tiny, old-fashioned houses for dolls.
          tiny   old-fashioned

1. They are unusual.
2. That house has three floors.
3. Some rooms, small and bright, are empty.
4. Little electric lights shine through clear windows.
5. This miniature house includes that fifty-year-old clock.

> ▸ An **adjective** modifies, or describes, a noun or a pronoun.
> ▸ An adjective can tell what kind, which one, or how many.

Independent Practice

A. Write each adjective. Then write the word it describes.

Example: That ten-speed bike is beautiful.
adj.: That ten-speed beautiful **word described:** *bike*

6. Two salespeople tried to sell us this green bike.
7. Other stores are selling three-speed bikes.
8. Good bikes are expensive.
9. Prices are high at all stores.
10. These bikes, shiny and bright, have different features.
11. This bike has handlebars with good leather.
12. Padded seats are comfortable.
13. This tri-colored bike has ten speeds.
14. Another bike, pretty and fast, has narrow tires.
15. That model is popular with many people.
16. You can go long distances with little effort.
17. I am happy with this new model.
18. Those bikes come in perfect sizes.

B. For each noun below, write one adjective that tells what kind, another that tells how many, and a third that tells which one.

Example: suit *wool suit one suit this suit*

19. stars
20. parrot
21. baby
22. sunset
23. computer
24. story
25. pet
26. songs
27. game
28. lunch

Writing Application: A Paragraph

Write a paragraph about something you would like to buy on an imaginary shopping trip. Use at least five adjectives that tell either what kind, which one(s), or how many.

For Extra Practice, see p. 247.

2 | Articles and Demonstratives

The words *a, an,* and *the* are special adjectives. They are called **articles**. An article can come before a noun or before another adjective.

> The ball hit an old shed.

The refers to a specific item. It can be used with singular nouns *(the dog)* or plural nouns *(the cats)*. A or *an* refers to any one item. Use *a* before words that begin with a consonant sound *(a helicopter, a knee)*. Use *an* before words that begin with a vowel sound *(an ankle, an hour)*.

Adjectives that tell *which one* are called **demonstrative adjectives**. They point out a specific person, place, or thing.

> This book is better than that magazine.

> These stories are more interesting than those articles.

This and *these* point out people, places, or things that are nearby. *That* and *those* point out people, places, or things that are farther away. Study the following chart.

Demonstrative Adjectives		
Singular	this	that
Plural	these	those

Guided Practice Which word in parentheses correctly completes each sentence?

Example: (A, An) windmill can give energy.   *A*

1. (A, The) windmill in our backyard is very old.
2. It once was (an, the) efficient tool.
3. (A, The) blades still turn in (a, an) unusually strong wind.
4. (This, These) form of energy has been replaced by newer forms.
5. (That, Those) new forms create more power.

▶ *A*, *an*, and *the* are special adjectives called **articles**. *The* refers to a specific item or items. *A* or *an* refers to any one item in a group.

▶ **Demonstrative adjectives** tell which one. Use *this* and *these* for things nearby. Use *that* and *those* for things farther away.

Independent Practice

A. Write the article that completes each sentence correctly.

Example: (A, An) lion called Homer escaped from (a, the) Bronx Zoo.   *A   the*

6. Did you hear about (a, the) excitement today?
7. Homer found (a, an) open car.
8. (A, The) lion got inside.
9. (A, An) passerby saw him and screamed.
10. (An, The) officials captured him quickly.
11. Homer is safely back in (a, an) cage.
12. What (a, an) day Homer had!
13. We had (a, an) exciting day too!

B. Write the demonstrative adjectives.

Example: Look at these paintings.   *these*

14. Do you know this artist's work?
15. Edward Hopper is that famous American painter.
16. I saw Hopper's work in this museum.
17. This exhibit includes some famous paintings.
18. These empty cafeterias and movie lobbies seem odd.
19. Those lonely figures show the beauty of ordinary things.
20. Hopper often uses that harsh light in his paintings.
21. This style has influenced many painters.
22. Among these pieces, I like this one best!

Writing Application: A Description

Describe a museum or a famous building that you once visited. What do you remember most about it? Use articles or demonstrative adjectives in each sentence of your paragraph.

For Extra Practice, see p. 248.   **Articles and Demonstratives   221**

3 | Comparing with Adjectives

You can use adjectives to compare two or more people, places, things, and ideas.

John is older than I am.   You made the wisest choice.

To show a difference between two things, use the **comparative** form of the adjective. Add *-er* to most one-syllable and some two-syllable adjectives to form the comparative. To show a difference among three or more things, use the **superlative** form of the adjective. Add *-est* to most one-syllable and some two-syllable adjectives to form the superlative.

COMPARATIVE: I am taller than Tom. (two things compared)

SUPERLATIVE: Peter is the tallest of all. (more than two compared)

Sometimes the spelling of an adjective changes when you add *-er* or *-est* to form the comparative or superlative.

Spelling Changes in Comparative and Superlative			
1. Adjectives ending in e: Do not add another e.	large nice	larger nicer	largest nicest
2. Adjectives ending in a consonant preceded by a single vowel: You usually double the final consonant.	flat sad big	flatter sadder bigger	flattest saddest biggest
3. Adjectives ending in y: Change the y to i.	busy happy	busier happier	busiest happiest

Guided Practice What are the comparative and superlative forms of each adjective?

Example: young *younger youngest*

1. old   **2.** thin   **3.** fat   **4.** cute   **5.** hungry

▶ Use the **comparative** form *(-er)* of an adjective to compare two people, places, things, or ideas.
▶ Use the **superlative** form *(-est)* to compare three or more.
▶ Sometimes the spelling of an adjective changes when *-er* or *-est* is added.

Independent Practice

Write the form of the adjective in parentheses that correctly completes each sentence.

Example: The ____ human bone of all is in the middle ear.   (small)
     smallest

6. Blue whales are ____ than right whales.   (large)
7. The ____ star we can see is known as the Dog Star.   (bright)
8. Where is the ____ place in the world?   (wet)
9. It is ____ in Mexico than in the United States.   (hot)
10. Arizona is ____ than Florida.   (dry)
11. The ____ mountain in the world is Mount Everest.   (high)
12. The ____ ocean is the Pacific Ocean.   (deep)
13. What is the ____ building in New York?   (tall)
14. Is English ____ to learn than Spanish?   (easy)
15. Diamonds are the ____ stone in the world.   (hard)
16. Is the Mississippi River ____ than the Rio Grande?   (long)
17. Is a pig ____ than a horse?   (smart)
18. Where has the ____ temperature been recorded?   (cold)
19. Alaska is the ____ state in the United States.   (big)
20. In Minnesota summer is ____ than winter.   (short)
21. Who is the ____ person in the world?   (rich)
22. The cheetah is the ____ animal on land.   (fast)
23. Is iron ____ than steel?   (strong)
24. China has the ____ population of any country.   (large)
25. In Australia the weather is ____ in July than in January.   (cool)

Writing Application: Comparison and Contrast

Think about two places you know that are different from each other. Write a paragraph about these places. In each sentence, use an adjective in its comparative or superlative form.

For Extra Practice, see p. 249.   **Comparing with Adjectives**

4 Comparing with *more* and *most*

You already know that you can add *-er* or *-est* to one-syllable adjectives to form the comparative or superlative. You can form the comparative and superlative of most adjectives of two or more syllables by adding the words *more* and *most*.

Adjective	Comparative	Superlative
honest	more honest	most honest
dangerous	more dangerous	most dangerous
plentiful	more plentiful	most plentiful

Be sure not to combine *-er* with the word *more* or *-est* with the word *most*.

INCORRECT: Peaches are <u>more sweeter</u> than lemons.

CORRECT: Peaches are sweeter than lemons.

INCORRECT: This is the <u>most ripest</u> peach in the basket.

CORRECT: This is the ripest peach in the basket.

Some adjectives are irregular. They have completely different forms to show the comparative and superlative.

Adjective	Comparative	Superlative
much	more	most
little	less	least
good	better	best
bad	worse	worst

Guided Practice What are the comparative and superlative forms of each adjective?

Example: serious   *more serious   most serious*

1. ridiculous   3. comfortable   5. pleasant
2. attractive   4. generous   6. comical

▶ Use *more* to form the comparative and *most* to form the superlative of most adjectives of two or more syllables.

▶ Some adjectives have completely different forms in the comparative and superlative.

Independent Practice   Write the form of the adjective in parentheses that correctly completes each sentence.

Example: Is the Library of Congress the world's
_____ library?   (good)   *best*

7. Rubies are _____ than diamonds.   (colorful)

8. We had _____ rain this year than last year.   (much)

9. Is America's _____ dog the poodle?   (popular)

10. This silk is the _____ of all these fabrics.   (delicate)

11. Where is the _____ scenery of all in Florida?   (beautiful)

12. The weather on Tuesday was _____ than today.   (bad)

13. What major country has the _____ crime?   (little)

14. Does Pikes Peak get _____ snow than Mount Washington?   (much)

15. The picnic this year was the _____ picnic ever.   (good)

16. The rainfall in Arizona is _____ than that in Oregon.   (little)

17. Which city in the world has the _____ museum?   (good)

18. We are having the _____ storm of the century.   (bad)

19. Snorkeling is _____ than water skiing.   (difficult)

20. Is the weeping willow the _____ tree?   (graceful)

21. The _____ word in the English language is *the*.   (common)

22. Firefighters have the _____ job.   (dangerous)

23. What is your _____ type of exercise?   (enjoyable)

24. Are mules _____ than donkeys?   (stubborn)

25. What country has the _____ rain?   (much)

Writing Application: A Newspaper Article

Imagine that you are a reporter for your school newspaper. Write an article comparing three movies you have seen. Use comparative and superlative adjectives. Underline the comparative form once and the superlative form twice.

For Extra Practice, see p. 250.   **Comparing with *more* and *most* 225**

5 | Proper Adjectives

An adjective formed from a proper noun is called a **proper adjective**. Like a proper noun, a proper adjective is capitalized.

Here is a Mexican silver bracelet.

The endings most often used to change proper nouns into proper adjectives are *-an, -ish,* and *-ese.* Notice the other spelling changes when the ending is added.

Proper noun	Ending	Proper adjective
Ireland Britain	-ish	Irish **seacoast** British **accent**
Italy Brazil	-an	Italian **painting** Brazilian **leather**
Japan China	-ese	Japanese **food** Chinese **language**

You will find other spelling changes in proper adjectives too.

 French cooking is popular in countries other than <u>France</u>.

 Norwegian sweaters are famous outside of <u>Norway</u>.

Guided Practice What proper adjective is formed from each underlined noun? Give each phrase.

Example: bullfighter from <u>Spain</u> *Spanish bullfighter*

1. ruins of <u>Rome</u>
2. pottery from <u>Mexico</u>
3. dances of <u>Poland</u>
4. hotels of <u>Europe</u>
5. imports from <u>China</u>
6. provinces of <u>Canada</u>
7. settlers from <u>England</u>
8. cars from <u>France</u>
9. cheese from <u>Denmark</u>

> ▶ A **proper adjective** is an adjective formed from a proper noun.
> ▶ A proper adjective begins with a capital letter.

Independent Practice

A. Write the proper adjective in each sentence. Remember to capitalize it.

Example: Some alaskan dogs are used to pull sleds. *Alaskan*

10. The dachshund, a german breed, was used to hunt badgers.
11. An english sheepdog has a long, shaggy coat.
12. Pictures of greyhounds were found in ancient egyptian temples.
13. The pug is a chinese breed that has a snub nose.
14. The australian dingo is a wild dog.
15. Our neighbors own an irish setter pup.
16. This spaniel looks like the dogs on japanese vases.

B. To complete each sentence, write a proper adjective made from the noun in parentheses. Use your dictionary if you need help.

Example: Have you ever eaten sweet _____ sausages? (Italy)
  Italian

17. Many _____ dishes use beans and rice. (Mexico)
18. My father's favorite cheese is _____ cheddar. (England)
19. We celebrated my birthday at a _____ restaurant. (China)
20. Vegetables fried with meat is a popular _____ dish. (Japan)
21. Pineapples are grown on _____ plantations. (Hawaii)
22. The first course of a _____ meal is often fish. (Sweden)
23. _____ food is very hot and spicy. (Korea)
24. The _____ language is very difficult. (Finland)

Writing Application: A Description

Write a paragraph about a certain animal, style of dress, or food. Use at least one proper adjective in each sentence. Check your dictionary if you need spelling help.

For Extra Practice, see p. 251.

6 | Adverbs That Modify Verbs

An **adverb** is a word that modifies a verb, an adjective, or another adverb. Adverbs that modify verbs answer these questions: *How? Where? When?* or *To what extent?*

HOW: Jackie left quickly.

WHERE: She arrived there.

WHEN: Then she returned.

TO WHAT EXTENT: She thoroughly explained.

Guided Practice Find adverbs and verbs they modify.

Example: Yesterday we packed. *Yesterday—packed*

1. I really enjoyed the trip.
2. Mom drove carefully and well.
3. Dad always checked the maps.
4. We usually headed north.
5. Finally, we arrived there.
6. Luckily, we returned safely.

Summing up

▸ An **adverb** can modify a verb, an adjective, or another adverb.
▸ An adverb can tell *how, where, when,* or *to what extent.*

Independent Practice Write adverbs and verbs they modify.

Example: Peanuts develop strangely. *strangely—develop*

7–12. First, the flowers wither. The stems slowly turn downward. Finally, they enter the ground. There they form seed pods. Farmers carefully harvest these pods. Then the sun dries the pods naturally.

Writing Application: Directions
Imagine that you are telling someone how to make something. Give directions. Underline each adverb.

For Extra Practice, see p. 252.

7 | Adverbs That Modify Adjectives and Adverbs

When an adverb modifies an adjective or another adverb, it tells *how* or *to what extent*.

adj.   adv.

A very large crowd gathered quite quickly.

Guided Practice What word does each adverb modify?

Example: perfectly simple life   *simple*

1. dreadfully long way
2. completely safe elevator
3. reads quite carefully
4. very realistic dreams
5. writes especially well
6. sing very beautifully

Summing up

▶ Adverbs that modify adjectives or other adverbs tell *how* or *to what extent*.

Independent Practice Write each underlined adverb.
Then write the word it modifies, and label it *adjective* or *adverb*.

Example: The photographer was very happy.
        very happy—adjective

7. She looked very thoroughly at all of her pictures.
8. One photograph had especially bright colors.
9. It showed a boy with a rather friendly grin.
10. A beautiful sea scene rather suddenly caught her eye.
11. She thought quite carefully about each photograph.
12. Ms. Hart wanted to win an extremely important photo contest.

Writing Application: A Paragraph
Write a paragraph that explains why you enjoy a hobby or sport. Use adverbs to modify adjectives and other adverbs.

For Extra Practice, see p. 253.   **Adverbs 229**

8 | Comparing with Adverbs

Like adjectives, adverbs can be used to make comparisons. To compare two things, use the comparative form *(-er)*. To compare more than two things, use the superlative form *(-est)*.

COMPARATIVE: Dan arrived later than Sidney.

SUPERLATIVE: I arrived latest of all.

If the adverb ends with *-ly,* add *more* or *most* to make comparisons.

Adverb	Comparative	Superlative
skillfully	more skillfully	most skillfully
frequently	more frequently	most frequently
heavily	more heavily	most heavily

Do not combine the *-er* ending with the word *more* or the *-est* ending with the word *most*.

INCORRECT: Sheila rows more better than Dan.

CORRECT: Sheila rows better than Dan.

INCORRECT: Of all the crew, she worked most hardest.

CORRECT: Of all the crew, she worked hardest .

Some adverbs become completely new words.

Adverb	Comparative	Superlative
well	better	best
badly	worse	worst
little	less	least
much	more	most

Guided Practice Give comparative and superlative forms.

Example: quickly *more quickly* *most quickly*

1. loudly   **2.** easily   **3.** little   **4.** bravely   **5.** thoroughly

▸ Add -er to form the comparative and -est to form the superlative of many adverbs.
▸ If the adverb ends with -ly, add more to form the comparative and most to form the superlative.
▸ Some adverbs have completely different forms of comparison.

Independent Practice

A. Write the adverb that correctly completes each sentence.

Example: Jay makes speeches (better, more better) than Beverly.
  better

6. Beverly speaks (more slowly, most slowly) than Jay.
7. Rudy was the (less, least) interesting of all the speakers.
8. We rehearsed (worse, more worse) today than yesterday.
9. Of all the students, Dee worked (hardest, harder).
10. We will practice (more, most) tomorrow.

B. Write the comparative or superlative form of the adverbs in parentheses to complete each sentence correctly.

Example: Grandpa tells stories even ____ than Dad.
  (wonderfully) *more wonderfully*

11. He visits us ____ now than in the past. (frequently)
12. Of all his stories, I listen ____ to tales of his boyhood adventures. (eagerly)
13. Did his pet frog really jump ____ than Gus's frog? (high)
14. Of all the places he saw, he recalled Iowa ____. (clearly)
15. Do you learn ____ from a story than from a lecture? (well)
16. He builds up suspense ____ than TV does. (skillfully)
17. His modern stories are ____ interesting of all. (little)
18. I listen ____ than my brother. (carefully)

Writing Application: A Story

Write a story about something that happened before you were born or make up a story. Use the comparative or superlative form of five different adverbs. Underline comparative forms once and superlative forms twice.

For Extra Practice, see p. 254.   **Comparing with Adverbs**

9 | Negatives

Some modifiers or other words mean "no." A word that means "no" is called a **negative**. A negative can reverse the meaning of a sentence.

Lynn is on the team.   Lynn is not on the team.

Some of the most common negatives are *no, none, not, no one, never, nothing, nowhere,* and *nobody.* Contractions using *not* are also negatives.

Don never mows the lawn.   Sid can't go with us.

Do not use two negatives together. Two negatives used together are called a **double negative**.

INCORRECT: I <u>can't</u> find <u>nothing</u> to wear.

CORRECT: I can find nothing to wear.

CORRECT: I can't   find   anything to wear.

The example above shows that you can avoid a double negative by dropping *not (n't)*. You can also substitute a positive word for a negative word. In the last sentence, *nothing* was changed to *anything*. Most negative words have matching positive words.

hardly – almost	never – ever	no – any
neither – either	nobody – anybody	none – some

Guided Practice Which word in parentheses makes each sentence negative?

Example: This flashlight has (no, some) batteries. *no*

1. There are (no, few) batteries in this drawer.
2. (Someone, No one) has gone to the store this week.
3. Batteries were (nowhere, everywhere) to be found.
4. These wax candles (never, always) fail.
5. We are (hardly, almost) ready for a storm.

> ▶ A **negative** is a word that means "no" and reverses the meaning of a sentence.
> ▶ Avoid using a **double negative,** two negatives together.

Independent Practice

A. Write the word in parentheses that completes each sentence correctly. Avoid double negatives.

Example: Kerry hadn't read (nothing, anything) about the Inca.   *anything*

6. (Nobody, Anybody) had told him about this great empire.
7. The Inca in South America don't exist (no more, anymore).
8. Nobody could (never, ever) wipe out their customs.
9. The civilization (hasn't, has) never been erased.
10. Nobody knows (nothing, anything) about the early history of the Inca.

B. Rewrite these sentences, correcting the double negatives.

Example: The Inca never had no system of writing.
   The Inca had no system of writing.

11. They didn't have a system of money neither.
12. Their group wasn't never very large.
13. Not none of the other Inca cities compared to Cuzco.
14. There weren't no individual landowners.
15. To the Inca, nothing wasn't more important than the clan.
16. There wasn't no unemployment.
17. The Inca never made no decision without careful thought.
18. There isn't nothing else in South America today to compare to the Inca civilization.
19. Kerry couldn't hardly wait to find out more about the Inca.
20. He didn't stop for nobody on his way to the library.

Writing Application: Persuasion

Choose something you dislike or disagree with. Write a paragraph that will convince a friend to share your view. Use at least five negatives. Check for double negatives.

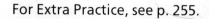

10 | Adjective or Adverb?

Sometimes it is easy to confuse adjectives and adverbs. When an adjective and an adverb are similar, you can usually tell which is the adverb because it ends in *-ly*.

ADJECTIVE:	slow	quick	bad	sweet
ADVERB:	slowly	quickly	badly	sweetly

Remember that adjectives modify nouns and pronouns. Adverbs modify verbs, adjectives, and other adverbs.

INCORRECT: We drove <u>slow</u> through the leaves.

CORRECT: We drove <u>slowly</u> through the leaves.

The words *good* and *well* are also sometimes confused. *Good* is an adjective. It modifies a noun or a pronoun.

It is a <u>good</u> day to take pictures.   Her pictures are always <u>good</u>.

Well is usually used as an adverb. However, when *well* means "healthy," it is an adjective and modifies a noun or a pronoun.

ADVERB: I played baseball <u>well</u>.

ADJECTIVE: I didn't feel <u>well</u> when I awoke.

Guided Practice   Choose the word in parentheses that completes each sentence correctly.

Example: The band played (loud, loudly).   *loudly*

1. They marched (bad, badly), however.
2. People waved (wild, wildly) from windows.
3. The hero gave a (good, well) speech.
4. He received (great, greatly) praise.
5. The hero was a (good, well) football player.
6. The hero thanked everyone (polite, politely).
7. Later, hundreds of people departed (slow, slowly) for home.
8. May didn't feel (good, well) after the excitement.
9. The events of the day had gone (good, well).

▶Use adjectives to modify nouns and pronouns.
▶Use adverbs to modify verbs, adjectives, and other adverbs.
▶*Good* is an adjective. *Well* is an adjective only when it means "healthy." Otherwise, *well* is an adverb.

Independent Practice

A. Write the word in parentheses that completes each sentence correctly. Then label the word *adjective* or *adverb*.

Example: That was a (good, well) story. *good* **adjective**

10. The author wrote (good, well) about a famous person.
11. The heroine was a (good, well) leader.
12. The trick of her double identity worked (good, well).
13. I didn't feel (good, well) when I read the scary parts.
14. I wonder if her other stories are also (good, well).

B. Write and label the adjective or the adverb in parentheses that completes each sentence correctly.

Example: Joan of Arc was (brave, bravely). *brave* **adjective**

15. When Joan of Arc was seventeen, the French army was losing (slow, slowly) to the English.
16. She (quick, quickly) went to the aid of France.
17. Wearing her white armor, she fought (good, well).
18. She showed (tremendous, tremendously) skill in battle.
19. Battles went (well, good) under her leadership.
20. Her leadership (gradual, gradually) united the French.
21. In the end the king treated her (bad, badly).
22. She was judged in court (unfair, unfairly) by the English.
23. Joan of Arc defended herself (good, well), but she was (eventual, eventually) put to death.
24. She showed (great, greatly) courage at the end.

Writing Application: A Story

Imagine that you are the hero of a great adventure. Write a story about your adventure. Use *good* or *well* in at least two sentences. Make sure you use adjectives and adverbs correctly.

For Extra Practice, see p. 256.   **Adjective or Adverb?**

11 | Combining Sentences: Expanding with Modifiers

You know that a simple subject and a simple predicate can make a sentence.

Stars shine.

By adding adjectives and adverbs, however, you can make the sentence clearer and more vivid.

Countless stars shine brightly tonight .

Adjectives and adverbs can also make your writing more interesting when you use them to combine short sentences.

The star is bright.
It is the North Star. ⟩ The bright star is the North Star.

A star fell from the sky.
   It fell quickly. ⟩ A star fell quickly from the sky.

You can place adverbs that modify verbs in different positions in a sentence. This can add variety to your writing.

I often watch the stars.

I watch the stars often .

Often I watch the stars.

Guided Practice How would you combine each pair of sentences?

Example: The balloons were green. They floated overhead.
The green balloons floated overhead.

1. The steak sizzled. It was juicy.
2. The leopards leaped. They leaped gracefully.
3. The soup spilled. It was hot.
4. The rain poured. It poured down suddenly.
5. The kitten was hungry. The kitten meowed.
6. The umpire yelled. He yelled loudly.

▶ Use modifiers to add meaning and interest to sentences.
▶ Use adjectives and adverbs to combine short sentences.

Independent Practice Write new sentences by combining each pair.

Example: Snow fell. It fell softly and quietly.
Snow fell quietly and softly.

7. Wheels screeched. They screeched suddenly.
8. The children played in the park. They were noisy.
9. The babies in the hospital cribs cried. They cried noisily.
10. The plums looked delicious. They were large and ripe.
11. Violet sang in the show. She sang loudly and clearly.
12. The horses were wild. They galloped across the plains.
13. Brian waited for the train. He waited impatiently.
14. The bride carried flowers. The flowers were white and purple.
15. The bulldozer pushed a load of dirt. The bulldozer was big.
16. Lee changed the subject. She changed the subject quickly.
17. The laundry was in the basket. The laundry was dirty.
18. The doctor studied the chart. He studied the chart thoughtfully.
19. The sailboats bobbed in the water. They were small and sleek.
20. The dog barked at the mail carrier. He barked fiercely.
21. The audience laughed at the clown. They laughed happily.
22. The branches were heavy. They were covered with snow.
23. The fish swam in the bowl. The fish were small and colorful.
24. The puppy was playful. It licked my hand.
25. This book is interesting. It is on sale.
26. The cat purred. It was striped and purred softly.
27. I had a ride in a helicopter. The ride was scary.
28. Margos erased his answer. The answer was incorrect.

Writing Application: A Paragraph

Write a paragraph about the chores you do at home. Use all simple sentences. Then exchange papers with a classmate, and combine each other's sentences. Add modifiers to make more interesting paragraphs.

For Extra Practice, see p. 257.   **Expanding with Modifiers 237**

Grammar-Writing Connection

Combining Sentences with Modifiers

You have learned that more than one adjective can modify a noun and that more than one adverb can modify a verb. This means that you can include several details in one sentence instead of writing a different sentence for each detail.

These sentences should be combined using modifiers.

The scientist Marie Curie and her husband discovered the element radium. Marie Curie was <u>famous</u>. She was from <u>Poland</u>. Her husband was from <u>France</u>.

The famous Polish scientist Marie Curie and her French husband discovered the element radium.

Notice that the proper nouns *Poland* and *France* become the proper adjectives *Polish* and *French* when the sentences above are combined.

You can sometimes combine details from different sentences by making adjectives into adverbs.

Over time radium decays. The decay is <u>slow</u>.

Over time, radium slowly decays.

Revising Sentences

Combine each set of sentences into one sentence using modifiers. Write the new sentence.

1. Some substances give off energy. The substances are natural.
2. Uranium is an element. Uranium is metallic.
3. Marie Curie won the Nobel Prize for her work. She won it twice. Her work was important.
4. Marie Curie did not know the effect that radium would have on her. The effect was harmful.
5. Today scientists use radium. They are careful.

Creative Writing

Stone City shows a landscape that looks as if it had been swept clean! Because Grant Wood loved the Iowa countryside, he exaggerated its neatness and beauty.

• How are the trees and hills in this painting unlike real ones?
• How do the shapes in *Stone City* add to its peaceful mood?

Stone City, Grant Wood, Joslyn Art Museum, Omaha, Nebraska

Activities

1. **Write a journal entry.** Suppose you could spend a day in this landscape. What would you choose to do: ride a horse? swim in the river? sit reading in the shade? Write a journal entry, describing your imaginary day in Stone City.

2. **Tell the legend of Stone City.** This place looks so peaceful that it almost seems frozen in time. Imagine that it really *is* a place where nothing moves or changes. Write a legend, explaining how and why Stone City became a place where time stopped.

Adjectives *(p. 218)* Write the adjective. (Do not include *a*, *an*, or *the*.) Then write the word that each adjective describes.

1. Edna is popular at parties.
2. She is a one-woman band.
3. She plays a small drum.
4. She plays two huge, flat cymbals.
5. She gives concerts, large and small.

Articles and Demonstratives *(p. 220)* Write the correct articles and demonstrative pronouns.

6. Do you own (a, an) poodle or (a, an) Irish setter?
7. I have (a, an) old mutt that is (a, an) wonderful friend to me.
8. (This, These) gray poodle is Jo's.
9. Did (the, an) dog win (a, an) award?
10. (Those, That) setters won in (the, a) annual competition.

Comparing with Adjectives *(p. 222)* Write each sentence, using the comparative or superlative form of the adjective in parentheses.

11. The ___ game was better than the earlier one. (late)
12. Even our ___ player scored. (weak)
13. It was the ___ game of all. (short)
14. It was also the ___. (hard)
15. This season was ___ for us than last season. (happy)

Comparing with *more* and *most* *(p. 224)* Write each sentence, using the comparative or superlative form of the adjective in parentheses.

16. Cara received the ___ applause in the talent show. (much)
17. The skiing today is ___ than it was yesterday. (good)
18. Which is the ___ camera of all? (expensive)
19. One of the ___ of all books is *Tom Sawyer*. (popular)
20. Are rubies ___ than diamonds? (valuable)
21. Does tomato juice have ___ vitamin C than orange juice? (much)
22. Which juice has the ___ vitamin C of all? (little)

Proper Adjectives *(p. 226)* Write a proper adjective for the proper noun in parentheses.

23. (China) vase
24. (Spain) lace
25. (Africa) art
26. (France) song
27. (Italy) food
28. (Mexico) fan

Adverbs That Modify Verbs *(p. 228)* Write each adverb and the verb it modifies.

29. The week passed slowly.
30. Lou waited patiently.
31. He often visits the zoo.
32. Today he ran there.
33. First, he saw the lions.
34. He usually watches them carefully.

Adverbs That Modify Adjectives and Adverbs (p. 229) Write each adverb that modifies an adjective or another adverb.

35. Lou watched the very playful birds.
36. One bird was remarkably graceful.
37. Lou sat especially quietly.
38. His movements were extremely cautious.
39. The bird chirped quite innocently.
40. Then it flew to a very high branch.

Comparing with Adverbs (p. 230) Write each sentence correctly, using the comparative or superlative form of the adverb in parentheses.

41. Gus draws ___ than Ron. (well)
42. Ron paints ___ than Gus. (fast)
43. Tim draws ___ of all three boys. (carefully)
44. Of all the students, Kim is the ___ interested in drawing. (little)
45. Rosemarie draws ___ than Jeanette does. (frequently)
46. I painted ___ today than I did yesterday. (badly)
47. However, I understand the problem ___ than I did yesterday. (clearly)

Negatives (p. 232) Rewrite the sentences to avoid double negatives.

48. Lee didn't see no clouds.
49. A wind didn't never blow.
50. No warning wasn't given.
51. She hadn't expected no rain.
52. There wasn't no shelter anywhere.
53. Not none of us stayed dry.

Adjective or Adverb? (p. 234) Write the correct adjective or adverb for each sentence.

54. Al likes (good, well) food.
55. He cooks (good, well).
56. He takes time to measure everything (careful, carefully).
57. He mixes (gradual, gradually).
58. He brings his homemade soups to a (slow, slowly) boil.
59. He doesn't work (quick, quickly).
60. He bakes (good, well) bread.
61. He bakes bread (good, well).
62. He also creates (delicious, deliciously) dishes of his own.
63. He can cook (wonderful, wonderfully) without following a recipe.

Combining Sentences: Expanding with Modifiers (p. 236) Write new sentences by combining each pair.

64. The man was Morris Frank. The man was blind.
65. His friends guided him around town. They guided him carefully.
66. He learned about Dorothy Eustis. He learned gratefully.
67. She was a dog trainer. She was very talented.
68. She said dogs could lead blind people on streets. The streets were busy.
69. Morris wrote a letter to Dorothy. He wrote eagerly.
70. Later Dorothy, Morris, and another man founded a school to train guide dogs. The school was successful.

Cumulative Review

Unit 1: The Sentence

Kinds of Sentences *(p. 14)* Add the correct end mark to each sentence. Label them *declarative, interrogative, imperative,* or *exclamatory.*

1. The cat and her kittens are playing
2. Would you like a kitten
3. How cute they are
4. Please keep them off the chair
5. I like the black kitten

Compound Subjects and Compound Predicates *(pp. 22, 24)* Write the parts of the compound subject or the compound predicate.

6. Carpenters pound nails or saw wood.
7. Jim measures a piece of wood and cuts it in half.
8. Jim and Russ are very experienced.
9. My brother and I help them.
10. I bring water or carry some tools.

Correcting Fragments and Run-ons *(p. 33)* Correct each sentence fragment or run-on sentence.

11. I belong to a book club I receive a new book each month.
12. I like mysteries and I like biographies and I have some of each.
13. Funny book with a good story.
14. The plot was good I liked it.
15. Solved the mystery.

Unit 3: Nouns

Plural Nouns *(p. 88)* Write the correct form of the noun given.

16. Three ___ from our street are coming to a barbecue. (family)
17. Everyone will bring two ___. (dish)
18. I sliced ___ for a salad. (apple)
19. All the ___ play volleyball. (child)
20. We make some great ___. (volley)

Possessive Nouns *(p. 91)* Write the correct form of the noun in parentheses.

21. The ___ chair is high. (lifeguard)
22. All the ___ swimming suits are bright orange. (lifeguards)
23. The ___ instructor is late. (girls)
24. ___ lesson will begin soon. (Tess)
25. The ___ lesson will be on the backstroke. (children)

Appositives *(p. 96)* Combine each sentence, using an appositive.

26. Mary is planting a garden. Mary is my older sister.
27. Bright flowers will grow. The flowers will be violets and pansies.
28. Some bulbs are tulips and crocuses. They grow every year.
29. My aunt is a good gardener. She gave my sister some advice.
30. I gave Mary a gift. The gift was a packet of sunflower seeds.

Unit 5: Verbs

Main Verbs and Auxiliaries *(p. 145)*
Write the verb phrase in each sentence. Underline the auxiliary verbs once and the main verbs twice.

31. Ali has studied color photography.
32. She will need a darkroom.
33. She must have learned about light meters and lens filters.
34. She has developed her photographs.
35. Should she exhibit her pictures?

Direct Objects *(p. 148)*
Write the action verb and the direct object in each sentence.

36. Today at school I learned the legend of Atlantis.
37. This mysterious island contained a great empire.
38. Earthquakes and floods destroyed the homeland.
39. The sea swallowed Atlantis in a single day and night.
40. People have written stories about this mystery.

Transitive and Intransitive Verbs *(p. 150)*
Write the verb in each sentence. Label the verb *transitive* or *intransitive.*

41. A jeweler repairs watches.
42. Mr. Milne cleaned my watch.
43. The watch ticks smoothly now.
44. The grandfather clock in the hall chimed.
45. Do you know the correct time?

Being Verbs and Linking Verbs *(p. 152)*
Write each linking verb and its predicate noun or predicate adjective.

46. Roy is a student at a cooking school.
47. Someday he will become a great chef.
48. Chefs are experienced cooks.
49. This wonderful vegetable dish seems nutritious.
50. The green vegetables look fresh.
51. The food tastes delicious.

Verb Tenses *(p. 154)*
Write each sentence. Use the correct tense of the verb in parentheses to complete each sentence.

52. Last year Jessie ___ her cousins in Japan. (visit)
53. Jessie ___ to use chopsticks before she went. (learn)
54. She ___ many new foods when she was in Japan. (taste)
55. Jessie's cousins ___ to America next year. (travel)
56. Jessie ___ her cousins around her country when they come. (guide)

Principal Parts of Verbs, Irregular Verbs *(pp. 156, 158)*
Write the four principal parts of each irregular verb.

57. freeze   60. make
58. fly   61. throw
59. swim   62. tear

Cumulative Review, *continued*

Subject-Verb Agreement *(pp. 160, 162)* Write the present tense of the verbs.

63. There ___ many kinds of dogs. (be)

64. Neither that poodle nor those Scottish terriers ___ very big. (be)

65. Watchdogs ___ houses and businesses from burglars. (protect)

66. This boxer and that German shepherd ___ good guard dogs. (make)

67. Olga ___ guide dogs. (train)

68. Either collies or sheepdogs ___ good herders of farm animals. (be)

69. Here ___ a St. Bernard. (be)

Contractions *(p. 164)* Write each contraction. Write each verb phrase.

70. We're studying about plants.

71. Plants can't live without light.

72. They'll bend toward the light.

73. My plants aren't getting enough water.

74. I've written my science report.

sit, set; lie, lay; rise, raise *(p. 166)* Write the verb in parentheses that completes each sentence correctly.

75. (Sit, Set) the cartons down.

76. I will (rise, raise) them up.

77. (Lay, Lie) those papers here.

78. Please don't (sit, set) on them.

79. You can (lie, lay) on the cushion.

lend, borrow; let, leave; teach, learn *(p. 168)* Write the verb in ( ) that completes each sentence correctly.

80. I will (teach, learn) Rita.

81. (Let, Leave) the game on my desk.

82. May I (lend, borrow) your rules?

83. Rita will (teach, learn) quickly.

84. Karl will (let, leave) us play too.

Unit 7: Modifiers

Adjectives *(pp. 218, 220)* Write each adjective. Include the articles.

85. This well-known music was written by an excellent musician.

86. That famous composer writes songs.

87. Some songs are cheerful and pretty.

88. Other songs, slow and sad, are nice.

89. A big concert was held in the gym.

Comparing with Adjectives *(pp. 222, 224)* Write the comparative or superlative form correctly.

90. Wheat is the world's ___ grain crop. (important)

91. Wheat fields cover ___ land than any other crop. (much)

92. Bread is one of the ___ products of wheat. (common)

93. The ___ part of the wheat kernel is made into flour. (useful)

94. Our crop is ___ this year than last year. (big)

Proper Adjectives *(p. 226)* Write a proper adjective from the noun in parentheses.

95. A ___ Blue cat has blue-gray hair. (Russia)
96. A ___ Blue cat has shorter legs. (Britain)
97. The ___ Shorthair can be many colors. (America)
98. A ___ cat has a curly tail. (China)
99. ___ art shows many cats. (Egypt)

Adverbs Modifying Verbs, Adjectives, Adverbs *(pp. 228, 229)* Write the adverbs.

100. Today a storyteller told a very strange story.
101. The audience listened very quietly.
102. The storyteller spoke rather softly.
103. The story was quite scary.
104. The storyteller often paused.
105. I was totally surprised at the end.

Comparing with Adverbs *(p. 230)* Write the comparative or superlative form of the adverbs.

106. The actors performed ___ tonight than last night. (good)
107. Sean said his lines the ___. (dramatically)
108. Claudia spoke ___ than Sean. (softly)
109. She was always the ___ prepared. (little)
110. The audience applauded ___ for Tom than for Shelley. (loudly)

Negatives *(p. 232)* Rewrite each sentence to avoid the double negative.

111. There wasn't no chalk.
112. No one couldn't write on the chalkboard.
113. The teacher hadn't found none in the supply closet.
114. We hardly never use any chalk.
115. There wasn't any chalk nowhere.

Adjective or Adverb? *(p. 234)* Write the correct adjective or adverb in each sentence.

116. Rose tells (good, well) stories.
117. She writes (good, well) too.
118. Her stories are (cheerful, cheerfully).
119. They end (happy, happily).
120. I listen (enthusiastic, enthusiastically) to Rose's stories.
121. They are often (funny, funnily).

Combining Sentences: Expanding with Modifiers *(p. 236)* Write new sentences by combining each pair.

122. The explorers discovered a city. The city was buried.
123. They had searched for this city. They had searched carefully.
124. The city was famous. It was called Troy.
125. A poet was Greek. He had written about this city.
126. Many tourists visit Troy. They visit eagerly.

Enrichment

Using Modifiers

Movie Ad

Imagine that you are asked to design a full-page newspaper ad for a new family film. First, think up a plot and title for your movie. On white paper, write the title in big letters. Then draw a picture to illustrate it. Next, write five favorable statements by reviewers of your movie. Include adjectives and adverbs. Have some of your adverbs modify the adjectives. Write adjectives in red and adverbs in green.

Cave Drawings

You are a reporter going back in time to prehistoric days. Make a cave drawing and write a news story to show what is going on. You might show people on a food-gathering expedition. On another sheet of paper, write a brief news story about what is happening in your picture. Use adjectives and adverbs to add interest. Underline adjectives in red, adverbs in blue, and articles in green.

Fabulous Fables

Create your own fable, using three or more animal characters. Show how bragging can make someone lose something valuable. Use comparisons with *much, bad, little, short, late,* and *plentiful.*

Extra! Illustrate your fable with drawings. Create a class book of your fables.

Extra Practice: Unit 7

● Write the adjectives in these sentences.

Example: This dog was lucky. *This   lucky*

1. He was lost.
2. Two children found Moon.
3. They helped dirty, scared Moon.
4. They brought him to that excellent shelter.
5. Moon stayed with some small dogs.
6. Moon was kept in this six-foot pen.
7. We saw that big friendly dog.
8. He was white and black.
9. I liked his happy bark.
10. We gave Moon this new home.

▲ Write adjectives to complete the sentences. Write the type of adjectives shown in parentheses.

Example: A castle is a ____ building. (what kind) *huge*

11. Most castles have only ____ main entrance. (how many) one
12. Life inside a castle must have been ____. (what kind)
13. ____ castles had towers, ____ ones. (which one, what kind)
14. They also had ____ windows. (what kind)
15. Each castle had ____ ____ hall. (how many, what kind)
16. ____ hall must have been ____. (which one, what kind)
17. ____ guards must have stood in front of the ____ gates. (how many, what kind)

■ Use the following adjectives in sentences. Draw an arrow to the noun that each adjective modifies.

Example: red-hot   *The red-hot peppers made my eyes water.*

18. twelve	22. tiny
19. suspicious	23. those
20. crisp	24. prize-winning
21. reckless	25. toothless

2 | Articles and Demonstratives (p. 220)

● Write the correct article or demonstrative pronoun.

Example: Clarence was (a, an) lion.   *a*

1. He became (a, an) movie star in 1965.
2. He starred in (the, an) film called *Clarence the Cross-eyed Lion*.
3. Many people enjoyed (that, those) film.
4. Clarence was (a, an) unusual animal.
5. He was (a, an) easygoing lion.
6. He later appeared in (a, an) television series.
7. (This, These) show was *Daktari*.
8. Clarence's co-star was (a, an) chimpanzee.
9. (That, Those) two seemed to be friends.

▲ Write each article and demonstrative adjective.

Example: That plane is a glider.   *That   a*

10. A glider does not have an engine.
11. This bigger plane will pull the glider into the air.
12. The big plane is called a tow plane.
13. That rope holds the glider.
14. When the planes get very high, the glider lets go.
15. Then it rides the air currents.
16. This glider is newer than that one.
17. Those pilots will control these gliders.

■ Read the story plot below. Then tell the story in your own words. Use articles and demonstrative adjectives. Underline the articles once and the demonstratives twice.

Example: Mouse bothers lion.   *Once upon a time when a lion was*
               asleep, a tiny mouse ran right up that lion's back.

18. Lion catches mouse.
19. Mouse pleads for life.
20. Mouse promises to return favor.
21. Lion lets mouse go.
22. Then lion gets caught in hunter's net.
23. Mouse hears lion roaring.
24. Mouse chews net and frees lion.

3 | Comparing with Adjectives (p. 222)

● Write the comparative or superlative adjective in each sentence.

Example: June has the longest day of the year.   *longest*

1. June days are longer than those in the fall.
2. The shortest day is in December.
3. The coldest weather comes soon after.
4. Chicago has been called the windiest city.
5. Many cities are windier, though.
6. Miami, Florida, is warmer than Chicago.
7. One of the chilliest spots is on Mount Washington.

▲ Write the correct form of each adjective in parentheses.

Example: The ____ land animal is the African elephant.   (large)
    largest

8. A giraffe, however, is ____ than an elephant.   (tall)
9. The ____ mammal is a kind of bat.   (small)
10. Bats also have the ____ hearing of any land mammal.   (sharp)
11. The ____ animal ever seen was a ribbon worm.   (long)
12. A turtle is ____ than a toad.   (slow)
13. A cheetah is ____ than a race horse.   (fast)
14. The ____ and ____ animal is the blue whale.   (large, heavy)

■ Write a sentence for each phrase. Use the comparative or superlative form of the adjective, as shown in parentheses.

Example: a bright color   (comparative)
    Yellow is a brighter color than gray.

15. the nice pet   (superlative)
16. a hot climate   (comparative)
17. the cold day   (superlative)
18. the happy time   (superlative)
19. the silly joke   (comparative)
20. the angry moment   (superlative)
21. an easy book   (comparative)
22. a sad story   (comparative)
23. the pretty scene   (superlative)
24. the long movie   (superlative)

4 | Comparing with *more* and *most* (p. 224)

● Write the words that complete each sentence correctly.

Example: One of the (more common, most common) hobbies is
stamp collecting.   *most common*

1. Collecting stamps is not the (good, best) way to get rich.
2. That is the (worse, worst) reason of all to start this hobby.
3. There are (better, best) reasons than that to collect stamps.
4. Stories about rare stamps are the (more popular, most popular)
   of all.
5. Rare stamps are (more unusual, most unusual) than people think.
6. This hobby is (less expensive, least expensive) than other hobbies.
7. It also makes trips to the post office (much, more) exciting.

▲ Write the correct comparative or superlative form of the adjective in parentheses to complete each sentence.

Example: Some animals are ____ than others.   (unusual)
              more unusual

8. Which animal is the ____ of them all?   (unusual)
9. Which animal is the ____ engineer of all?   (good)
10. Beavers are ____ engineers than mice.   (good)
11. The beaver is ____ for its dams.   (famous)
12. Beavers spend ____ time in water than on land.   (much)
13. Gorillas may be the ____ appreciated animals.   (little)
14. Gorillas are really ____ than other animals.   (gentle)

■ Write the comparative or superlative form of an adjective to
complete each sentence. Do not use the same adjective more
than once.

Example: Which is the ____ camera?   *least expensive*

15. This is the ____ camera made today.
16. Is that a ____ camera than my old one?
17. I would like to take ____ pictures than I usually do.
18. I am the ____ photographer of all my friends.
19. Karen is ____ with a camera than Leroy.
20. Background is ____ to a photograph than many people think.

5 | Proper Adjectives (p. 226)

● Write the proper adjective in each sentence.

Example: My family is Mexican.   *Mexican*

1. For breakfast we had Irish soda bread.
2. I ate Scottish oatmeal.
3. We also enjoyed Italian cheese.
4. For lunch I ate Swedish meatballs.
5. Dad served them on German noodles.
6. I also had crisp Chinese vegetables.
7. With dinner we ate English cheese.
8. I toasted the cheese on French bread.
9. American meals come from many countries.
10. The meals are very European.

▲ Write a proper adjective from each noun in parentheses.

Example: The ____ language has words from many other languages.
(England)   *English*

11. We have taken the ____ word *pronto*.   (Spain)
12. The word *coupon* is a ____ word.   (France)
13. When someone sneezes, we often say a ____ word.   (German)
14. People in other countries also use ____ words.   (England)
15. ____ people say *il weekend*.   (Italy)
16. ____ citizens know what rock-and-roll is.   (China)
17. Our word *hi* means *yes* to a ____ person.   (Japan)
18. The ____ word for *was* sounds like the name *Bill*.   (Russia)
19. The ____ word for *word* sounds like *so*.   (Hungary)
20. The words *moose, raccoon,* and *woodchuck* are Native ____
    words.   (America)

■ For each proper noun, write a proper adjective. Then write a
sentence, using it as an adjective.

Example: Scotland   *Scottish   Do you like Scottish bagpipes?*

21. England	25. Italy	29. Canada
22. Norway	26. Brazil	30. Mexico
23. France	27. China	31. Hawaii
24. Ireland	28. Japan	32. Alaska

6 | Adverbs That Modify Verbs (p. 228)

● Write the adverb in each sentence.

Example: Yesterday Alan picked his first tomato.   *Yesterday*

1. Alan grows tomatoes anywhere.
2. He lives in the city now.
3. Alan carefully planted two plants in pots.
4. He watered them daily.
5. The plants grew quickly.
6. Finally, he picked four ripe tomatoes.
7. He served them proudly.
8. Everyone thoroughly enjoyed them.

▲ Write all the adverbs that modify verbs in these sentences.

Example: Five little bats hung upside-down.   *upside-down*

9. Susan looked at them nervously.
10. Finally, she asked if they were alive.
11. She had never seen bats.
12. Now she and her uncle were staring at some.
13. He knew they would fly away.
14. Bats live everywhere, but most people never see them.
15. Susan looked quietly at the tiny creatures.
16. She really wanted to see them fly.

■ Write each adverb and the verb or verb phrase it modifies. Underline the adverb once and the verb twice.

Example: Ana was cheerfully washing her bicycle.
      cheerfully   was washing

17. Suddenly she saw a cat.
18. The cat was staring hard at a sparrow.
19. The sparrow was pecking carelessly at some seeds.
20. The cat crept steadily toward the bird.
21. The cat's tail twitched nervously.
22. Ana shouted loudly at the cat.
23. Immediately the cat stopped.
24. The sparrow flew high into a tree.
25. The hungry cat ran away.

7 | Adverbs Modifying Adj. and Adv. (p. 229)

● Write the underlined adverb and the adjective or the adverb that it modifies.

Example: Luis took a <u>very</u> long hike. *very long*

1. At first, he walked <u>quite</u> slowly.
2. Then Luis saw some <u>very</u> dark clouds.
3. Luis became <u>rather</u> nervous.
4. He walked <u>more</u> quickly.
5. Luis stayed <u>really</u> calm.
6. He looked for a <u>completely</u> safe place.
7. He saw a <u>truly</u> perfect shelter ahead.

▲ Write the adverb in each sentence that modifies an adjective or an adverb. Then write the word that it modifies.

Example: Most sharks are very good swimmers. *very good*

8. Some sharks, such as the nurse shark, are rather small.
9. Others, including the whale shark, are really huge.
10. Sharks have an especially good sense of smell.
11. They most often eat other fish.
12. Some sharks will swallow almost any object.
13. They have eaten very old ropes and boots.
14. About ten percent of sharks are extremely dangerous to people.
15. The other ninety percent are more harmful to other fish.

■ Write an adverb to modify the adjective or the adverb that follows it. Label the modified word *adjective* or *adverb*.

Example: A magnet is a ____ important tool. *very **adjective***

16. For hundreds of years, magnets guided sailors ____ accurately.
17. A horseshoe magnet is ____ stronger than a straight magnet.
18. It is stronger because the two points are ____ closer together.
19. Nails become magnets ____ quickly.
20. You hold them ____ close to a magnet.
21. Steel becomes a magnet ____ slowly than nails.
22. No one is ____ sure what makes magnets work.
23. Some types of magnets are ____ useful in scientific research.
24. These magnets are often ____ powerful.

8 | Comparing with Adverbs (p. 230)

● Write the form of the adverb that is correct in each sentence.

Example: Tuesday I ran (better, more better) than I usually do.
better

1. I study (best, bestest) in the library.
2. Now I worry (littler, less) than I used to about Field Day.
3. Robin always ran the (best, most best) in our class.
4. She (most frequentliest, most frequently) won the Field Day race.
5. This year I practiced (more often, more oftener) than ever before.
6. Tomorrow I want to run (more better, better) than ever.
7. What I fear (mostest, most) is the heat.
8. I am (littler, less) worried about losing than I used to be.
9. It is (more, morer) important to run as fast as I can.

▲ Write the form of the adverb in parentheses that correctly completes each sentence.

Example: My brother Bob rides ___ than I do. (well) *better*

10. The horses obey him ___ than they obey me. (quick)
11. This year he worked ___ than he did last year. (hard)
12. He wants to run the barrel races ___ than anyone. (fast)
13. Last year he ran the course ___ than he does now. (bad)
14. He trained ___ this year than last year. (often)
15. Of all the horses, Pepper runs ___. (enthusiastically)
16. Bob trains him ___ than he trains the others. (frequently)
17. Bob and Pepper will not race ___ than any other pair. (badly)
18. I think they will enjoy themselves ___ of all. (much)

■ Use the phrases below in complete sentences.

Example: reads more slowly
Sally reads more slowly than Liz, but she also reads more carefully.

19. sings better
20. are most easily lost
21. answered most quickly
22. laughed longer
23. asked most often

24. painted most creatively
25. felt best
26. sews more skillfully
27. studies more thoughtfully
28. answers most promptly

9 ‖ Negatives (p. 232)

● Write the words that make these sentences negative.

Example: Last summer nobody wanted to stay home. *nobody*

1. Mark wanted to do something he had never done before.
2. None of us had ever tried camping.
3. Dad made lists to make sure that nothing would be left behind.
4. We chose a place that was not crowded.
5. The place was nowhere we had ever been.
6. I had never slept in a tent before.
7. We had no stove, and we cooked over a fire.
8. Later no one wanted to go home.

▲ Write the word in parentheses that completes each sentence correctly.

Example: Natalie didn't see (no, any) grocery store. *any*

9. Nobody (was, wasn't) paying attention.
10. No one (never, ever) bought much at the store.
11. Your store isn't (anything, nothing) like my store.
12. The store no longer carries (no, any) frozen food.
13. No one (ever, never) bought frozen food here.
14. The store didn't (never, ever) have a bakery.
15. Natalie couldn't find fresh fruit (nowhere, anywhere).
16. This store isn't in business (no more, anymore).

■ Write each sentence correctly, avoiding double negatives.

Example: No one uses picture writing no more.
        No one uses picture writing anymore.

17. Once many people didn't use nothing else.
18. Until 1821 the Cherokees didn't have no alphabet.
19. There wasn't no way they could write certain ideas.
20. Sequoya didn't let nothing stop him.
21. No one never invented a writing system alone before.
22. Before 1828 Cherokee writing wasn't published nowhere.
23. Sequoya's alphabet wasn't hard for no one to learn.
24. Cherokees had never read no Cherokee newspaper before.
25. Now there wasn't nothing they couldn't read.

10 | Adjective or Adverb? (p. 234)

● Write the correct word to complete each sentence.

Example: Last year I got a (good, well) camera.   *good*

1. I (quick, quickly) learned how to use it.
2. My pictures were not (good, well), though.
3. I took pictures (bad, badly).
4. My friend Sal takes (good, well) pictures.
5. He (careful, carefully) showed me what to do.
6. On Sunday I didn't feel (good, well).
7. I read (good, well), and I have many books.
8. I read one (good, well) book about cameras.

▲ Complete each sentence by writing the correct word: *good, well, quick,* or *quickly.*

Example: My older sister Cheryl cooks very ____.   *well*

9. Someday she will be a ____ chef.
10. Last year she took a class at a ____ cooking school.
11. The school was French, and Cheryl has spoken French ____ for many years.
12. She ____ learned to cook many dishes.
13. A few wonderful dishes are also ____ and easy to make.
14. This dish tastes very ____.
15. Once I ate too fast and didn't feel ____ later.
16. Now I don't eat so ____.

■ Write a sentence using each pair of phrases. Underline the phrases.

Example: good music   plays well
          Andy loves good music and plays the clarinet well.

17. bad handwriting   writes badly
18. slow eater   talked slowly
19. looks good   feels well
20. looked bad   threw badly
21. tasted sweet   sweetly asked
22. good performer   juggles well
23. quick wink   quickly saw
24. happy song   sings happily

11 | Combining Sentences (p. 236)

● Combine each pair of sentences below to form one complete sentence.

Example: The terrible storm struck. It struck quickly.
The terrible storm struck quickly.

1. Clouds gathered. They gathered overhead.
2. Thunder crashed. It was loud.
3. Lightning flashed. It flashed often.
4. Marion pointed outside. She pointed suddenly.
5. Clouds appeared. They were funnel-shaped.
6. Everyone raced downstairs. They raced quickly.
7. They waited in the cellar. They waited anxiously.
8. A roaring sound filled the cellar. The cellar was damp.
9. Then the noise stopped. It stopped suddenly.
10. The house was big. It remained untouched.

▲ Add at least one adjective and one adverb to each sentence below. Write each new sentence.

Example: Panthers climb. *Sleek black panthers climb gracefully.*

11. Tigers swim.
12. Antelope graze.
13. Lions hunt.
14. Zebras gallop.
15. People approach.
16. Cubs run.
17. Leaves rustle.
18. Birds fly.
19. Hippos wade.
20. Visitors whisper.

■ Combine each pair of sentences, adding at least one adjective or one adverb to each new sentence. Underline the adjectives once and the adverbs twice.

Example: Boris and Tia completed a map. The map was large.
Boris and Tia carefully completed a large map.

21. They drew a map of an island. They drew neatly.
22. The island had a treasure. The treasure was buried.
23. Clues were hidden on the map. There were many clues.
24. Boris and Tia planned the clues. They planned cleverly.
25. No one had been to this island. The island was undiscovered.
26. They talked about the pirate's treasure. They talked excitedly.

● ▲ ■ **Three levels of practice 257**

S ail-
boats on the sea:
white butterflies, winging
across a watery meadow of blue.

Carlota Cárdenas de Dwyer
"Cinquain: An Image"

Description

Getting Ready Imagine that you are standing underneath a large, hollow, brass object, looking up into its interior. Its circumference is ten feet, but its sides taper and curve inward to meet at the top. In the center, suspended from the top and hanging down to the bottom, is a very narrow rod with a solid ball at the end. This part of the object swings freely when the entire object is tipped. Each time the object is tipped, a loud noise is made. What is this object? From which point of view was it described? Think of an object you would like to describe. In this unit, you will learn to write descriptions.

ACTIVITIES

Listening
Listen to the poem as it is read. Are the boats moving or still? Which words tell you that? What are the boats being compared to? What is the sea being compared to?

Speaking
Look at this picture. What is your overall impression? Which details would you include in a description? Select those that back up your impressions.

Writing
Pick a scene of your own. In your journal, describe your overall impression. List the details that back up your impression.

LITERATURE

The Women's 400 Meters

By Lillian Morrison

Skittish,
they flex knees, drum heels and
shiver at the starting line

waiting the gun
to pour them over the stretch
like a breaking wave.

Bang! they're off
careening down the lanes,
each chased by her own bright tiger.

Think and Discuss

1. What event is described in this poem? What part of that event is described in detail?
2. Lines of poetry that are arranged in sections are called **stanzas**. Like a paragraph, a stanza has one main idea. How many stanzas are there in "The Women's 400 Meters"? What part of the action is described in each stanza?
3. The first stanza uses **literal language** to tell what the runners are doing. Literal language describes exactly what is happening or what can be seen. We picture the runners flexing their knees as they wait for the starting gun.

   In the next stanzas, the poet uses **figurative language**. Figurative language uses words in a way that suggests something other than their exact or usual meaning. A **simile** is a type of figurative language. A simile uses *like* or *as* to compare things in an unexpected way to create forceful, dramatic images. What is the simile in the second stanza? To what does the poet compare the movement of the runners?
4. What other titles would suit this poem? Write a different title for the poem—one that uses figurative language.

Can new shoes make you feel like a different person?

New Sneakers

By Ray Bradbury

Old Mr. Sanderson moved through his shoe store as the proprietor of a pet shop must move through his shop where are kenneled animals from everywhere in the world, touching each one briefly along the way. Mr. Sanderson brushed his hands over the shoes in the window, and some of them were like cats to him and some were like dogs; he touched each pair with concern, adjusting laces, fixing tongues. Then he stood in the exact center of the carpet and looked around, nodding.

There was a sound of growing thunder.

One moment, the door to Sanderson's Shoe Emporium was empty. The next, Douglas Spaulding stood clumsily there, staring down at his leather shoes as if these heavy things could not be pulled up out of the cement. The thunder had stopped when his shoes stopped. Now, with painful slowness, daring to look only at the money in his cupped hand, Douglas moved out of the bright sunlight of Saturday noon. He made careful stacks of nickels, dimes, and quarters on the counter, like someone playing chess and worried if the next move carried him out into sun or deep into shadow.

"Don't say a word!" said Mr. Sanderson.

Douglas froze.

"First, I know just what you want to buy," said Mr. Sanderson. "Second, I see you every afternoon at my window; you think I don't see? You're wrong. Third, to give it its full name, you want the Royal Crown Cream-

Sponge Para Litefoot Tennis Shoes: 'LIKE MENTHOL ON YOUR FEET!' Fourth, you want credit."

"No!" cried Douglas, breathing hard, as if he'd run all night in his dreams. "I got something better than credit to offer!" he gasped. "Before I tell, Mr. Sanderson, you got to do me one small favor. Can you remember when was the last time you yourself wore a pair of Litefoot sneakers, sir?"

Mr. Sanderson's face darkened. "Oh, ten, twenty, say, thirty years ago. Why . . . ?"

"Mr. Sanderson, don't you think you owe it to your customers, sir, to at least try the tennis shoes you sell, for just one minute, so you know how they feel? People forget if they don't keep testing things. United Cigar Store man smokes cigars, don't he? Candy store man samples his own stuff, I should think. So . . ."

"You may have noticed," said the old man, "I'm wearing shoes."

"But not sneakers, sir! How you going to sell sneakers unless you can rave about them and how you going to rave about them unless you know them?"

Mr. Sanderson backed off a little distance from the boy's fever, one hand to his chin. "Well . . ."

"Mr. Sanderson," said Douglas, "you sell me something and I'll sell you something just as valuable."

"Is it absolutely necessary to the sale that I put on a pair of the sneakers, boy?" said the old man.

"I sure wish you could, sir!"

The old man sighed. A minute later, seated panting quietly, he laced the tennis shoes to his long narrow feet. They looked detached and alien down there next to the dark cuffs of his business suit. Mr. Sanderson stood up.

"How do they *feel*?" asked the boy.

"How do they feel, he asks; they feel fine." He started to sit down.

"Please!" Douglas held out his hand. "Mr. Sanderson, now could you kind of rock back and forth a little, sponge around, bounce kind of, while I tell you the rest? It's this: I give you my money, you give me the shoes, I owe you a dollar. But, Mr. Sanderson, *but*—soon as I get those shoes on, you know what *happens*?"

"What?"

"Bang! I deliver your packages, pick up packages, bring you coffee, burn your trash, run to the post office, telegraph office, library! You'll see twelve of me in and out, in and out, every minute. Feel those shoes, Mr. Sanderson, *feel* how fast they'd take me? All those springs inside? Feel all the running inside? Feel how they kind of grab hold and can't let you alone and don't like you just *standing* there? Feel how quick I'd be doing the things you'd rather not bother with? You stay in the nice cool store while I'm jumping all around town! But it's not me really, it's the shoes. They're going like mad down alleys, cutting corners, and back! There they go!"

Mr. Sanderson stood amazed with the rush of words. When the words got going the flow carried him; he began to sink deep in the shoes, to flex his toes, limber his arches, test his ankles. He rocked softly, secretly, back and forth in a small breeze from the open door. The tennis shoes silently hushed themselves deep in the carpet, sank as in a jungle grass, in loam and resilient clay. He gave one solemn bounce of his heels in the yeasty dough, in the yielding and welcoming earth. Emotions hurried over his face as if many colored lights had been switched on and off. His mouth hung slightly open. Slowly he gentled and rocked himself to a halt, and the boy's voice faded and they stood there looking at each other in a tremendous and natural silence.

A few people drifted by on the sidewalk outside, in the hot sun.

264

Still the man and boy stood there, the boy glowing, the man with revelation in his face.

"Boy," said the old man at last, "in ive years, how would you like a job selling shoes in this emporium?"

"Gosh, thanks, Mr. Sanderson, but I don't know what I'm going to be yet."

"Anything you want to be, son," said the old man, "you'll be. No one will ever stop you."

The old man walked lightly across the store to the wall of ten thousand boxes, came back with some shoes for the boy, and wrote up a list on some paper while the boy was lacing the shoes on his feet and then standing there, waiting.

The old man held out his list. "A dozen things you got to do for me this afternoon. Finish them, we're even Stephen, and you're fired."

"Thanks, Mr. Sanderson!" Douglas bounded away.

"Stop!" cried the old man.

Douglas pulled up and turned.

Mr. Sanderson leaned forward. "How do they *feel*?"

The boy looked down at his feet deep in the rivers, in the

265

fields of wheat, in the wind that already was rushing him out of the town. He looked up at the old man, his eyes burning, his mouth moving, but no sound came out.

"Antelopes?" said the old man, looking from the boy's face to his shoes. "Gazelles?"

The boy thought about it, hesitated, and nodded a quick nod. Almost immediately he vanished. He just spun about with a whisper and went off. The door stood empty. The sound of the tennis shoes faded in the jungle heat.

Mr. Sanderson stood in the sun-blazed door, listening. From a long time ago, when he dreamed as a boy, he remembered the sound. Beautiful creatures leaping under the sky, gone through brush, under trees, away, and only the soft echo their running left behind.

"Antelopes," said Mr. Sanderson. "Gazelles."

He bent to pick up the boy's abandoned winter shoes, heavy with forgotten rains and long-melted snows. Moving out of the blazing sun, walking softly, lightly, slowly, he headed back toward civilization. . . .

Think and Discuss

1. What happens to Mr. Sanderson when he puts on a pair of sneakers for the first time in thirty years?
2. How does Douglas propose to pay for his sneakers?
3. The **characters** in "New Sneakers" are two people, Mr. Sanderson and Douglas. The author does not tell us what Douglas and Mr. Sanderson are like. He *shows* us what they are like by what they do and say. How do we learn that Mr. Sanderson is observant? What details show that both characters have vivid imaginations?
4. "New Sneakers" is the story of an encounter between a young boy and an old man. What does each of them gain from the encounter? Do you think each is likely to remember the other long after their meeting? Why or why not?

RESPONDING TO LITERATURE

The Reading and Writing Connection

Personal Response Have you ever figured out a creative way to get something you wanted very badly? Write a paragraph telling what you wanted and how you got or tried to get it.

Creative Writing Use figurative language to imaginatively describe your favorite sport or hobby. Make an unexpected comparison. Then write a poem, using your comparison.

Creative Activities

Read Aloud With a partner, read the roles of Douglas and Mr. Sanderson. Read aloud just the dialogue from the time Mr. Sanderson says, "Don't say a word!" to the time Douglas says, "I sure wish you could, sir!" Practice expressing the feelings and mood of each character.

Make an Ad Pretend that the Litefoot Shoe Company has hired you to design a new ad for Royal Crown Cream-Sponge Para Litefoot Tennis Shoes. Illustrate the ad. Write the words that will go on the ad, and create a slogan.

Vocabulary

At the end of "New Sneakers," Mr. Sanderson heads "back toward civilization." The word *civilization* comes from the Latin word *civis*, which means citizen. Use a dictionary to discover how the Latin root is related to the meaning of these terms: *civilian, civics, civility.*

Looking Ahead

Description In the following unit, you will be writing a description. Look at the third paragraph of "New Sneakers." How does the author create a vivid word picture of Douglas's arrival at the store?

VOCABULARY CONNECTION

Word Connotations

The words you use can often create feelings and reactions. The associations that a word brings to mind are called its **connotation.** Read the passage below.

> Mr. Sanderson stood **amazed** with the rush of words. When the words got going the flow carried him. . . .
> *from "New Sneakers" by Ray Bradbury*

- Does *amazed* bring to mind a positive or a negative feeling?
- If you replace *amazed* with *shocked* in the passage above, what connotation comes to mind?

Amazed has a positive connotation. It suggests that Mr. Sanderson is pleasantly surprised. *Shocked* has a negative connotation. *Shocked* suggests that Mr. Sanderson is upset. It is important to know the connotations of the words you use.

Connotations			
Positive	clever	curious	cautious
Negative	tricky	nosy	timid

Vocabulary Practice

A. The positive words in each pair are from "New Sneakers." Write the words with the more negative connotations.

1. dreams   nightmares
2. frigid   cool
3. breathing   panting
4. blazing   bright

B. Write five words from "New Sneakers" that have a positive or a negative connotation. For each of these words, think of a word that has the opposite connotation. Use the words in each pair in sentences of your own.

Prewriting
Description

Listening and Speaking: Poetry

Poets often use "sound effects" to help create the meaning and the rhythm of a poem. Understanding how these sounds work can help you with all kinds of descriptive writing.

One kind of sound effect is **onomatopoeia**. The word comes from two Greek words that mean "to make a name." It is used to describe words whose sounds imitate or suggest the sound that the words stand for. Words like *buzz, thud, hiss, meow,* and *crackle* are all onomatopoetic. In the lines below, which word creates a sound effect?

> Bang! they're off
> careening down the lanes,
> each chased by her own bright tiger.
> *from "The Women's 400 Meters" by Lillian Morrison*

Sometimes a poet repeats the beginning sounds of words for their effect. This is called **alliteration**. Alliteration links together the words that sound alike. How does repetition of sounds in these lines affect the meaning?

> In a summer season when soft was the sun
> *from* Piers Plowman *by William Langland*
>
> Over the cobbles he clattered and clashed.
> *from "The Highwayman" by Alfred Noyes*

- Which line would you read slowly and quietly?
- What do you hear in the second line?

When lines in a poem have the same last sounds, they **rhyme**. The pattern of the rhyme is different in different poems. In the poem on the next page, the pattern of the rhyme follows an *a, b, a, b* pattern.

> By the rude bridge that arched the flood,   *a*
> Their flag to April's breeze unfurled,   *b*
> Here once the embattled farmers stood   *a*
> And fired the shot heard round the world.   *b*
> *from "Concord Hymn" by Ralph Waldo Emerson*

Notice that lines 1 and 3 do not have an exact rhyme. The poet pairs similar vowel sounds. Rhymes don't have to be exact.

The sounds in a poem help create the **rhythm**. Rhythm is the number of beats in a line. A **beat** is an accented syllable or a stressed word. In poetry rhythm gives added meaning to the words. Sometimes you can feel danger. Sometimes you can hear the clatter of horses' hoofs. Some poems have a very distinct rhythm that follows a pattern of regular beats. Read the following lines aloud.

> I sprang to the stirrup, and Joris, and he;
> I galloped, Dirck galloped, we galloped all three;
> "Good speed!" cried the watch, as the gate-bolts undrew;
> "Speed!" echoed the wall to us galloping through.
> *from "How They Brought the Good News*
> *from Ghent to Aix" by Robert Browning*

- How does the rhythm help you emphasize certain words?
- How does the rhythm create the effect of galloping?

Other poems do not follow a regular pattern. Their rhythm is more like that of speech. The rhythm does not come from the number of beats per line. The lines do not have to rhyme.

> people always ask what
> am i going to be
> when i grow
> up and i always
> just think
> i'd like to grow
> up
>
> *"poem for rodney"*
> *by Nikki Giovanni*

- Do the line breaks make you emphasize certain words?
- Do these lines have any rhythm?

Prewriting Practice

A. Listen as your teacher reads you this part of a poem.
   Then read the questions that follow and listen
   again. Answer the questions.

> Hear the sledges with the bells—
>   Silver bells!
> What a world of merriment their melody foretells!
>   How they tinkle, tinkle, tinkle,
>   In the icy air of night!
>   While the stars that oversprinkle
>   All the heavens seem to twinkle
>   With a crystalline delight;
>   Keeping time, time, time,
>   In a sort of Runic rhyme,
> To the tintinnabulation that so musically wells
>   From the bells, bells, bells, bells,
>   Bells, bells, bells—
> From the jingling and the tinkling of the bells.
>   *from "The Bells" by Edgar Allan Poe*

1. What are some of the onomatopoetic words in this poem?
   What sounds do they imitate?
2. Find two examples of alliteration in this poem. Which
   consonant sounds are repeated?
3. What are some of the rhyming words in this poem?
4. Does this poem have a regular, repeated rhythm, or is its
   rhythm irregular like speech?

B. Work with a partner. Take turns reading these lines aloud.

> The saddest noise, the sweetest noise,
> The maddest noise that grows,—
> The birds, they make it in the spring,
> At night's delicious close.
>   *by Emily Dickinson*

1. What sounds are repeated in the first two lines?
2. What lines rhyme at the end?
3. How many beats are in each line?

Thinking: Determining Point of View ☑

When you describe something, you must first determine your **point of view.** Point of view is your attitude toward the thing that you are describing. The details you choose should support your point of view. They should show *why* you feel or think the way you do.

Here are two descriptions of the same pair of sneakers— one from the point of view of a student named Jason and one from the point of view of Jason's mother.

1. These sneakers are ready for the garbage can. They are a filthy shade of gray. The strings are frayed on the ends, and they've been broken and tied back together in several places. The rubber soles are cracked around the edges. There are holes in the canvas tops, and someone has scribbled all over them in ink.

2. These are the best sneakers I've ever had. They're finally broken in and they don't make me feel like Bigfoot when I walk down the street. They are the perfect shade of gray—just like the sidewalk. They have molded themselves to the exact shape of my feet, and they bend in all the right places. On top of everything else, they have sentimental value. They have the autographs of the whole basketball team.

Notice that each paragraph has a topic sentence that states the writer's attitude toward the sneakers. The topic sentence is followed by supporting details that show *why* the writer feels the way he or she does.

Prewriting Practice

Choose a person, a place, or an object that you could describe. Decide on two different points of view toward it. Write a topic sentence for each, one on the left side of your paper and one on the right side. List at least four supporting details under each topic sentence.

Composition Skills
Description

Using Descriptive Language ☑

Read these sentences. The second sentence in each pair is from "New Sneakers" by Ray Bradbury.

> 1. Douglas <u>stopped</u>.
> 2. Douglas <u>froze</u>.
>
> 1. Mr. Sanderson stood in the <u>sunny</u> door.
> 2. Mr. Sanderson stood in the <u>sun-blazed</u> door.

Look at the difference between the underlined words in each pair. The second version is more interesting because the author chose **exact words**. Exact words give precise information. They paint a clear word picture. In the first pair of sentences, for example, *froze* is better than *stopped* because it describes *how* Douglas stopped—suddenly and completely.

As you can see, an exact word is not necessarily long or difficult or unusual. An exact word is the one that helps your readers picture just what you want them to.

Figurative language can create word pictures that are even more vivid. You have learned that figurative language compares two things in an unexpected way. A simile uses *like* or *as* to make the comparison. A **metaphor**, however, does not use *like* or *as*. Instead of saying that one thing is *like* another, a metaphor says that one thing *is* another.

SIMILE: The carpet felt like jungle grass.
METAPHOR: The carpet was jungle grass.

The author of "New Sneakers" uses a metaphor to describe how the tennis shoes feel. Mr. Sanderson "gave one solemn bounce of his heels in the yeasty dough." Instead of saying the floor suddenly felt *like* dough (simile), the author says the floor *was* dough (metaphor).

➡

Prewriting Practice

A. Replace each underlined word with a more exact word. Then write a second version of each sentence, using another exact word that creates a different picture.

1. The horse <u>went</u> down the road.
2. I <u>looked</u> at the painting.
3. Her clothes were <u>old</u>.
4. The cat crept <u>slowly</u>.

B. Find the metaphors in these lines of poetry.

The wind was a torrent of darkness among the gusty trees.
The moon was a ghostly galleon tossed upon cloudy seas.
The road was a ribbon of moonlight over the purple moor. . . .

from "The Highwayman" by Alfred Noyes

The Grammar Connection

Adjectives and Adverbs

Strong, exact adjectives and adverbs can make your writing come alive.

The excited crowd cheered wildly as Jesse Owens sped around the Olympic track.

The descriptive adjective **excited** and the adverb **wildly** add meaning to the sentence.

Practice Expand each sentence by adding up to three adjectives and adverbs. Write two versions of each sentence. In the second versions, use modifiers that will change the meaning of the sentences.

1. Mom said, "It's time you cleaned your room!"
2. Erin danced in the contest.
3. Joy and Bryan laughed and woke up their baby sister.
4. The car went down the street.
5. The waves broke against the rocks and the beach.
6. The customer asked the salesclerk for assistance.

Organizing a Descriptive Paragraph ☑

Suppose you were asked to write a description of a shoe store's window display. How would you present your information so that your reader could picture the window? You might use **spatial order** to arrange the information. To do this, you would organize your description in one of these ways.

1. Left to right or right to left
2. Top to bottom or lowest to highest
3. Near to far or far to near

The same information might also be organized in **order of importance.** This involves listing details in order of most to least important or least to most important.

Which organization is used in each of the following paragraphs?

1. Next to the glass is a row of children's school shoes. Behind them on the right are dozens of pairs of women's shoes of all different kinds and colors. Men's shoes, mostly black and brown, are on the left side. The whole back row is made up of winter boots—men's, women's, children's, rubber, and leather. A few brightly colored boots stand out among the black and brown boots.

2. The first thing you notice about this window is that it is designed to remind people that fall is almost here. All the shoes are dark and sturdy-looking compared with the sandals and sneakers that were here a few days ago. Colored leaves are scattered around the floor and many of the shoes are displayed with matching wool socks.

Prewriting Practice

Plan a description of your classroom or a room at home. First decide what kind of organization will be most effective for the information you want to present. Then list the details you will include in the description. Arrange them according to the organization you have chosen.

The Writing Process
How to Write a Description

Step 1: Prewriting—Choose a Topic

Rosa jotted down several ideas for writing a description. Then she thought about each one.

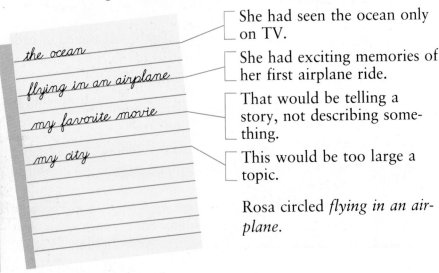

the ocean — She had seen the ocean only on TV.

flying in an airplane — She had exciting memories of her first airplane ride.

my favorite movie — That would be telling a story, not describing something.

my city — This would be too large a topic.

Rosa circled *flying in an airplane*.

On Your Own

1. **Think and discuss** List several things you can describe. Use the Ideas page for help. Discuss your ideas with a partner.
2. **Choose** Ask yourself these questions about the topics on your list.
   Which ones have I seen or done myself?
   Which ones bring to mind many interesting details?
   Which ones would I like to share with others?
   Circle the topic you want to write about.
3. **Explore** How will you describe your topic? Do one of the activities under "Exploring Your Topic" on the Ideas page.

Ideas for Getting Started

Choosing Your Topic

Topic Ideas

Crossing the finish line

A prized possession

A peaceful place

My aunt's new baby

The sounds of a basketball game

Diving

My favorite store

The hottest day of summer

Riding a subway

Eating a watermelon

Idea Gathering

To come up with ideas of your own, try writing each of these headings on a piece of paper and listing three ideas for each.

People, places, or things . . .
   that I find beautiful
   that I think are strange
   that I find thrilling
   that strike me funny
   that I dislike

Exploring Your Topic

A Sense Chart

Draw five large boxes on a sheet of paper. Label each with one of the five senses: sight, sound, taste, touch, smell. Then jot down details about your topic in the proper boxes. Which senses are most important for your topic?

Talk About It

With a partner, choose a detail from your Sense Chart. Using figurative language, write an exaggerated description of the detail. Be as creative as possible.

Step 2: Write a First Draft

Rosa decided to write her description for her best friend, Terry. Terry had never ridden in an airplane.

Rosa wrote her first draft. She did not stop to correct her mistakes as she wrote. She would have time to fix them later. She wrote on every other line.

Rosa's first draft

> Riding in an airaplane is like a dream come true. Right below your window ~~is~~ are beautiful clouds they change color ~~in~~ at night. As you take off, the engine grows loud and you fly through the sky like a bird. When you start to land, you think your going to crash into a miniture city, but soon the plane lands safely.

On Your Own

1. **Think about purpose and audience** Ask yourself these questions.

    Will my reader be a child? an adult? How much does the person already know about my topic?

    What is my purpose?

    What feelings do I want to share?

2. **Write** Write your first draft. Remember to use exact words and vivid details. Write on every other line to leave room for changes. Do not worry about mistakes. Just keep your mind on your topic and let your ideas flow.

Step 3: Revise

Rosa read her first draft. She noticed that the airplane's takeoff came too late in the paragraph. It would make more sense to describe the takeoff before she described the clouds.

Rosa read her description to Joshua. She hoped he would see how exciting an airplane ride could be.

Reading and responding

Rosa thought about how the clouds had looked and how the landing had felt. She pictured the takeoff more clearly too. Then she replaced some parts of her description.

Rosa's revised draft

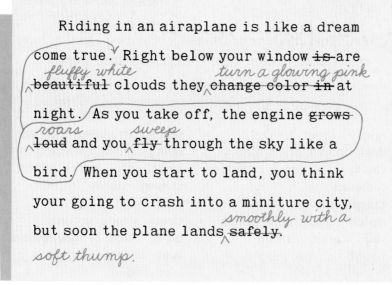

Think and Discuss ✓

- Why did Rosa change the order of her sentences?
- Which words did she replace with new words? Why?

On Your Own

Revising Checklist
- ☑ Have I used exact words and figurative language?
- ☑ Have I used enough details?
- ☑ Are my details organized effectively?
- ☑ Do my details support my point of view?

1. **Revise** Make changes in your first draft. Replace words that are not exact and vivid. Use the thesaurus below or the one in the back of this book to help you find just the word you want. Reorganize your details if necessary. To move a sentence, circle it and use an arrow to show where it goes.

2. **Have a conference** Read your description to a partner.

WRITING CONFERENCE

Ask your listener:	As you listen:
"Where is my description the clearest?"	I must pay close attention.
"Do any parts seem out of order?"	Can I picture this clearly? Which parts are really sparking my interest?
"Where do I need more details or more vivid words?"	What would I like to know more about?

3. **Revise** Think about your listener's remarks. Do you have any other ideas? Make these changes on your paper.

Thesaurus

angry upset, furious
dark dusky, black, gloomy
funny amusing, humorous, comical
laugh chuckle, snicker
quick fast, nimble, speedy
red scarlet, maroon
rough coarse, ragged, uneven, jagged

scared frightened, afraid
shiny glossy, gleaming
small little, petite, minor
strong sturdy, forceful, powerful
tired sleepy, drowsy
walk stroll, browse, amble
wet drenched, soggy, soaked

Step 4: Proofread

Rosa proofread her description for mistakes in spelling, capitalization, and punctuation. She checked her spellings in a dictionary. She used proofreading marks to make her changes.

Here is the way Rosa's proofread description looked.

Part of Rosa's proofread description

Riding in an airplane is like a dream

come true. Right below your window ~~is~~ are

fluffy white
beautiful clouds they ~~change color in~~ *turn a glowing pink* at

night. As you take off, the engine ~~grows~~
roars   *sweep*
loud and you ~~fly~~ through the sky like a

bird. When you start to land, you think
you're
~~your~~ going to crash into a *a* miniture city,
          smoothly with a
but soon the plane lands ~~safely~~.

Think and Discuss

- What words did Rosa correct for spelling?
- What punctuation did she add? Why?

On Your Own

1. **Proofreading Practice** Proofread this paragraph
for mistakes in grammar and spelling. There are
four grammar mistakes and two spelling mistakes. There is one sentence fragment and one
error in the possessive form.

> My sisters room look like a pet
> store. She have two green turtles
> and three pink and white angel fishs.
> There is also two bright yellow
> canarys that sing good. And a brown
> hamster named Sam.

Proofreading Marks

- ⁋ Indent
- ∧ Add
- ⩘ Add a comma
- ᐥᐥ Add quotation marks
- ⊙ Add a period
- ℓ Take out
- ≡ Capitalize
- / Make a small letter
- ∿ Reverse order

➡

2. Proofreading Application Now read your paper. Use the Proofreading Checklist and the Grammar and Spelling Hints below. You may want to use a colored pencil to make your corrections. Check your spellings in a dictionary.

Proofreading Checklist

Did I

- ☑ **1.** indent the first line?
- ☑ **2.** begin each sentence and proper noun with a capital?
- ☑ **3.** make sure all my sentences are complete?
- ☑ **4.** end each sentence with the correct punctuation?
- ☑ **5.** use adjectives and adverbs correctly?
- ☑ **6.** spell all words correctly?

The Grammar/Spelling Connection

Grammar Hints
Remember these rules from Unit 7.

- Use adverbs to modify verbs. *(run quickly)*
- Use adjectives to modify nouns. *(a quick beat)*
- *Good* is an adjective and *well* is an adverb. *(plays well, a good meal)*

Spelling Hints
Remember these rules from Unit 3 when forming plurals.

- To most nouns, add *s* or *es*. *(pet–pets, dish–dishes)*
- Some nouns remain the same in the singular and plural. *(moose–moose, salmon–salmon)*

Step 5: Publish

Rosa drew three views from an airplane—one from the runway, one above the clouds, and one just before landing. She put her description and the pictures in a booklet for Terry.

On Your Own

1. **Copy** Write or type your description as neatly as you can.
2. **Add a title** Think of a title to catch your reader's interest. Remember to capitalize the first, last, and all important words.
3. **Check** Read over your description again to make sure you have not left out anything or made any mistakes in copying.
4. **Share** Think of a special way to share your description.

Ideas for Sharing

- In small groups, read your descriptions aloud. Draw a picture of what *someone else* has described.
- Make your description a puzzle by leaving blanks for key words. List the key words on the side.

Applying Description

Literature and Creative Writing

In "New Sneakers" Douglas is determined to get a pair of Litefoot tennis shoes. Because he doesn't have enough money, he offers to do errands for Mr. Sanderson. Before Mr. Sanderson can say no, Douglas persuades him to try on a pair of the sneakers. Like Douglas, Mr. Sanderson feels lifted out of the ordinary world when he wears the sneakers.

Have fun using what you have learned in this unit about writing descriptions to complete one or more of the following activities.

> **Remember these things** ☑
> Use exact words and figurative language.
> Organize your details so that your reader can picture what you are describing.

1. **Can you find comfort in your old shoes?** Write a paragraph describing a favorite pair of shoes you have owned—slippers, sneakers, hiking boots, ballet slippers. Describe how they looked either when they were brand-new or when you stopped wearing them.

2. **Describe a character.** Write a paragraph describing what you think Douglas or Mr. Sanderson looked like.

3. **What was Mr. Sanderson's store like?** Write a paragraph describing Sanderson's Shoe Emporium. Is it old or new? clean or messy? cheerful or gloomy? What does it smell like?

Writing Across the Curriculum
Music

Music has been called the universal language. Although people have different tastes, everyone enjoys some type of music. In the same way that describing a picture makes you see more, so too can describing music make you more aware of what you hear and feel.

Choose one or more of the following activities.

1. **Can you feel the music?** Music can affect your moods and feelings. Listen to some music that has no words. Describe the way the music makes you feel. What images does the music make you think of? Play the music for your classmates, and share your reactions.

Writing Steps
1. Choose a topic
2. Write a first draft
3. Revise
4. Proofread
5. Publish

2. **Lights! Camera! Action! Music!** Imagine that you are going to compose music for a movie. Decide what kind of movie it will be—a mystery? a romance? an adventure? Describe the kind of music you will need for the background. Make the music fit the mood.

Word Bank
tempo
harmony
rhythm
beat
melody

3. **Sound off.** Imagine that you are a music critic for a newspaper. Listen to one of your favorite pieces of music. Write a description of the music, giving its good and bad points. Tell why you like the piece.

Adam liked "New Sneakers," and he decided to look for more stories by its author, Ray Bradbury. One of the stories Adam found was called "All Summer in a Day." Adam decided to write a letter about this story to the author and share the letter with his class. Here is the letter Adam wrote.

> 4632 Samsoa Street
> Everett, Washington 98203
> April 15, 1990
>
> Dear Mr. Bradbury,
>
> I am a boy about the age of Douglas Spaulding, the main character in "New Sneakers." I really like the way you describe things so that they come alive!
> When I read your story "All Summer in a Day," I could almost believe I was on a planet where the sun shone only once in seven years. You made me see, feel, smell, and even taste that rainy world! I could even understand how the children felt about Margot, the only one who knew what the sun was like. But I would never have guessed what would happen on the day the sun was supposed to shine.
> Thanks for writing such a great story.
>
> Sincerely,
> Adam Cassidy

Think and Discuss

- What do you find out about the story from Adam's letter?
- What did Adam especially like about the story?
- Why is this a good way to share a story?

Share Your Book

Write to an Author

1. Choose something about your book that you particularly liked. Talk about this in your letter. Tell enough about what happened without giving away the story.
2. You may ask a question about why the author created a certain kind of character or decided how the story would end. Be careful not to tell the end of the story.
3. Write your letter in correct friendly letter form. Be sure you include the author's name and the title of the book somewhere in the letter.
4. Display your letter on a bulletin board in your classroom.

Other Activities

• Mail your letter to the author. Send it in care of the publisher and ask that it be forwarded.
• Pretend that you live in a time or place where something is very different. Perhaps it never rains there or perhaps there are strange plants and animals. Draw a picture of this place. List words that describe what it is like.
• Write a letter from your imaginary place describing what you see, hear, smell, and feel. Address the letter to your class.

 # The Book Nook

The Borrowers	A Wrinkle in Time
by Mary Norton Tiny people live in an old house, "borrowing" things that full-sized people drop or lose.	*by Madeleine L'Engle* Meg and her friends step through a "wrinkle" in time, in search of her father, lost on an expedition.

A short pause,
like waiting for the traffic light to change,
and looking at the person next to you
until the green comes on
and you move along
and he turns into a stranger once again,
the same as you.

Eve Merriam "Markings: The Comma"

288

Capitalization and Punctuation

Getting Ready Just as an athlete or a dancer practices old plays and steps and continues to learn new ones, you polish and practice old language skills while continuing to learn new ones. You have already learned many capitalization and punctuation skills. In this unit, you will practice and polish skills you know and learn new ones.

ACTIVITIES

Listening
Listen to the poem "Markings: The Comma." This poem shows how a comma is like a real life situation. Which line tells what a comma signals?

Speaking
Look at the photograph on the opposite page. Choose two people from the picture and make up a conversation between them. Write it on the board, using correct capitalization and punctuation.

Writing
If a comma is "like waiting for the traffic light to change," what real life situation is like a period? a question mark? an exclamation mark? Write your ideas in your journal.

1 | Reviewing End Punctuation

When will it open?

You know that a sentence begins with a capital letter and ends with an end mark. End marks tell whether you are making a statement (.), asking a question (?), giving a command (.), or showing strong feeling (!).

We'll land at noon.   Please check your speed.
Do you take flying lessons?   What a small plane this is!

Soon, I hope!

Guided Practice What are the correct end marks?

Example: I shall cook dinner *period*

1. Are you cooking it tonight
2. We like cooked greens
3. Will you make the biscuits
4. Let's have some pecans
5. You can shell them first
6. How tasty the soup is

Summing up

▶ Use a **period** to end a declarative or an imperative sentence.
▶ Use a **question mark** to end an interrogative sentence.
▶ Use an **exclamation point** to end an exclamatory sentence.

Independent Practice Write the sentences. Add end marks.

Example: Look at the flag *Look at the flag.*

7. The flag of the United States has one star for each state
8. How many stars are on the flag
9. What an interesting history the flag has
10. When was the last star added to the flag
11. The stripes stand for the original thirteen colonies
12. Please write the names of the colonies on the board

Writing Application: Personal Narrative
Write a story about a meal that you made yourself or helped prepare. Use each end mark at least once.

  For Extra Practice, see p. 310.

2 | Proper Nouns and Proper Adjectives

You have learned that a proper noun names a particular person, place, or thing. A proper noun begins with a capital letter. If a proper noun has more than one word, capitalize only the important words.

Capitalizing Proper Nouns		
People	Carol B. Cohen	Uncle Hank
Places and things	Montana Mount Mansfield Pine Road	India Rio Grande Oak Street
Days, months, and holidays	Thursday Fourth of July	October Thanksgiving
Buildings and companies	White House Ace Shoe Company	Fisk Art Museum Clay's Food Store

You have also learned that a proper adjective is an adjective made from a proper noun. You should capitalize proper adjectives as well as proper nouns.

France   French bread
Greece   Greek dances
North America   North American animals

Guided Practice Which nouns and adjectives should be capitalized?

Example: Did dr. alice hamilton take many european trips?
Dr. Alice Hamilton   European

1. She was born in new york and lived in fort wayne, indiana.
2. She entered the university of michigan in march 1892.
3. The hamiltons had dutch, irish, and english ancestors.
4. Did dr. hamilton live and work at hull house in chicago?
5. She treated italian children in her clinic there.

> ▶ Capitalize proper nouns and proper adjectives.
> ▶ If a proper noun consists of more than one word, capitalize just the important words.

Independent Practice Write the proper nouns and the proper adjectives. Capitalize them correctly.

Example: Did alice hamilton investigate factories for the united states bureau of labor?
Alice Hamilton   United States Bureau of Labor

6. She studied german and british factories.
7. In 1925 she published the first book about industrial poisons in the united states.
8. She became the american expert on lead poisoning.
9. Always interested in peace, she met with swiss, french, and belgian women in europe.
10. She was the first woman to become a teacher at harvard university.
11. Her older sister, edith hamilton, also became famous.
12. She wrote books about greek and roman myths.
13. She was born in dresden, germany.
14. Both edith and alice hamilton went to a school called miss porter's school in farmington, connecticut.
15. The fort wayne public library and radcliffe college have letters and papers about these two famous sisters.

Writing Application: Descriptions

Think of people from different countries, or invent them. Write a sentence about each person, naming the country. Then change the name of the country into a proper adjective by writing about customs, food, or products.

> My friend Daranee lives in Thailand.
> She wrote to me about spicy Thai food.

If you need help with the spelling of some proper adjectives, you may use your dictionary.

3 | Interjections

An **interjection** is a word or words that show feeling. If the interjection stands alone, it is followed by an exclamation point. If it begins a sentence, it is set off by a comma.

Hooray! They won the game.   Oh, I knew they would!

Oh, no! I can't believe it.   Well, I wasn't sure.

Guided Practice What is the interjection in each sentence?

Example: Goodness! Both teams want to play again.   *Goodness*

1. Amazing! They don't know when to stop.
2. Well, that team won't win again.
3. Good grief! Are they having a winning streak?
4. Oh, I don't think so.
5. Phew! They won by just one point.

Summing up

▸ An **interjection** is a word or words that show feeling.
▸ Use an exclamation point or a comma after an interjection.

Independent Practice Write each sentence. Add the punctuation.

Example: Oh we're late.   *Oh, we're late.*

6. Wow Next time look at the clock.
7. Hey we still have a chance.
8. Hooray We didn't miss the train after all!
9. Oh, dear did you remember the theater tickets?
10. Whew They're here in my jacket pocket.

Writing Application: A Newspaper Article

Write a newspaper article about an exciting school game or event. Use interjections in some of your sentences.

For Extra Practice, see p. 312.

4 | Commas in a Series

You often use three or more similar words together in a sentence. These words form a **series**.

A fork , a knife , and a spoon came in a package.

Use commas to separate the items in a series. The commas tell your reader to pause between words. Notice how commas change the meaning of a sentence.

I bought fruit salad, tuna sandwiches, and juice.
I bought fruit, salad, tuna, sandwiches, and juice.

A conjunction such as *or* or *and* usually appears before the last item in the series. The conjunction connects the items.

Do I use one, two, or three teaspoons of parsley?

My mom taught me to ski, to scuba dive, and to play chess.

Guided Practice

A. Where do commas belong in these sentences?

Example: Red is the color used for stop signs traffic lights and some fire hydrants. *after signs and lights*

1. Red yellow orange green and blue are five of the colors in the rainbow.
2. Green reminds me of marbles lettuce and spring.
3. Colors can make you sleepy wake you up or help you think.
4. Advertisers designers florists and chefs use many colors.

B. Use each list of items as a series in a sentence. Where do commas belong?

Example: six pencils   two erasers   a pen   three rulers
    I lost six pencils, two erasers, a pen, and three rulers.

5. soccer	baseball	tennis	basketball
6. cars	buses	trains	planes
7. flowers	trees	grass	bushes
8. walk	run	skip	jump

▶ Use a comma to separate items in a series. The commas tell your reader to pause between items.

▶ Use a comma before the conjunction that connects the items.

Independent Practice Write each sentence, adding a series. Insert commas and conjunctions where they are needed.

Example: The four seasons are ____.
The four seasons are spring, summer, fall, and winter.

9. Three musical instruments are ____.
10. The four whole numbers following *one* are ____.
11. The three basic meals of the day are ____.
12. Three different kinds of flowers are ____.
13. Three countries located in Europe are ____.
14. Four of the world's rivers are ____.
15. Five kinds of wild animals are ____.
16. Three of my favorite foods are ____.
17. Three things I do before school are ____.
18. Four past Presidents of the United States are ____.
19. The first three months of the year are ____.
20. Three skills of a basketball player are ____.
21. Four of my favorite holidays are ____.
22. Three things I use in class are ____.
23. Four points on a compass are ____.
24. Four things a cat does are ____.
25. Three ways an audience shows approval are ____.
26. Four coins are ____.
27. Five states in the United States are ____.
28. Three of my past teachers are ____.
29. The seven days of the week are ____.
30. Five of my favorite names are ____.

Writing Application: Creative Writing

Make five lists of your favorite things. Include three or more items in each list. Then write a sentence for each list, using all the items. Check that you have used commas correctly.

For Extra Practice, see p. 313.

5 | More Uses for Commas

You have already learned that a comma separates the simple sentences that make up a compound sentence.

Whales live in the ocean, but they are not fish.
A female whale is called a cow, and a baby whale is a calf.

You have also learned that an appositive is a word or group of words that identify or explain the noun that they follow. Commas separate an appositive from the rest of the sentence.

Blue whales, the fastest kind, are found in all oceans.
Mr. Gilmore, an expert on whales, works at an aquarium.

Commas are also used to set off certain introductory words such as *well, yes,* and *no* at the beginning of a sentence.

Yes, I have seen a finback whale.
Well, we actually saw its spout first.

Finally, commas are used to set off a noun in direct address, the name of a person who is directly spoken to.

From this distance, Sue, that looks like a blue whale.
Jerry, have you read *Island of the Blue Dolphins*?

Guided Practice Where do commas belong in each of the following sentences?

Example: Class who invented the first workable steamboat?
           after Class

1. Yes, it was Robert Fulton.
2. He was a well-known portrait painter, but he became more and more interested in engineering.
3. He ran his first steamboat on the Seine a river in France.
4. No, that was not the only boat Fulton built.
5. The *Clermont* another steamboat, traveled the Hudson River.
6. Well, the steamboat was only one of his projects.
7. Have you ever seen a steamboat Tim?
8. Yes I saw one last year.

▶ Use a comma to separate simple sentences in a compound sentence.
▶ Use commas to set off an appositive.
▶ Use a comma after introductory words like *well*, *yes*, and *no*.
▶ Use commas to set off a noun in direct address.

Independent Practice Copy these sentences and add commas where needed.

Example: The hornet a common insect is like the yellow jacket.
The hornet, a common insect, is like the yellow jacket.

9. How many parts does an insect's body have, Paul?
10. Well, there are three main sections.
11. Some insects help humans but, others are very harmful.
12. The honeybee, a stinging insect makes honey.
13. Mosquitoes, disease-carrying insects can pass along more than twenty different viruses.
14. Valerie, can you name other insects that have wings?
15. Moths and flies have wings, Mr. Jensen.
16. Butterflies, members of the moth family also have wings.
17. Moths fly at night but, butterflies fly in the daytime.
18. Many butterflies live in the tropics, and other kinds live near the North Pole.
19. An ant, a very small insect, can lift large weights.
20. No, ants cannot live at the North Pole.
21. Ants can breathe fresh air, but they do not have lungs.
22. Can you describe an ant colony, Jeffrey?
23. Some ant colonies are small but, other colonies may have hundreds of thousands of ants.
24. Did you know Jules, that all insects have three pairs of legs?
25. Yes, Mr. Jensen I knew that.

Writing Application: A Speech

Imagine that you are running for class president. Write a speech, explaining what you will do as president. Use commas in the four ways taught in this lesson.

For Extra Practice, see p. 314.   **More Uses for Commas   297**

6 | Abbreviations

An **abbreviation** is a shortened form of a word. It usually ends with a period. Abbreviations are often used in addresses or to save space. Study the chart of common abbreviations. Notice that not all abbreviations have capital letters or periods. If you need help with an abbreviation, use your dictionary.

Common Abbreviations

Place names:

Apt.	Apartment	Mt.	Mount or Mountain
Ave.	Avenue	Pkwy.	Parkway
Expy.	Expressway	P.O.	Post Office

Businesses and titles:

Co.	Company	P.D.	Police Department
Inc.	Incorporated	R.N.	Registered Nurse
Ltd.	Limited	J.P.	Justice of the Peace

Measurements:

in.	inch	hp	horsepower
ft	feet	mph	miles per hour

State abbreviations:

CA	California	IN	Indiana
NY	New York	MI	Michigan

Agencies and organizations:

SBA	Small Business Administration
NPR	National Public Radio
NATO	North Atlantic Treaty Organization

Guided Practice How would you abbreviate the following groups of words?

Example: Pearly Piano Company   *Pearly Piano Co.*

1. Fifth Avenue
2. Fun Games, Incorporated
3. Garden State Parkway
4. Apartment 3-A
5. Mount Washington
6. Post Office Box 871

> ▶ Abbreviations are shortened forms of words.
> ▶ Most abbreviations begin with capital letters and end with periods.
> ▶ Some abbreviations have capital letters but no periods.
> ▶ Other abbreviations have no capital letters or periods.

Independent Practice

A. Write each item, using abbreviations correctly.

Example: Missouri   *MO*

7. National Public Radio
8. Mount Snow
9. 55 miles per hour
10. Main Street
11. Bright Company
12. Indiana

13. Brook Parkway
14. Simon and Lane, Incorporated
15. yard
16. inch
17. Madison Avenue
18. Justice of the Peace

B. Copy this bicycle registration form. Then fill it in, using abbreviations wherever you can.

DEPARTMENT OF PUBLIC SAFETY
APPLICATION FOR REGISTRATION OF BICYCLE

Name _____
Address _____ City _____ State _____
ZIP _____
Telephone Number _____
Make of Bicycle _____ Color(s) _____
Serial Number _____

Signature _____
Date _____

Writing Application: An Advertisement
Write a newspaper advertisement to sell something that you own. Include a description of the item and your name and address. Use at least three abbreviations in your advertisement.

For Extra Practice, see p. 315.

When you write someone's exact words, you are writing **dialogue**. Dialogue is written conversation. The speaker's words are set apart from the rest of the sentence with **quotation marks**. Begin the first word of the quotation with a capital letter. Place end punctuation inside the quotation marks.

> Terry said, "Let's go swimming."
> "This beach is closing," the lifeguard announced.

Notice that a comma separates the speaker from the quotation.

When a quotation ends in a question mark or an exclamation point, however, do not add a comma.

> "What time will the beach open?" I asked.

A quotation is sometimes interrupted in the middle. End the first part of the quotation with quotation marks. Begin the second part with quotation marks. Use commas to separate the quotation from the speaker.

> "Do you realize," asked Rob, "that we forgot the raft?"

If the second part of the interrupted quotation begins a new sentence, start it with a capital letter. Use a period after the speaker.

> "It's too late now," I said. "We'll have to come back later."

Guided Practice How would you punctuate these sentences? Which letters should be capitalized?

Example: What time Tim asked does Mom's train arrive?
"What time," Tim asked, "does Mom's train arrive?"

1. Dad answered it will arrive at noon.
2. I'm sure she missed the city Tim said.
3. Marta sighed it will be good to have her home.
4. She'll have photos replied Dad and probably movies.
5. Maybe she'll have presents for us too said Tim I want to hear her stories about her trip to the ranch.

▶ Use **quotation marks** to set off dialogue from the rest of the sentence. Place punctuation inside the closing quotation marks.
▶ Begin the first word of a quotation with a capital letter.
▶ Use commas to separate most quotations from the rest of the sentence.

Independent Practice Write these sentences, using correct punctuation and capitalization.

Example: Little strokes Benjamin Franklin said fell great oaks.
"Little strokes," Benjamin Franklin said, "fell great oaks."

6. If our American way of life fails the child, it fails us all said Pearl S. Buck.
7. I have a dream! said Martin Luther King, Jr.
8. One has to grow up with good talk in order to form the habit of it Helen Hayes said.
9. Sherlock Holmes said it's elementary, my dear Watson.
10. A poem begins with a lump in the throat said Robert Frost.
11. Walt Whitman said I hear America singing.
12. Mark Twain said when a teacher calls a boy by his entire name, it means trouble.
13. The mere absence of war is not peace said John F. Kennedy.
14. I am not a Virginian Patrick Henry said but an American.
15. D. H. Lawrence said the living moment is everything.
16. The road to ignorance said George Bernard Shaw is paved with good intentions.
17. Anything you're good at contributes to happiness said Bertrand Russell.
18. Thoughts Thomas Mann said come clearly while one walks.

Writing Application: A Conversation

Imagine that you are talking to a person whom you admire. The person can be someone you know or someone who is famous. Write a conversation that you would like to have. Use at least five quotations. Then check to see that you have punctuated and capitalized your quotations correctly.

For Extra Practice, see p. 316.   **Punctuating Dialogue**

8 | Titles

When you write the titles of books, magazines, newspapers, songs, and other works, you must treat them in special ways. Capitalize the nouns, verbs, and other important words in a title. Do not capitalize short words such as *a, an, the, and, or, at, to, up,* and *for* unless they begin or end a title.

"The Mouse That Won the Race"

Titles of books, magazines, newspapers, and movies are underlined in writing. In print, such titles appear in slanted type called *italics.*

IN WRITING: She reads the Washington Post on the train.
IN PRINT: We started a magazine called *The Sport Report.*

Titles of short stories, articles, songs, book chapters, and most poems should be enclosed in quotation marks. Place punctuation that follows a title inside the quotation marks.

The third chapter is called "Planting Your Garden."
My first song, "Butterflies in the Snow," was not published.

Guided Practice

A. How would you write these titles correctly?

Example: chicago sun times (newspaper) *Chicago Sun Times*

1. the necklace (short story)
2. to be a clown (article)
3. live it up (book)
4. the raven (poem)
5. travel news (magazine)
6. flying kites (book chapter)

B. How would you punctuate and capitalize the titles in these sentences?

Example: I wrote a poem called outside at recess.
I wrote a poem called "Outside at Recess."

7. A magazine for young writers, cricket, published it.
8. New york times readers live all over the world.
9. I read an article called today's american family.
10. At the school festival, we sang moon river.

Summing up

▶ Capitalize the first, last, and all important words in a title.
▶ Underline the titles of books, magazines, newspapers, and movies.
▶ Use quotation marks around titles of short stories, articles, songs, book chapters, and most poems. Punctuation that follows a title usually goes inside the quotation marks.

Independent Practice Write these sentences, correcting each title.

Example: An evening herald reporter interviewed the mayor about her article in this month's post.

An <u>Evening Herald</u> reporter interviewed the mayor about her article in this month's <u>Post</u>.

11. In our card catalog, I found a book called aesop's fables.
12. My favorite American short story is the man without a country.
13. Willie Nelson and Waylon Jennings sang pick up the tempo.
14. I have just discovered the magazine smithsonian.
15. Our social studies teacher read Archibald MacLeish's poem voyage to the moon.
16. A new poet, Carol Wenger, read her poem spring pools.
17. In what weekly magazine did the article ending world hunger appear?
18. The first chapter of this book is entitled off again.
19. A review of his book appeared in today's chicago tribune.
20. Sharon recited concord hymn, a poem by Ralph Waldo Emerson.
21. The last song on the album is the rainbow connection.
22. Charles Dickens edited a magazine called household words.
23. Evening chronicle published his articles.
24. Oliver twist, hard times, and a tale of two cities are three of Dickens's novels.

Writing Application: Titles

Make a list of five of your favorite songs, poems, books, magazines, or short stories. Write a sentence for each title. Capitalize and punctuate the titles correctly.

For Extra Practice, see p. 317.

Grammar-Writing Connection

Writing Dialogue

You can make your writing more vivid and interesting by using dialogue. Dialogue gives the exact words of the people or the characters you are writing about. However, you must make it clear to your reader who is speaking and exactly what the speaker's words are. This dialogue is not clear.

> May I borrow your geography book? asked Lani. One of my pages is missing. I forgot mine I said. why don't you ask Chris if you can borrow his?

You can point out the speakers and their words clearly by using correct capitalization and punctuation. Use quotation marks around the speaker's words. In addition, you should begin a new paragraph every time a different person begins to speak.

> "May I borrow your geography book?" asked Lani. "One of my pages is missing."
>
> "I forgot mine," I said. "**Why** don't you ask Chris if you can borrow his?"

Revising Sentences

(1–6) Write the following sentences as dialogue, using correct punctuation and capitalization. Remember to begin a new paragraph whenever the speaker changes.

Did you read the chapter on climate in our geography book asked Lani it tells some interesting facts. Yes I learned that height affects climate I replied. I was surprised to find out that Mount Everest and New Orleans are the same distance from the equator. That is true said Lani but New Orleans is at sea level, and Mount Everest is over twenty-nine thousand feet high. That explains I added why the top of Mount Everest is always covered with snow. That is also why the temperature in New Orleans hardly ever gets below freezing.

Creative Writing

Could such a strange, dramatic landscape as this truly exist? The answer is yes—and no. *View of Toledo,* painted around 1600, shows Toledo, Spain. Yet El Greco painted the city as it never really looked. He moved a tower and added buildings. This, plus his whirling brush strokes, make the scene seem more imagined than real.

- How does the sky affect the picture's mood?
- Why does the landscape seem full of movement?

View of Toledo, El Greco
Metropolitan Museum of Art
The H. O. Havemeyer Collection

Activities

1. **Write a travel poster.** How would you tempt tourists to visit the city shown in this painting? What would you say about the weather and the view? Write a travel poster for Toledo.
2. **Write a poem.** Imagine that you are sitting on the hill in this painting. The dark clouds over the city signal an approaching storm. Write a poem describing the sounds, smells, and sights you experience as the sunny weather changes into a thunderstorm.
3. **Describe your view.** El Greco has managed to capture a special feeling in this portrait of his home city. If you were to paint a view of the area where you live, what mood would you try to capture? Describe how you would portray your home town or city.

Check-up: Unit 9

Reviewing End Punctuation (p. 290)
Write these sentences. Add the correct end punctuation.

1. Stop at this campsite for the day
2. What a large bird that is
3. Is its nest near
4. Please carry the binoculars
5. Do we have time for a hike now
6. I see different kinds of birds
7. Do you recognize these tracks
8. We can stop here for a rest
9. Please hand me the canteen

Proper Nouns and Proper Adjectives (p. 291)
Write each proper noun and proper adjective. Capitalize them correctly.

10. The capital of canada is ottawa.
11. It is on the ottawa river in the province of ontario.
12. The area was settled by french traders.
13. Many tourists visit the national gallery of canada.
14. It has european and canadian art.

Interjections (p. 293)
Write each sentence. Add the punctuation that is missing.

15. Hey these are wonderful seats.
16. Well that was a funny play.
17. Gracious My sides hurt from laughing.
18. Wow That was a terrible play.
19. Oh, my The audience laughed too.
20. Oh, well I guess we'll never agree.

Commas in a Series (p. 294)
Write the sentences. Add commas where needed.

21. Greg Bob and Cynthia visited us.
22. We took them to a museum a beach and a TV studio.
23. We found stones shells seaweed and driftwood on the beach.
24. Greg took photographs wrote postcards and bought souvenirs.
25. Did he buy one two or three gifts?
26. Cynthia enjoys scuba diving watching sea animals and doing underwater photography.

More Uses for Commas (p. 296)
Write the sentences. Add commas where needed.

27. Kay please set the timer to develop the film.
28. Well how much time do we need?
29. The directions call for two minutes but we will need six.
30. I think that the developer this strong-smelling chemical is too cool right now.
31. Check the temperature now Jim.
32. Kay will pour out the developer and Jim will refill the tank with clean water.
33. After the film is washed Kay will put it on this line to dry.
34. Well what happens next?
35. This negative should make a good print but I can't tell for sure yet.

Abbreviations (*p. 298*) Write the correct abbreviation for each of the following items.

36. The Goldenrod Company
37. 26 Fairfield Street
38. Post Office Box 542
39. Apartment 356
40. Buffalo, New York

Punctuating Dialogue (*p. 300*) Write each sentence below, punctuating and capitalizing the quotation correctly.

41. This train goes to the airport said the guard.
42. The customer asked do you sell magazines at this newsstand?
43. Buy your paper here shouted the news seller.
44. Please give me your ticket the conductor said.
45. Buy two tickets now urged the passenger you will save time.
46. Which train asked the tourist do I take to the art museum?
47. Take the north train the conductor answered get off at the third stop.
48. What a beautiful museum this is exclaimed the visitors.
49. Where is the Greek sculpture they asked we especially want to go and see that.
50. Walk down the hall explained the guide and turn right.
51. I see a large room ahead said the visitor the sculptures must be there.
52. How lovely these statues are everyone exclaimed.

Titles (*p. 302*) Write each sentence, correcting the title.

53. Have you read tonight's buffalo evening news?
54. I have just written a short story called the revolving door.
55. The poem snow is very short.
56. The book I am reading now is why the tides ebb and flow.
57. On our bus trip, the class sang the impossible dream.
58. My mom reads the magazine modern life every Saturday.
59. Did you read the article smart shoes?
60. The first chapter of this book is called my friend rufus.
61. I've just finished reading the short story strangers that came to town.
62. This chapter is called fuels.
63. David McCord read his beautiful poem take sky.
64. A review of a new play is in today's springfield daily news.
65. The first song my sister sang was row, row, row your boat.
66. I have read twice the book wind in the willows.
67. In which magazine did the article computers and language appear?
68. I have not read the short story two were left.
69. A magazine that my family often reads is popular machinery.
70. My favorite poem is sea fever.
71. We enjoyed the song heroes and villains.
72. I recited the poem the raven.

Enrichment

Using Capitalization and Punctuation

Design a Museum

Imagine that your town or city is building a museum. It will exhibit things that represent your community. Write a letter to the editor of the local paper, explaining what should be in the museum. List some items and use modifiers to describe them. Be sure to use commas in a series correctly.

Extra! Draw a floor plan of the museum. Show where the things you suggest should be displayed.

Reading File

Do you ever have trouble finding interesting books to read? Get together with classmates and make a reading catalog. First, think of your five favorite books that you read in the past year. On five index cards, write the titles and authors of the books. On each card, write several compound sentences that explain why others would enjoy the book. Be sure to punctuate these sentences correctly. One student should collect the cards and start a reading file for your classroom. Divide the books by subject, such as drama, biography, and history.

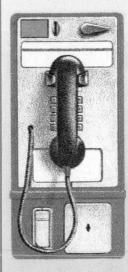

TELEPHONE TALK

Write a telephone conversation between two friends who are talking about some exciting news. In your conversation, use the three types of end marks: periods, question marks, and exclamation points. Use commas with nouns of direct address. Write the conversation as dialogue, using quotation marks correctly with other punctuation.

"Hi, Jenny, it's Alex," said Alex.

"How are you, Alex?" Jenny asked.

"I'm fine," said Alex. "What great news I have to tell you!"

Credit for Kids

Imagine that a store in your local shopping area is letting teen-agers apply for their own credit cards. Make up a store and create a credit card application that asks for the following information: name, address, city, state, ZIP code, telephone number, name of parent or legal guardian, and guardian's business address. The form should also request the names and addresses of two references, people who know you well. Fill out a sample application, using abbreviations wherever possible.

Extra! Your application has been approved! Design an official credit card for yourself.

Extra Practice: Unit 9

● Write each sentence. Add the correct end punctuation.

Example: We sing a song about the flag of the United States
We sing a song about the flag of the United States.

1. Do you know the name of the song
2. Think of the stars on the flag
3. Francis Scott Key wrote the song in 1814
4. The song is about a real flag
5. Do you know where the flag is displayed
6. Go see it in a museum in Washington
7. What a big flag it is

▲ Write each sentence, using correct end punctuation. Label each sentence *declarative, interrogative, imperative,* or *exclamatory.*

Example: Nations have flags   *Nations have flags.*   **declarative**

8. Do you know about state flags of the United States
9. Each state in the nation has its own flag
10. Look at this one from one of the largest states
11. What a pretty flag it is
12. Why does it have only one star
13. Think about another name for the state
14. Is it the flag of the Lone Star State

■ Rewrite each sentence as a different kind of sentence. Use correct end punctuation. You may add or change some words.

Example: Flags were once used to give weather forecasts.
What interesting flags were used to give weather forecasts!

15. The National Weather Bureau had many different flags.
16. A white flag meant clear weather.
17. Did a blue one mean rain or snow?
18. Please show me the warning flags.
19. They are square with another square in the center.
20. A red flag with a black square meant that a storm was coming.

2 | Proper Nouns, Proper Adjectives (p. 291)

● Write the underlined proper nouns and proper adjectives. Capitalize them correctly.

Example: Many people are interested in egypt.   *Egypt*

1. Egypt is on the african coast.
2. Each year people visit the great pyramid and the valley of tombs.
3. Many ancient tombs were discovered by british explorers.
4. Howard carter worked with the egyptian exploration fund.
5. One of the most famous egyptian kings was king tutankhamen.
6. Objects from his tomb are in the metropolitan museum of art.
7. Others are in the national museum at cairo.

▲ Write the proper nouns and proper adjectives. Capitalize them correctly.

Example: People from many countries have come to america.
   America

8. The british colonists were among the first settlers.
9. They started a colony in plymouth, massachusetts.
10. Other early settlers came from france.
11. Many traders settled in what is now canadian territory.
12. Immigrants from ireland arrived in large numbers.
13. Many european citizens left their native lands.
14. They came to ellis island in new york bay.
15. Thousands of people in california have asian ancestors.

■ Write each sentence. Capitalize all the proper nouns and proper adjectives.

Example: Is james herriot a famous veterinarian?
   Is James Herriot a famous veterinarian?

16. His books about life in yorkshire, england, are popular.
17. The doctor and his partner, siegfried, are likable.
18. They visit many farms in the english countryside.
19. Among their patients are german shepherds.
20. They also treat farm animals such as swiss cows.
21. Their more unusual patients include arabian horses.
22. Herriot's books appeal to people in big cities like new york.

3 | Interjections (p. 293)

● Write the interjection and the punctuation that follows it in each sentence.

Example: Oh, no! I forgot about the math quiz.   *Oh, no!*

1. Well, you don't have to worry.
2. Gracious, I certainly do!
3. Wow! This test is so difficult.
4. Oh, Pete never has trouble with math.
5. Whew! I finished just before the final bell.
6. Oh, my! I'm glad that's over.
7. Hooray! I received a perfect score.
8. Hey! You must be so happy.

▲ Write each sentence, punctuating the interjection correctly.

Example: Oh, my It can't be you.   *Oh, my! It can't be you.*

9. Well it is.
10. Goodness You've really changed.
11. Oops I hope I didn't offend you.
12. Oh, no You couldn't ever do that.
13. Wow We haven't seen each other in a year.
14. Well how have you been?
15. Alas I have felt better.

■ Rewrite each sentence, using an interjection.

Example: What's all the excitement?
          Hey! What's all the excitement?

16. My sister's hamster escaped from its cage.
17. Where can it be?
18. I'll help you find it.
19. We can't let the cat find it.
20. We found the hamster in your room.
21. It was in your model race car.
22. How could it have climbed in there?
23. That's quite an accomplishment for a hamster.
24. I'm glad that we found it so quickly.
25. Don't let your hamster escape again.

4 | Commas in a Series (p. 294)

● Write each of the following sentences. Add commas where they are needed.

Example: Kate invited Mary Joe and me.
Kate invited Mary, Joe, and me.

1. We went swimming bike riding and walking.
2. Kate brought food a blanket and a jug to the park.
3. She served chicken carrot sticks celery and rolls.
4. I brought apples juice and peanuts.
5. Kate Joe and I cleared away the picnic.
6. We put the paper plates cups and napkins into the trash barrel.
7. Then we played games jumped rope and walked home.

▲ Write a sentence with items in a series for each group of words. Separate the items in each series with commas.

Example: lamps – table – vases
I dusted the lamps, the table, and the vases.

8. sheets – towels – blankets
9. dishes – glasses – silverware
10. washed – scraped – painted
11. paint – wallpaper – rugs – curtains
12. painting – calendar – poster – photograph
13. chair – table – desk – bookcase

■ Use each pair of words in two sentences. In the first sentence, use the two words as one item. In the second sentence, use each word as part of a series of items. Underline the words and punctuate the sentences correctly.

Example: gold rings
We found three <u>gold rings</u> buried in the garden.
Silver, <u>gold</u>, <u>rings</u>, and bracelets were brought up from the sunken ship.

14. spinach salad	17. tomato soup	20. milk bottles
15. banana bread	18. water pipes	21. orange juice
16. paper bags	19. glass jar	22. sports news

5 | More Uses for Commas (p. 296)

● Each sentence contains a question mark in parentheses. Write *yes* if a comma belongs in that place. Write *no* if it does not.

Example: Jon (?) tell us about salmon.   *yes*

1. Salmon, a kind of fish (?) is very special.
2. Most fish live (?) in fresh water or salt water.
3. Salmon live in salt water (?) and they live in fresh water too.
4. Yes (?) it does sound strange.
5. Salmon eggs (?) hatch in streams.
6. The fish swim to the sea (?) and they grow up there.
7. Kim (?) did you know that the salmon later return to the same stream?

▲ Write each sentence, adding the missing commas.

Example: In 1931 a boat the *Baychimo* headed north.
　　　　In 1931 a boat, the *Baychimo*, headed north.

8. A bad storm came and the boat was caught in ice.
9. John Cornwell the captain told the crew to leave.
10. The people moved to shore and they built a shelter.
11. During an awful storm a blizzard the boat disappeared.
12. Yes it floated off with no one on board.
13. People tried to catch it but no one succeeded for long.
14. That ship was spotted Carol as late as 1969.

■ Write each sentence, adding each missing comma. Then tell why the commas are needed.

Example: Tell us about swordfish Kim.
　　　　Tell us about swordfish, Kim.   direct address

15. Swordfish rapid and powerful swimmers sometimes drive their swords into the ocean floor.
16. They often swim fast but they move slowly in calm weather.
17. Are sailfish similar to swordfish Jim?
18. Yes they have the same long, sharp upper jaw.
19. The sword is used for obtaining food and it is also used for protection.
20. Do you know Dave how much sailfish weigh?

6 | Abbreviations (p. 298)

● Write the abbreviation from the Word Box that has the same meaning as the underlined word or words.

Example: Police Department *P.D.*

1. Brook Road
2. Elm Street
3. miles per hour
4. Registered Nurse
5. New Jersey
6. Post Office Box 242
7. twenty feet
8. Indiana

| mph | P.O. | St. | R.N. | ft | Rd. | P.D. | NJ | IN |

▲ Write the following names and addresses, using abbreviations from the Word Box.

Example: Mount Rushmore *Mt. Rushmore*

9. Webster Company
10. 111 Orchard Parkway
11. Barton and Jones, Limited
12. Columbia, South Carolina
13. Apartment 3
14. Avis Holmes, Justice of the Peace
15. Small Business Administration
16. sixty inches
17. Federal Bureau of Investigation
18. twenty yards

| yd |
| Co. |
| in. |
| SBA |
| Pkwy. |
| FBI |
| J.P. |
| SC |
| Apt. |
| Ltd. |
| Mt. |

■ Rewrite the following items, using abbreviations.

Example: 1004 Halton Street *1004 Halton St.*

19. the temperature on Mount Washington
20. the purpose of the Small Business Administration
21. the training of a Registered Nurse
22. Santa Fe, New Mexico
23. Route 66
24. The Theatre Network, Incorporated
25. 55 miles per hour
26. the Southeast Expressway

● ▲ ■ **Three levels of practice   315**

7 | Punctuating Dialogue (p. 300)

● Write the following sentences. Add quotation marks where they are needed.

Example: Look at me! said Ben.
"Look at me!" said Ben.

1. Ned asked, What are you doing?
2. Look quickly, said Ben, before I fall down.
3. Are you really standing on your hands? Ned said.
4. Yes, I am, said Ben. Do you want to try?
5. I will if you'll help me, said Ned.
6. Will you hold my feet? he asked.
7. Yes, said Ben, and I'll tell you how to do it too.

▲ Write the following sentences. Capitalize and punctuate them correctly.

Example: What are you writing asked Lara
"What are you writing?" asked Lara.

8. I am making a day book answered Marie
9. Lara asked what's a day book
10. A day book said Marie is a book of quotations
11. Where do you get a quotation a day Lara asked
12. It's not hard said Marie books have many quotations
13. I just read a poem that I enjoyed said Lara
14. Well said Marie why don't you start a day book

■ Write each sentence below as dialogue. Put the authors' names in different places in your sentences. Use correct punctuation and capitalization.

Example: The impossible is often the untried.   Jim Goodwin
"The impossible," said Jim Goodwin, "is often the untried."

15. We are tomorrow's past.   Mary Webb
16. The pen is mightier than the sword.   Edward Bulwer-Lytton
17. Nothing in life is to be feared.   Marie Curie
18. I have not yet begun to fight.   John Paul Jones
19. It takes all sorts of people to make a world.   Douglas Jerrold
20. There is no substitute for hard work.   Thomas Edison

8 | Titles (p. 302)

● Each title below should be underlined or enclosed in quotation marks. Write each title correctly.

Example: Washington Post (newspaper)   *Washington Post*

1. The Rush for Gold (article)
2. When You Talk to a Monkey (poem)
3. Penny Power (magazine)
4. The Lion and the Mouse (story)
5. Codes and Secret Writing (book)
6. Father and Son Mystery (book chapter)
7. City of New Orleans (song)
8. Library News (newspaper)

▲ Write and punctuate each sentence correctly.

Example: Mollie Hunter wrote the book the haunted mountain.
Mollie Hunter wrote the book The Haunted Mountain.

9. Mollie Hunter also wrote the book the kelpie's pearls.
10. We laughed at the poem called what a funny bird the frog are.
11. My brother is a reporter for the local newspaper the examiner.
12. My aunt wrote an article called the great chiefs.
13. Paul McCartney wrote the beautiful song yesterday.
14. The open window is a story with a surprise ending.
15. I read the chapter called old two toes.
16. The magazine children's digest had a report on bicycles.

■ Complete the following sentences by adding titles.

Example: Kim enjoys reading books like ____. (book title)
Kim enjoys reading books like The Trumpet of the Swan.

17. She has a book called ____ that lists things. (book title)
18. Of all the song titles listed, Kim thought that ____ would be the most popular. (song title)
19. She had read about the song in the ____. (newspaper title)
20. Kim is writing a review of the book for the school magazine ____. (magazine title)
21. The name comes from the poem ____. (poem title)
22. An article called ____ will be in the next issue. (article title)

Literature and Writing

Dear Mr. Henshaw,
I was surprised to get your postcard from Wyoming, because I thought you lived in Alaska. . . .

Beverly Cleary
from *Dear Mr. Henshaw*

Persuasive Letter

Getting Ready In this unit, you will learn to write a persuasive letter. You can urge someone to help a worthy cause, encourage a friend to try harder to reach a goal, or complain about a faulty item you purchased and ask for a replacement. In other words, you can write a letter that might persuade the receiver to do something.

ACTIVITIES

Listening

Listen to the letter as it is read. Do you think the writer knows Mr. Henshaw very well? Explain why or why not.

Speaking

Look at the picture. Imagine that you have the chance to go here on a vacation. List the reasons you would or would not like to go to this place.

Writing

Write a letter in your journal to a well-known author whom you have never met. Try to persuade this person to write a new book with you as the main character.

LITERATURE

Have you ever made plans for a special day and then had everything go wrong? What went wrong for Stuart?

An Evening on the River

By E. B. White

Mr. and Mrs. Frederick C. Little's second son not only looked like a mouse, he was only two inches tall. The doctor was delighted. It was unusual for a family to have a mouse. Stuart's adventures are described in the book *Stuart Little.* When Stuart was growing up and traveling about, he saw a girl who was just his size. Stuart bought a souvenir-size canoe and wrote a letter inviting Harriet to go canoeing.

When Stuart arrived at his camp site by the river, he was tired and hot. He put the canoe in the water and was sorry to see that it leaked badly. The birch bark at the stern was held together by a lacing, and the water came in through the seam. In a very few seconds the canoe was half full of water.

"Darn it!" said Stuart, "I've been swindled." He had paid seventy-six cents for a genuine Indian birchbark canoe, only to find that it leaked.

"Darn, darn, darn," he muttered.

Then he bailed out his canoe and hauled it up on the

beach for repairs. He knew he couldn't take Harriet out in a leaky boat—she wouldn't like it. Tired though he was, he climbed a spruce tree and found some spruce gum. With this he plugged the seam and stopped the leak. Even so, the canoe turned out to be a cranky little craft. If Stuart had not had plenty of experience on the water, he would have got into serious trouble with it. It was a tippy boat even for a souvenir. Stuart carried stones from the beach down to the water's edge and ballasted the canoe with the stones until it floated evenly and steadily. He made a back-rest so that Harriet would be able to lean back and trail her fingers in the water if she wished. He also made a pillow by tying one of his clean handkerchiefs around some moss. Then he went for a paddle to practise his stroke. He was angry that he didn't have anything better than a paper spoon for a paddle, but he decided that there was nothing he could do about it. He wondered whether Harriet would notice that his paddle was really just an ice cream spoon.

All that afternoon Stuart worked on the canoe, adjusting ballast, filling seams, and getting everything shipshape for the morrow. He could think of nothing else but his date with Harriet. At suppertime he took his ax, felled a dandelion, opened a can of deviled ham, and had a light supper of ham and dande-lion milk. After supper, he propped himself up against a fern, bit off some spruce gum for a chew, and lay there on the bank dreaming and chewing gum. In his imagination he went over every detail of tomorrow's trip with Harriet. With his eyes shut he seemed to see the whole occasion plainly—how she would look when she came down the path to the water, how calm and peaceful the river was going to be in the twilight, how graceful the canoe would seem, drawn up on the shore. In imagination he lived every minute of their evening together. They would paddle to a large water-lily pad upstream, and he would invite Harriet to step out on the pad and sit awhile. Stuart planned to wear his swimming trunks under his clothes so that he could dive off the lily pad into the cool stream. He would swim the crawl stroke, up and down and all around the lily pad, while Harriet watched, admiring his ability as a swim-mer. (Stuart chewed the spruce gum very rapidly as he thought about this part of the episode.)

Suddenly Stuart opened his eyes and sat up. He thought about the letter he had sent and he wondered whether it had ever been delivered. It was an unusually small letter, of course, and might have gone unnoticed in the letterbox. This idea filled him with fears and worries. But soon he let his thoughts return to the river, and as he lay there a whippoorwill began to sing on the opposite shore, darkness spread over the land, and Stuart dropped off to sleep.

The next day dawned cloudy. Stuart had to go up to the village to have the oil changed in his car, so he hid the canoe under some leaves, tied it firmly to a stone, and went off on his errand, still thinking about Harriet and wishing it were a nicer day. The sky looked rainy.

Stuart returned from the village with a headache, but he hoped that it would be better before five o'clock. He felt rather nervous, as he had never taken a girl canoeing before. He spent the afternoon lying around camp, trying on different shirts to see which looked best on him and combing his whiskers. He would no sooner get a clean shirt on than he would discover that it was wet under the arms, from nervous perspiration, and he would have to change it for a dry one. He put on a clean shirt at two o'clock, another at three o'clock, and another at quarter past four. This took up most of the afternoon. As five o'clock drew near, Stuart grew more and more nervous. He kept looking at his watch, glancing up the path, combing his hair, talking to himself, and fidgeting. The day had turned chilly and Stuart was almost sure that there was going to be rain. He couldn't imagine what he would do if it should rain just as Harriet Ames showed up to go canoeing.

At last five o'clock arrived. Stuart heard someone coming down the path. It was Harriet. She had accepted his invitation. Stuart threw himself down against a stump and tried to strike an easy attitude, as though he were accustomed to taking girls out. He waited till Harriet was within a few feet of him, then got up.

"Hello there," he said, trying to keep his voice from trembling.

"Are you Mr. Little?" asked Harriet.

"Yes," said Stuart. "It's nice of you to come."

"Well, it was very good of you to ask me," replied Harriet. She was wearing a white sweater, a tweed skirt, short white wool socks, and sneakers. Her hair was tied with a bright colored handkerchief, and Stuart noticed that she carried a box of peppermints in her hand.

"Not at all, glad to do it," said Stuart. "I only wish we had better weather. Looks rather sticky, don't you think?" Stuart was trying to make his voice sound as though he had an English accent.

Harriet looked at the sky and nodded. "Oh, well," she said, "if it rains, it rains."

"Sure," repeated Stuart, "if it rains, it rains. My canoe is a short distance up the shore. May I help you over the rough places in the path?" Stuart was a courteous mouse by nature, but Harriet said she didn't need any help. She was an active girl and not at all inclined to stumble or fall. Stuart led the way to where he had hidden the canoe, and Harriet followed, but when they reached the spot Stuart was horrified to discover that the canoe was not there. It had disappeared.

Stuart's heart sank. He felt like crying.

"The canoe is gone," he groaned.

Then he began racing wildly up and down the bank, looking everywhere. Harriet joined in the search, and after a while they found the canoe—but it was a mess. Some one had been playing with it. A long piece of heavy string was tied to one end. The ballast rocks were gone. The pillow was gone. The back-rest was gone. The spruce gum had come out of the seam. Mud was all over everything, and one of the paddles was all bent and twisted. It was just a mess. It looked just the way a birchbark canoe looks after some big boys are finished playing with it.

Stuart was heartbroken. He did not know what to do. He sat down on a twig and buried his head in his hands. "Oh, gee," he kept saying, "oh, gee whiz."

324

"What's the trouble?" asked Harriet.

"Miss Ames," said Stuart in a trembling voice, "I assure you I had everything beautifully arranged—*everything*. And now look!"

Harriet was for fixing the canoe up and going out on the river anyway, but Stuart couldn't stand that idea.

"It's no use," he said bitterly, "it wouldn't be the same."

"The same as what?" asked Harriet.

"The same as the way it was going to be, when I was thinking about it yesterday. I'm afraid a woman can't understand these things. Look at that string! It's tied on so tight I could never get it off."

"Well," suggested Harriet, "couldn't we just let it hang over in the water and trail along after us?"

Stuart looked at her in despair. "Did you ever see an Indian paddling along some quiet unspoiled river with a great big piece of rope dragging astern?" he asked.

"We could pretend we were fishing," said Harriet, who didn't realize that some people are fussy about boats.

"I don't *want* to pretend I'm fishing," cried Stuart, desperately. "Besides, look at that mud! *Look* at it!" He was screaming now.

Harriet sat down on the twig beside Stuart. She offered him a peppermint but he shook his head.

"Well," she said, "it's starting to rain, and I guess I'd better be running along if you are not going to take me paddling in your canoe. I don't see why you have to sit here and sulk."

Would you like to come up to my house? After dinner you could take me to the dance at the Country Club. It might cheer you up."

"No, thank you," replied Stuart. "I don't know how to dance. Besides, I plan to make an early start in the morning. I'll probably be on the road at daybreak."

"Are you going to sleep out in all this rain?" asked Harriet.

"Certainly," said Stuart. "I'll crawl in under the canoe."

Harriet shrugged her shoulders. "Well," she said, "good-by, Mr. Little."

"Good-by, Miss Ames," said Stuart. "I am sorry our evening on the river had to end like this."

"So am I," said Harriet. And she walked away along the wet path toward Tracy's Lane, leaving Stuart alone with his broken dreams and his damaged canoe.

Think and Discuss

1. What things happened to spoil Stuart's plans?

2. The two characters in this story had very different reactions to their bad luck. What differences do you see between Stuart's and Harriet's reactions? Why do you think Stuart behaved as he did?

3. A hint that gives you a clue about what is to come is called **foreshadowing**. Foreshadowing helps you to predict the outcome of a story. It also prepares you for the ending. What foreshadowing can you find that Stuart's date with Harriet will not have a happy outcome?

4. Careful, precise language, usually in complete sentences, is called **formal language**. Casual speech, often used with friends or in relaxed settings, is called **informal language**. When Stuart and Harriet first meet, whose language is more formal? What other examples of formal and informal language can you find in the story?

Have you ever wondered how authors get ideas for their stories? How might E. B. White have gotten the idea to write about a mouse?

Letter to His Readers

By E. B. White

Where did I get the idea for *Stuart Little* and for *Charlotte's Web*? Well, many years ago I went to bed one night in a railway sleeping car, and during the night I dreamed about a tiny boy who acted rather like a mouse. That's how the story of Stuart Little got started.

As for *Charlotte's Web,* I like animals and my barn is a very pleasant place to be, at all hours. One day when I was on my way to feed the pig, I began feeling sorry for the pig because, like most pigs, he was doomed to die. This made me sad. So I started thinking of ways to save a pig's life. I had been watching a big grey spider at her work and was impressed by how clever she was at weaving. Gradually I worked the spider into the story that you know, a story of friendship and salvation on a farm. Three years after I started writing it, it was published. (I am not a fast worker, as you can see.)

I don't know how or when the idea for *The Trumpet of the Swan* occurred to me. I guess I must have wondered what it would be like to be a Trumpeter Swan and not be able to make a noise.

Sometimes I'm asked how old I was when I started to write, and what made me want to write. I started early—as soon as I could spell. In fact, I can't remember any time in my life when I wasn't busy writing. I don't know what caused me to do it, or why I enjoyed it, but I think children often find pleasure and satisfaction in trying to set their thoughts down on paper, either in words or in pictures. I was no good at drawing, so I used words instead. As I grew older, I found that writing can be a way of earning a living.

Are my stories true, you ask? No, they are imaginary tales, containing fantastic characters and events. In *real* life, a family doesn't have a child who looks like a mouse; in *real* life, a spider doesn't spin words in her web. In *real* life, a swan doesn't blow a trumpet. But real life is only one kind of life—there is also the life of the imagination. And although my stories are imaginary, I like to think that there is some truth in them, too—truth about the way people and animals feel and think and act.

Think and Discuss

1. How did E. B. White get the idea for *Stuart Little*?

2. In this letter the author says, "although my stories are imaginary, I like to think that there is some truth in them, too—truth about the way people and animals feel and think and act." What do you think he meant? What truths did you find in "An Evening on the River"?

3. E. B. White wrote this letter to the many children who wrote to him because they liked his books. Judging from what he wrote, what questions do you think he was asked most often by his fans? What other things would you like to know about the author?

4. The attitude a writer has toward a subject is called the **tone**. A speaker can show attitude in the tone of voice. A writer, however, must express tone through the choice of words and details. Tone can be serious, humorous, angry, or sad. What is the tone of E. B. White's letter? Is the tone formal and cold or conversational and warm? Explain your answer.

RESPONDING TO LITERATURE

The Reading and Writing Connection

Personal Response Have you ever had a day when *everything* went wrong? Does it seem funny now or do you still get mad when you think about it? Write a paragraph telling what happened. Use dialogue to show how you felt about the events.

Creative Writing We know that Stuart wrote a letter to Harriet asking her to come canoeing with him, but the author does not tell us what he said. Pretend you are Stuart. You want very much to impress Harriet. Write a letter to persuade her to come canoeing.

Creative Activities

Draw Choose a moment in "An Evening on the River" that is not illustrated in your book. Draw a picture of that scene. Use a quote from the story as a caption for your illustration.

Act Out With a partner, script, rehearse, and then act out the scene in which Stuart and Harriet discuss fixing the canoe. Begin with Harriet saying, "What's the trouble?" and end with Stuart saying, "*Look* at it!" Add lines that show Harriet's and Stuart's attitudes.

Vocabulary

What does the author mean when he says "Stuart was a very courteous mouse"? What does the word *courteous* have to do with the word *court*? Use a dictionary to find out.

Looking Ahead

Persuasive Letter In this unit you will be writing a persuasive letter. Look back at page 325 of "An Evening on the River." What are Stuart's reasons for not trying to fix the canoe? Are his reasons persuasive?

VOCABULARY CONNECTION

Homophones

Homophones are words that are pronounced the same way but have different meanings. Homophones can be confusing because they have different spellings.

> The birch bark at the stern was held together by a lacing, and the water came in **through** the seam.
>
> Stuart **threw** himself down against a stump. . . .
> *from "An Evening on the River" by E. B. White*

The homophones *threw* (hurled with a swift motion) and *through* (in one side and out the opposite) are pronounced the same way but are spelled differently and have different meanings. Here are some other homophones.

heard (listened to)   site (a place)
herd (group of animals)   sight (ability to see)

Vocabulary Practice

A. Write each sentence, using the correct homophone in parentheses. Check your dictionary if you need help.

1. A river can overflow during a heavy (reign, rain).
2. (It's, Its) a dangerous time for animals living nearby.
3. Otters abandon (their, there) homes in the riverbanks.
4. A burrowing frog leaves its (whole, hole) quickly.

B. Each of these words from "An Evening on the River" is part of a homophone pair. Write another homophone to complete each pair. Use the words in each pair in sentences.

5. for   **6.** would   **7.** here   **8.** one

Prewriting
Persuasive Letter

Listening: For a Speaker's Motive and Bias

Most speakers have one of these purposes in mind.

1. To share an experience
2. To inform
3. To give instructions or directions
4. To persuade
5. To amuse

What is this speaker's purpose?

The book *Stuart Little* is really fantastic! You ought to read it.

Obviously, the speaker's purpose is to persuade you to read *Stuart Little*. What if the speaker added this?

Pick up a copy today at the Old Book Shoppe.

The speaker's purpose hasn't changed. However, the added sentence shows the speaker's **motive**. That motive—the real reason for persuading you to read *Stuart Little*—is to sell books. Detecting motives can help you judge persuasion.

Also listen for bias. Bias is an attitude that keeps someone from seeing both sides of an issue. Suppose you heard these statements.

Books about animals are boring. Don't read *Stuart Little*.

This speaker is biased against animals in books. The speaker doesn't consider how funny a book might be, how many other people have loved it, or what the book is really about. Bias keeps the speaker from being able to make a judgment about the book itself.

Prewriting Practice

Listen as your teacher reads a letter to a newspaper editor. Discuss the writer's purpose, motive, and bias.

Thinking: Evaluating and Making Judgments

When Stuart Little's canoe began to leak, he declared, "I've been swindled!" Stuart was **evaluating** the canoe's condition and **making a judgment** about it. When you evaluate something, you study or test it against certain standards. Then you make a judgment about its value.

Guidelines for Evaluating and Making Judgments

1. **Identify the stated facts and opinions.** Facts give information that can be proved to be true. Opinions state feelings or thoughts. Facts make better reasons for agreeing to do something.

    FACT: The canoe is made of fiberglass.

    OPINION: Canoes should be made of fiberglass.

2. **Look for facts that support the opinions.** The opinion above would be stronger if it were backed up with facts.

    FACT: Fiberglass is strong but lightweight.

    FACT: Fiberglass needs less care than wood.

3. **Check the statements for accuracy.** Check at the library or with an expert to be sure all statements are correct. Which of these statements is accurate?

    Harriet was a little mouse, just like Stuart.

    Harriet was a little girl, just Stuart's size.

4. **Look for overgeneralization.** E. B. White started to write as a small child. You may know of other writers who began at an early age. Knowing these facts, you could make a **generalization,** or a broad statement, about writers.

    GENERALIZATION: Some writers began writing as children.

    However, beware of **overgeneralization,** in which a statement goes beyond the facts.

    OVERGENERALIZATION: Most writers began writing as children.

5. Check to see if any statements are exaggerations. An exaggeration stretches the truth.

The book will make you laugh until you explode.

Now evaluate and make a judgment about this letter.

Dear Aunt Elizabeth,

    I just had the greatest idea in the world for a children's book. It will be easy for you to turn this idea into a story.
    I dreamed that some numbers came to life. They even had personalities, like the dwarves in "Cinderella"! Children will just love a book about walking, talking numbers.
    Good writers always get their best ideas in dreams. Maybe I should sleep more!

          Your nephew,

- What opinions does Adam state? What facts?
- Are Adam's opinions backed up with facts?
- Which statement is not accurate?
- What overgeneralization has Adam made?
- What exaggeration can you find?

Prewriting Practice

Work with a partner. Think of a good idea you have had. Try to persuade each other that your idea is great. Then evaluate each argument and make a judgment about it.

Composition Skills
Persuasive Letter

Writing Business Letters ☑

You can write a business letter to order a product, to apply for a job, to ask for information, or to persuade someone to do something. You usually will write a business letter to someone you do not know.

The body of a business letter should be brief and to the point. The language should be formal and polite, or **business-like.** A business letter should include all necessary details but no personal information.

HEADING	P.S. 2 112 Henry Street New York, NY 10002 January 10, 1990
INSIDE ADDRESS	Harper & Row, Publishers, Inc. 10 E. 53 Street New York, NY 10022
GREETING	Dear Sir or Madam:
BODY	I am in the sixth grade at P.S. 2. My class and I just read Stuart Little. We were wondering whether an editor who worked with E. B. White would come to talk to us. It would be thrilling to meet someone who knew E. B. White. Most of us have read and loved his other books. Also, we would enjoy meeting a professional editor.
CLOSING	Sincerely,
SIGNATURE	*Amanda Daley* Amanda Daley

- What are the six parts of a business letter?
- What information does each part of the letter give?
- What is the purpose of the letter?
- Is Amanda's language businesslike? Why or why not?
- Would you have used a closing such as "Your friend" in a business letter? Why or why not?
- Notice that Amanda signed her full name. Why didn't she use just her first name?

Use these guidelines when you write business letters.

Guidelines for Writing Business Letters

Form of a business letter

1. **Heading** Write a three-line heading in the upper right-hand corner. Write your address on the first two lines and the date on the third line.
2. **Inside address** At the left margin, write the same address as you will use on the envelope.
3. **Greeting** Skip a line and write a greeting, ending with a colon. If you do not know whose name to use, write *Dear Sir or Madam* or *Dear [Business Name]*.
4. **Body** Write your message. Indent each paragraph.
5. **Closing** Skip a line and write a formal closing such as *Yours truly*. Line up the closing at the left with the heading. Capitalize the first word and end with a comma.
6. **Signature** Write your full name below the closing. Then print or type your name below your signature.

Content of a business letter

1. State your message briefly but clearly. Use polite, formal language. Be businesslike.
2. Include all necessary details. If you want information, fully explain what you need. If you are ordering, tell exactly what you want and mention the amount you are enclosing. If you are giving an opinion, state it clearly and support it with good reasons.

Prewriting Practice

Rewrite the following section of a business letter. Take out anything that does not belong in the letter. Change any language that is not businesslike.

Dear Representative Waldman:

   My friends and I would sure like you to support the bill to clean up the river. It is a real mess! We often go canoeing, and we are afraid that our canoes might tip over. Many kids also swim in the river. Will they get sick because of that? Do you ever swim there?

                                    Your pal,

                                    Kevin Wright
                                    Kevin Wright

The Grammar Connection

Abbreviations

   Abbreviations are often used in addresses and within business letters to save space. Place names, titles, names of businesses, and names of agencies and organizations are commonly abbreviated.

High St.   Dr. Edgar Luna
Video, Inc.   Creative Costume Co.
United Nations—UN   Federal Trade Commission—FTC

Practice Rewrite this section of a business letter, using abbreviations where possible.

Dear Mister Freed:
   Congratulations on receiving your Certified Professional Secretary rating! Your many hours of hard work have paid off. We hope you will attend the National Secretaries Association convention as the speaker for Holley, Biggs Company, Incorporated.

Stating and Supporting an Opinion ☑

If Harriet Ames had expressed her opinion of Stuart Little after their disastrous date, here is what she might have said.

> Mr. Little is a very disagreeable person. He invited me to go canoeing with him, but when I arrived, he didn't seem glad to see me. I'm sure he saw me coming from a long way off, but he didn't greet me until I was standing right in front of him. When he found that the canoe had been damaged, he went to pieces. I wanted to fix it, but he just kept saying very rudely that everything was spoiled. He actually screamed at me! Finally, I asked him to take me to the dance, but he refused. Apparently he preferred to lie out on a rainy river bank and sulk about his canoe.

- What is the topic sentence of this paragraph?
- What supporting details, or reasons, does Harriet give for holding this opinion?

If all you knew about Stuart was what Harriet told you in this paragraph, would you be likely to agree with her that Stuart was a disagreeable person? A clearly stated opinion makes a good topic sentence for a persuasive paragraph.

A topic sentence that states an opinion needs strong facts to back it up to persuade the reader to agree with the opinion. Now read the following paragraph. It has the same topic sentence, but its supporting details are different.

> Mr. Little is a very disagreeable person. He invited me to go canoeing with him, but when I got there it was about to rain. Then he found that some big boys had played in the canoe and ruined it. When it started to rain, I decided I might as well go home. Stuart wasn't interested in coming with me.

- Do any details support the opinion in the topic sentence?
- Which paragraph is more persuasive? Why?

Prewriting Practice

Complete each sentence to express an opinion. List supporting reasons that back up your opinion.

1. A(n) ＿＿ is an ideal pet.
2. ＿＿ is the best time of year.
3. The hardest chore you'll ever have to do is ＿＿.

Ordering Your Reasons ☑

You can order your reasons in several ways. The order you choose depends on your audience. Always prepare your argument to suit your audience.

Order of Importance Imagine that you want your parents to buy you a fiberglass canoe. Before you ask your parents, you make a list of your reasons for wanting a canoe. You put the reasons in order of importance to you, from most to least important.

1. I could have a lot of fun in a canoe.
2. I love the outdoors.
3. If I had a canoe, I could make new friends.
4. Because paddling is hard work, canoeing will help me to build muscles.
5. I can learn a lot about the river by exploring it.

- How persuasive would these reasons be to a parent?
- Which reasons would be the most persuasive to a parent?

Now read this list. The same basic reasons are presented, but the order is different.

1. My canoe explorations will give me facts for science reports on river currents, wildlife, and plant life.
2. The exercise I get canoeing will help me to keep fit.
3. Canoeing with my friends will help me to learn cooperation.

4. Having a canoe will give me a chance to meet people who share my interests.
5. Spending a lot of the summer outdoors in the fresh air will be healthier than watching TV inside.

- How is this list different from the first one?
- Which reasons have been worded differently?
- Why might this list be more persuasive to parents?

In addition to the change in order, some words have been added to the second list. These words change reasons that would not have been persuasive to parents to reasons that *are* persuasive. Remember, when you are trying to be persuasive, make your case from the other person's point of view.

Sometimes you may want to go from less important reasons to the most important ones. Follow this order if the listener needs to be "warmed up" before you reach your most important reason or if the listener will not understand the most important reason without knowing the less important reasons.

Answering Objections Suppose that the people you are trying to persuade have a single strong objection. They may not be open to any of your arguments until that objection is overcome. In this case begin your argument with reasons that answer the objection.

"I know you are probably thinking that I'll get bored with a canoe the way I did with my tuba, but this is different. . . ."

Ordering by Subject Suppose two of your reasons for wanting a canoe are related to your health. Two are ways the canoe would help you to improve socially. The most effective way of ordering your reasons might be to group them by subject in two groups.

HEALTH BENEFITS: 1. The exercise will keep me fit.
                  2. I'll be healthier if I spend time outdoors.
SOCIAL BENEFITS: 3. I'll learn cooperation.
                  4. I'll meet friends who share my interests.

Prewriting Practice

Choose one of the following topics. List at least five persuasive reasons to support your topic. Number your reasons in the order that you think will be the most effective.

1. Persuade your teacher to give your class a longer lunch period.
2. Persuade a friend to take dance lessons with you.
3. Persuade your sister or brother to help you build a tree house.
4. Ask your parents to buy you a bicycle.
5. Convince your mother that you should be allowed to leave your bedroom messy if you want to.

Choosing Words to Persuade ☑️

When you want to persuade someone to do (or not to do) something, use words that express your ideas most convincingly. Strong, exact words that appeal to the five senses are usually more persuasive. These words help the reader or listener form mental pictures or feelings. Which of these sentences would do a better job of persuading you to take a raincoat on a canoe trip?

1. Take your raincoat. It could rain.
2. Take your raincoat. It could pour.

Rain and *pour* have similar meanings, but *pour* sounds a lot worse. You might think, "I don't mind canoeing in the rain," but you probably would not think "I don't mind canoeing in the pouring rain."

Now read these sentences. Which one better persuades you to help repair canoes for your school's Boating Club?

1. *Sign up!* Help fix canoes this Saturday.
2. *Join us* for Canoe Fix-It Day this Saturday!

- Which phrase gives you a better mental picture or feeling—*sign up* or *join us*?

When you choose your words, think about the person or people whom you are trying to persuade. Use words that will be especially appealing to them. Suppose you want to sell used books to make money for your club. Here are three sets of words you might use to get people to come.

1. book fair
2. bargain book sale
3. recycled books

- Which would appeal to people who like to save money?
- Which sounds like it would be the most fun?
- Which would appeal to people who are concerned about the environment?

Prewriting Practice

A. Write each sentence, using the word in parentheses that will make the statement more persuasive.

1. Try on these rain boots. They are a good ____.
(price, bargain)

2. Come out for a walk along the river. The air is ____.
(bracing, cold)

3. I need a new raincoat. My old one is ____.
(worn, ragged)

4. Won't you have some of these ____ berries?
(good, luscious)

5. This ____ lamp is worth a lot of money.
(antique, old)

6. Read this book. The story is very ____.
(interesting, exciting)

B. For each person described below, write two descriptive words about a glass of milk that would persuade the person to drink it. Think of words that would appeal to each person.

1. a hot, thirsty traveler
2. a little child
3. a person who is ill
4. a tired athlete
5. a teen-ager

Step 1: Prewriting—Choose a Topic

Daniel wrote down several ideas that he might want to persuade someone about. Then he thought about each one.

finding sponsors for a charity race — Daniel was going to run in such a race, and it would be for a very good cause.

inviting friends to a picnic — He would not really need to do much persuading.

getting people to improve the environment — This seemed too general. To whom would he write the letter?

asking friends to help with a book sale — He was not very interested in this idea.

Daniel circled *race*.

On Your Own

1. **Think and discuss** Make a list of ideas for a persuasive letter. Use the Ideas page to help you. Discuss your ideas with a classmate.
2. **Choose** Ask yourself these questions about each of your ideas.
    To whom will I write?
    Can I think of several good reasons to support my idea?
    Do I really care about this matter?
3. **Explore** Before you begin writing, do one of the "Exploring Your Topic" activities on the Ideas page.

Ideas for Getting Started

Choosing Your Topic

Topic Ideas

Persuade someone to—

come on a long hike
talk to your class
    about careers
recycle paper
vote for you
set up a bike path
continue a canceled
    TV series
come to a road race
come to a car wash
display safe driving
    posters
add wheelchair ramps

Deal Out Ideas

Make ten playing cards with these labels:

Please take my advice and . . .
Please donate . . .
Something I'd like changed is . . .
Give me my money back because . . .
Please help with . . .

Form small groups of two or three and deal the cards. Each person turns the phrase on his or her card into an idea for a persuasive letter. Then shuffle the cards and play again.

Exploring Your Topic

Come to Order

List all the reasons you will use to persuade your reader. You should have at least three. Decide which is the strongest and mark it *A.* Mark the next strongest *B,* and so on. Now number your reasons to show in what order you will use them. You must go either from strongest to weakest or weakest to strongest.

Talk About It

Pick one of the reasons that supports your topic. Using only that reason, try to persuade a classmate. As you talk, try to make your reason stronger by adding details and examples.

Step 2: Write a First Draft

Daniel decided to send his letter to Mr. Carelli at the neighborhood grocery, where he often stopped after running practice.

Daniel wrote his first draft. He did not worry about spelling and grammar mistakes for now. Later he would go back and make corrections.

Daniel's first draft

Think and Discuss

- How many reasons did Daniel use?
- Where could he have used more detail to make his reasons clear?
- What persuasive words did he use?

> Dear Mr. Carelli
>
> On April 19, I will be running in the Boys and Girls Club Road Race. ~~We~~ It is being run to raise money for a charity ~~cause~~ fund. It is a very good cause. Please take part by being my sponsor. Any pledge you make will be a big help.
>
> Sincerely,

On Your Own

1. **Think about purpose and audience** Ask yourself the following questions.

   To whom am I writing this letter?

   What is my purpose? What results am I hoping to get?

   What reasons will appeal to my audience?

2. **Write** Write your first draft. State your reasons in order and use persuasive words. Write down all your ideas without stopping to correct spelling and grammar mistakes. Write on every other line so you can make changes later.

Step 3: Revise

Daniel read his first draft. He noticed that he had not said exactly what the charity fund was for. Mr. Carelli might be more interested if he knew that. Daniel added a sentence to explain whom the money would help.

Daniel wanted to find out how persuasive his letter was. He read it to Sara.

Reading and responding

Daniel thought of two more reasons why the race was worth sponsoring. He also added some more persuasive words.

Part of Daniel's revised draft

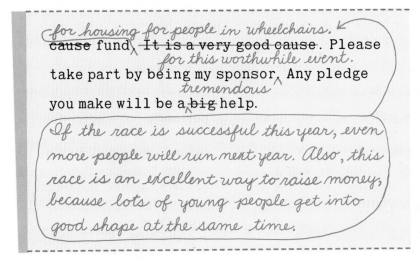

for housing for people in wheelchairs.

~~cause~~ fund. ~~It is a very good cause~~. Please

for this worthwhile event.

take part by being my sponsor. Any pledge

tremendous

you make will be a ~~big~~ help.

If the race is successful this year, even more people will run next year. Also, this race is an excellent way to raise money, because lots of young people get into good shape at the same time.

Think and Discuss ✓

- What reasons for sponsoring the race did Daniel add?
- How did he order his reasons?
- What persuasive words did he add?

The Writing Process 345

On Your Own

Revising Checklist
☑ How many reasons have I used to support my ideas?
☑ Have I stated my reasons in the best order?
☑ Are there parts I could make stronger by adding details or persuasive words?

1. **Revise** Make changes in your first draft. If you need to find persuasive words, use the thesaurus below or the one at the back of this book. If you need extra room to add something, use the margins. Draw an arrow to show where that part should go.

2. **Have a conference** Read your letter to a partner.

Ask your listener:	As you listen:
"Can you see very clearly what I am asking?" "Are my reasons good ones? Can you think of any others?" "Where do I need more persuasive words?"	I must pay close attention. Do I understand clearly what is being asked? What more do I want to know? Would I be persuaded by this letter? Why?

3. **Revise** Has your partner pointed out any ways of making your letter more persuasive? Do you have any other new ideas? Make these changes on your paper.

Thesaurus

capable able, efficient, qualified
eager keen, interested
give provide, supply, donate
grateful appreciative, thankful
join enroll, sign up

persuade convince, convert
refuse deny, decline, turn down
respect admire, appreciate
sure positive, confident, certain
worthy valuable, admirable

Step 4: Proofread

Daniel proofread his letter for mistakes in spelling, grammar, and letter form. He used a dictionary to check his spellings. He used proofreading marks to make his changes.

Here is how the opening looked after he proofread it.

Daniel's proofread letter opening

Mr. Albert Carelli

Carelli's Variety Store

28A East First Street

Petersville, Md 12345

On Your Own

1. **Proofreading Practice** Proofread the opening of this business letter. Correct the mistakes in spelling and business letter form. There are three mistakes in capitalization, four mistakes in punctuation, and three misspelled words.

1151 east Park Street
Waterford Mi. 48095

Director of sales
Red Balloon Enterprizes
90 Highland Boullevard
Kansas City, KS, 66106

Dear Directer of Sales.

2. **Proofreading Application** Now proofread your letter. Use the Proofreading Checklist and the Grammar and Spelling Hints below. If you wish, make your corrections with a colored pencil. Use a dictionary to check your spellings.

Proofreading Checklist

Did I

☑ **1.** use the proper format for my letter?

☑ **2.** use capital letters correctly?

☑ **3.** use punctuation marks correctly?

☑ **4.** spell all words correctly?

☑ **5.** sign my full name?

The Grammar/Spelling Connection

Grammar Hints

Remember these rules from Unit 9 when you use commas.

- Use commas between words in a series.   *(red, blue, and green)*
- Use commas to set off the name of a person being spoken to directly.   *(Thank you, Janet, for your thoughtful letter.)*

Spelling Hints

- The pronunciation of an unstressed final ending does not always give a clue to the way it is spelled. The final (īz) sounds may be spelled **ize** or **ise**.   *(exercise, realize)*

Step 5: Publish

Daniel wrote out a neat copy of his letter on plain stationary. He centered the letter nicely on the page. Then he addressed an envelope to Mr. Carelli, put a stamp on the envelope, and mailed the letter.

On Your Own

1. **Copy** Write or type your letter as neatly as possible.
2. **Check** Read over your letter again to make sure you have not left out anything or made any mistakes in copying.
3. **Share** Address your letter carefully and mail it!

Ideas for Sharing

- With your classmates, make a thesaurus of persuasive words. Include the ones from your letters.
- Write a reply to a classmate's letter.

Literature and Creative Writing

"An Evening on the River" was the story of Stuart Little's disastrous date with Harriet Ames. Stuart was very anxious to have the evening go smoothly, but instead, everything went wrong. E. B. White's letter to his readers told how he got the ideas for each of his three children's books.

Use what you have learned about persuasion and letter writing to complete one or more of the following activities.

Remember these things ☑
Include all appropriate letter parts.
State your opinions clearly.
Put your reasons in the most persuasive order.
Use reasons that appeal to your audience.

1. **Ask for a replacement canoe.** Pretend you are Stuart. Since your new, genuine birchbark canoe leaks, you think the store where you bought it should replace it. Write to the store manager. Persuade the manager to replace your canoe.

2. **Write to a canoe expert.** Persuade the expert to come to a pond or lake in your town to give lessons in canoe handling and safety.

3. **Write to a house builder.** Pretend you are Stuart's size, just two inches tall. Write to a house builder. Persuade the builder to make a house for you, just right for your size. Think of some good reasons why the builder should take time away from bigger projects to work on your house.

Writing Across the Curriculum
Mathematics

People use math often, both on and off the job. You may even find math necessary when you write letters.

Choose one or more of the following activities. Use businesslike language.

1. **Place your order.** If you could send away for anything, what would it be? Write a letter to the company that makes the item you want. Order the item and include the price, tax, and the address to which the material is to be sent.

2. **Clear up the confusion.** Imagine that this sales slip is incorrect. You were overcharged for an item that was supposed to be on sale. Write a letter to the store, explaining that the store owes you a refund. Be sure to make your explanation clear.

Writing Steps
1. Choose a topic
2. Write a first draft
3. Revise
4. Proofread
5. Publish

Sound City 5th and Main Street			
QUANTITY	DESCRIPTION	PRICE	AMOUNT
1	AM-FM radio	$24 99	$24 99
SALES SLIP Customer's Copy	Subtotal	24 99	
	Sales Tax	1 25	
	Total	$26 24	

Word Bank
refund
error
credit
overcharge
reputation

3. **Explore career opportunities.** Write a letter, asking a local businessperson to visit your class. Explain that you would like this person to speak about ways that the employees use math on the job.

Kristen really enjoyed reading "An Evening on the River." She loved fantasy of all kinds. The next book she chose, *Mrs. Frisby and the Rats of NIMH* by Robert C. O'Brien, was a very different kind of story. Kristen decided to share her book by interviewing Nicodemus, an important character in the book. She asked a classmate to be the interviewer and she was Nicodemus. Here is the interview that she presented.

INTERVIEWER: This is Nicodemus from the book <u>Mrs. Frisby and the Rats of NIMH</u> by Robert C. O'Brien. Nicodemus, just what is NIMH?

NICODEMUS: NIMH is the National Institute of Mental Health. Psychologists there study the mind, emotions, and behavior of animals in order to understand people.

INTERVIEWER: What was your life like at NIMH?

NICODEMUS: We lived in cages. It seems that we were part of an experiment. We had to learn how to get out of a maze. But the terrible part was living as a prisoner!

INTERVIEWER: Is it really true that you learned to read?

NICODEMUS: It certainly is. Jenner and I became friends with Justin, who was a very smart rat. He was the first to figure out what the letters meant. In fact, reading saved our lives!

INTERVIEWER: How could reading save the lives of laboratory rats? To find out more about Nicodemus, you must read the book.

Think and Discuss
- What did you find out about the characters in the book?
- What did you learn about the setting of the story?
- Why is this a good way to share a book?

Share Your Book

Interview a Book Character

1. Decide which character in the book to interview. Choose an important character who knows what happens in the story.
2. Decide which parts of the book you will tell about. Choose exciting or interesting incidents that will make others want to read the book themselves. Ask your character questions about those parts of the story.
3. Write down what the interviewer and the character will say. Ask a classmate to read the part of the interviewer and you be the book character. Be careful not to tell too much.
4. Start your interview by having the interviewer introduce the character. Tell the author and title of your book.

Other Activities

- Interview the illustrator of your book. Ask the illustrator how he or she decided which parts of the story to illustrate.
- Write an imaginary letter from your book character to the author of the book. The character might complain about some of the problems or thank the author for the solution.
- Draw a map or diagram of some important part of the setting for your story. Label the locations of important incidents.

The Book Nook

Time Cat *by Lloyd Alexander* Gareth is a remarkable cat who needs only to blink an eye to transport himself and his owner, Jason, back in time.	**The Wind in the Willows** *by Kenneth Grahame* Water Rat and Mole share a great life by the river, but trying to keep Toad out of trouble keeps them busy.

I'm not too sure that all I've read
Is under my hat or over my head;
What I've forgotten, so far as I see,
Is a matter between myself and me.

David McCord from "Forget It"

Pronouns

Getting Ready Pronouns are the best shortcuts in our language. We save a lot of time and space by using them instead of repeating nouns again and again. It is much easier to say "They lost their scarves," than to say "Abigail and Annie lost Abigail's and Annie's scarves." Pronouns can do many different language jobs, and there are special pronouns for each job. In this unit, you will be introduced to some new pronouns and learn more about others.

ACTIVITIES

Listening Listen as the poem on the opposite page is read. There are eight pronouns in the poem that refer to *I*. List them all on the board. (Note: *myself* is a pronoun that you will learn about in seventh grade. Be sure to count it.)

Speaking Look at the photograph. On the board, make a list of nouns to name the things in the picture. Beside each noun write a pronoun that might take its place.

Writing In your journal, rewrite the poem in your own words. Then write a response to the poem. Do you like it? What do you think it means?

1 | Pronouns and Antecedents

You have already learned how to use nouns in sentences. A **pronoun** is a word that takes the place of one or more nouns. Pronouns keep us from having to repeat the same noun.

James owns an ax, but James needs a log splitter.

James owns an ax, but he needs a log splitter.

Singular pronouns refer to one person or thing. Plural pronouns refer to more than one.

SINGULAR PRONOUNS: I   you   he   she   it
  PLURAL PRONOUNS: we   you   they

A pronoun makes sense only if you know which noun it replaces. The noun that the pronoun refers to is called the **antecedent**. Make sure that you have a clear antecedent for every pronoun. A pronoun can have more than one antecedent.

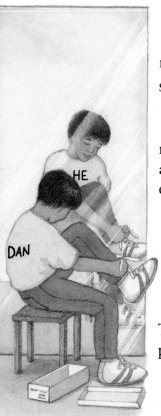

When George had enough money, he bought a bike.

George left the bike out in the rain, and it rusted.

After Brian and Carla had collected many recipes, they decided to write a cookbook.

The antecedent does not have to be in the same sentence as the pronoun.

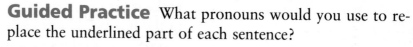

Brian and Carla wrote the cookbook. Carla illustrated it.

Guided Practice What pronouns would you use to replace the underlined part of each sentence?

Example: Tom and Wendy walked home quickly. *They*

1. Nancy walked fast too.
2. The streets were empty.
3. Bruce answered the door.
4. Ruth looked at the sky.
5. The friends went inside.
6. The rainstorm began.
7. Telephone wires fell down.
8. The road was flooded.

> ▸ A **pronoun** is a word that takes the place of one or more nouns.
> ▸ The **antecedent** of a pronoun is the noun or nouns to which the pronoun refers.
> ▸ Provide a clear antecedent for every pronoun.

Independent Practice

A. Write the pronouns. Then write their antecedents.

Example: The fans cheered when they saw the touchdown.
they—fans

9. The seats were too far from the field. They were uncomfortable too.
10. Judy knew the cheers. She shouted them from the stands.
11. Danny bought a sandwich. He shared it with Judy.
12. The musicians played the school song. Then they played it again.

B. Write each pronoun and its antecedent. The pronoun and its antecedent may not always be in the same sentence.

Example: Henry was lonely until he met Joey. *he—Henry*

13. He and Joey found a tree in Joey's backyard.
14. They climbed the tree every day.
15. It was very tall and had thick branches.
16. Joey loved the tree, and he wanted to build a treehouse.
17. He and Henry built the treehouse in a week.
18. They put sleeping bags and a chair in it.
19. Joey's mother said that they had to pay rent to live in it.
20. Joey wanted to know if she was serious, but she told him that she wasn't.
21. He said that he would sleep in it that night.
22. Henry said that he would sleep in it too.

Writing Application: A Paragraph

Imagine that you are on a camping trip with some friends. Write a paragraph about your activities on the trip. Include pronouns in some of your sentences and underline them.

For Extra Practice, see p. 376.   **Pronouns and Antecedents** 357

2 | Pronouns as Subjects and Objects

You know that nouns can be subjects or direct objects. A pronoun that replaces a subject is a **subject pronoun**.

Bob Phillips hit the ball. He hit the ball.

A pronoun that replaces a direct object is an **object pronoun**. An object pronoun receives the action of a verb. Object pronouns are used after words such as *to*, *in*, *for*, and *at*.

Dad knows Sue Fox. Dad knows her .

Kevin threw the ball to Joan. Kevin threw the ball to her .

The chart shows how singular and plural pronouns change their forms according to their use.

Subject pronouns		Object pronouns	
Singular	Plural	Singular	Plural
I	we	me	us
you	you	you	you
he, she, it	they	him, her, it	them

Guided Practice

Are the underlined pronouns subject or object pronouns?

Example: I am learning about the eagle.   *subject*

1. It is a very powerful and unusual bird.
2. The Great Seal of the United States displays it.
3. Eagles are important to us.
4. Years ago people hunted them.
5. Now they are protected by strict laws.
6. They are still very scarce.
7. Pollution affects them.
8. We must save the eagles.

> ▶ Use a subject pronoun to replace a noun used as a subject.
> ▶ Use an object pronoun to replace a noun used as a direct object or after words such as *to, in, for,* and *at.*

Independent Practice Write these sentences, using the correct pronouns in parentheses. Label each pronoun *subject* or *object.*

Example: (I, me) saw some eagles in the mountains.
         I saw some eagles in the mountains.   **subject**

9. (They, Them) soared high in the sky.
10. Elliot has only seen (they, them) in pictures.
11. I thought that one eagle might swoop down on (I, me).
12. It did stare fiercely at (we, us).
13. (They, Them) appeared very powerful to (we, us).
14. (They, Them) dive to the earth to catch their prey.
15. Benjamin Franklin did not like (they, them).
16. (He, Him) preferred turkeys.
17. (They, Them) are more useful, peaceful birds.
18. Others did not want (they, them) on the Great Seal.
19. (We, Us) now have an eagle on the Great Seal.
20. It represents (we, us) as a nation.
21. (I, Me) think that the eagle is a good symbol of courage.
22. The eagle also reminds (I, me) of power.
23. My sister says that eagles inspire (she, her).
24. (They, Them) are beautiful birds to (she, her).
25. (She, Her) knows many facts about bald eagles.
26. (They, Them) live for as long as thirty years.
27. (They, Them) have powerful wings that spread to seven feet.
28. (We, Us) can see (they, them) in the wilderness in the United States and Canada.

Writing Application: A Description
Pretend that you visited a zoo and saw several different kinds of birds. Write a description of what you saw and heard. Use six subject and object pronouns. Underline them.

For Extra Practice, see p. 377.
     Pronouns as Subjects and Objects   359

3 | Possessive Pronouns

You know that possessive nouns show ownership. A pronoun that shows ownership is called a **possessive pronoun**.

My mug is on the table. Its handle is broken.

Some possessive pronouns always come before nouns. Other possessive pronouns always stand alone.

BEFORE NOUNS: Her *mug* is red.   Our *glasses* are clean.

STAND ALONE: That mug is theirs . This is mine , not hers .

The chart shows the singular and plural possessive pronouns. Notice that *his* and *its* can come before nouns or can stand alone.

Possessive Pronouns			
Used before nouns		**Used alone**	
my	our	mine	ours
your	your	yours	yours
his, her, its	their	his, hers, its	theirs

Do not confuse possessive pronouns with contractions. Possessive pronouns do not have apostrophes.

POSSESSIVE PRONOUNS:	its	their	your
CONTRACTION:	it's	they're	you're
	(it is)	(they are)	(you are)

Guided Practice What possessive pronoun correctly completes each sentence?

Example: A glove that belongs to me is ___. *mine*

1. A house that belongs to us is ___.
2. A dog that belongs to them is ___.
3. A hat that belongs to Karen is ___.
4. A memory that belongs to you is ___.
5. A book that belongs to James is ___.

▸ Use a **possessive pronoun** to show ownership, replacing a possessive noun.

▸ Some possessive pronouns come before nouns, and some stand alone.

▸ Never use an apostrophe in a possessive pronoun.

Independent Practice Write these sentences, using the correct words in parentheses.

Example: The snake had already shed (it's, its) skin.
The snake had already shed its skin.

6. The poster on the bulletin board is (my, mine).

7. (Its, It's) colors are very bright.

8. (They're, Their) house has more windows than (your's, yours).

9. Do you know where (your, you're) friends are?

10. (Its, It's) time to give the cat (its, it's) medicine.

11. (Your, You're) skates are too tight, aren't they?

12. This brand new camp stove is all (our's, ours).

13. (My, Mine) desk needs more work than (you're, your) desk.

14. I'll paint (my, mine), and you paint (your's, yours).

15. Somehow I knew that desk was (her, hers).

16. (Your, You're) umbrella is not as old as (my, mine).

17. Can this entire building be (their's, theirs)?

18. (Your, You're) assignment is harder than (my, mine).

19. (My, Mine) coat looks longer than (her, hers).

20. (They're, Their) work looks better than (our, ours).

21. (Your, You're) doing (your, you're) homework early.

22. Did the boys finish (their, theirs)?

23. I put (my, mine) paper on (her, hers) desk.

24. Is (my, mine) work better than (her, hers)?

25. (Her, Hers) directions were more difficult than (their, theirs).

Writing Application: Comparison and Contrast

Imagine that your school drama club is holding tryouts for a play. Compare and contrast the actors' performances. Use at least five different possessive pronouns in your sentences.

For Extra Practice, see p. 378.

4 | Pronouns After Linking Verbs

You have learned that a linking verb joins the subject of a sentence with a predicate noun. A pronoun can replace a predicate noun. Always use subject pronouns after linking verbs.

The champions <u>were</u> they . The team members <u>were</u> she and I .

To check that the pronoun is correct, reverse the order of the sentence. *They were* is correct. *Them were* is not.

Guided Practice Which pronoun is correct?

Example: It was (they, them) who found the boat. *they*

1. It was (I, me) who saw the wreck.
2. The owners of the boat are (they, them).
3. The rescuers were Jake and (we, us).
4. The bravest ones were (her, she) and (him, he).
5. The heroes are (they, them).

Summing up

▶ A subject pronoun is used after a linking verb.

Independent Practice Write each sentence correctly.

Example: The woman with the prettiest garden is (she, her).
The woman with the prettiest garden is she.

6. It was (I, me) who planted the roses.
7. That is (he, him) now.
8. Our friends are (they, them).
9. The man in the garden is (he, him).
10. The gardeners with the best ideas are (him, he) and (her, she).

Writing Application: A Description
Pretend you are a detective. Describe the suspects in a case.
Use subject pronouns after linking verbs in some sentences.

     For Extra Practice, see p. 379.

5 | Pronouns in Compound Subjects and Objects

You know that two or more simple subjects joined by *and* or *or* make up a compound subject. The pronouns in compound subjects are subject pronouns. If you want to include yourself as part of the compound subject, use the subject pronoun *I*. It is polite to mention yourself last.

Pam or I will water the plants.

She and he took a walk.

To check that the pronoun is correct, try using it alone as the subject. For example, drop the words *Pam or*. *I will water the plants* is correct. *Me will water the plants* is not.

You know that a direct object receives the action of a verb. Any pronoun in a compound direct object must be an object pronoun. Here, too, it is polite to mention yourself last.

The dog followed Tom and me .

The class invited her , him , and me .

To be sure that the pronoun is correct, ask yourself which pronoun fits when used alone. For example, drop *Tom and*. *The dog followed me* is correct. *The dog followed I* is not.

Guided Practice Which pronoun is correct?

Example: You and (me, I) are studying the French Revolution. *I*

1. Marie Antoinette and Louis XVI interest you and (I, me).
2. She and (he, him) ruled France.
3. Many French people thought that (she, her) and he were cruel.
4. The people criticized the king and (she, her).
5. You and (I, me) understand their reasons.
6. She and (he, him) lived a life of luxury.
7. (They, Them) and the people lived very different lives.
8. A huge gap separated the people and (they, them).

> ▶ Use a subject pronoun in a compound subject.
> ▶ Use an object pronoun in a compound object.
> ▶ When you include yourself as part of a compound subject or compound object, mention yourself last.

Independent Practice Write each sentence, using the correct subjects and objects in parentheses.

Example: Max and (I, me) have studied Nicholas and Alexandra.
Max and I have studied Nicholas and Alexandra.

9. (He and she, Him and her) ruled Russia before the Revolution.
10. The people of Russia forced (him and her, he and she) to give up the throne.
11. The people asked (him and her, he and she) for better laws.
12. Nicholas and (she, her) made some new laws, but the new laws weren't enough.
13. (He and she, Him and her) lost their power in the Revolution.
14. (He, Him) and his family did not escape from Russia.
15. This surprised (Max and I, Max and me).
16. We thought that (he, him) and Alexandra had fled Russia.
17. My teacher and (I, me) checked on the facts.
18. (She and I, Her and me) looked in two books.
19. The books said that (she and he, her and him) had tried to escape.
20. The teacher, Max, and (I, me) decided to read more.
21. (Max and I, Max and me) asked the librarian for help.
22. She gave (Max and I, Max and me) some books.
23. She also told (Max and I, Max and me) about a movie.
24. The librarian, Max, and (I, me) ordered the movie.
25. (Max and I, Max and me) learned a lot from it.

Writing Application: A Letter
Write a letter to a friend or a relative about a school project that you have done with your classmates. Use one or more pronouns in compound subjects and compound objects in your sentences.

  For Extra Practice, see p. 380.

6 Using *who, whom, whose*

The words *who*, *whom*, and *whose* are forms of the pronoun *who*. Questions often include *who*, *whom*, or *whose*. Use *who* as a subject pronoun.

> Who is running for office?

> Who voted this morning?

Use *whom* as an object pronoun.

> Whom do you believe? (You do believe *whom*.)

> Whom has Barry chosen? (Barry has chosen *whom*.)

To check that *whom* is correct, make a statement out of the question, as shown in the examples above. *Whom*, not *who*, is correct because it works as a direct object in both examples.

Whose is the possessive form of the pronoun *who*. You often use the pronoun *whose* when you ask questions about ownership.

> Whose ideas are better?

> Whose vote will decide?

Do not confuse *whose* and *who's*. *Whose* is a possessive pronoun. *Who's* is a contraction of the words *who is*. Remember that a possessive pronoun never has an apostrophe.

> Who's the best person for the job? (Who is)

> Whose sister is she?

Guided Practice Which pronoun is correct?

Example: (Who, Whom) did you see at the store? *Whom*

1. (Who, Whom) loads the produce?
2. (Who's, Whose) groceries are these?
3. (Who, Whom) will she ask for the crates?
4. (Who, Whom) manages the store for Bobbie?
5. (Who, Whom) will drive you home after work?

► Use the pronoun *who* as a subject.
► Use the pronoun *whom* as a direct object.
► Use the possessive pronoun *whose* to show ownership.

Independent Practice

A. Write *who* or *whom* to complete each sentence. You can check your answer by rearranging the sentence.

Example: ____ turned out the light?   *Who*

6. ____ do you like?
7. ____ ordered the fishing pole?
8. ____ will you contact at the newspaper?
9. ____ wants to go to the movie with me?
10. ____ can answer this question?
11. ____ will we ask for another glass of water?
12. ____ did you see at the gym?

B. Write the pronoun that completes each sentence correctly.

Example: (Who's, Whose) skateboard is red?   *Whose*

13. (Who, Whom) did you race last Tuesday?
14. (Who, Whom) should I tell about your surprise?
15. (Who, Whom) wrote me that thank-you note?
16. (Who's, Whose) brother was here?
17. (Who, Whom) brought you flowers?
18. (Who, Whom) did she invite to the concert?
19. (Who, Whom) has a minibike?
20. (Who's, Whose) bike is parked outside?
21. (Who's, Whose) riding my bike?
22. (Who's, Whose) coming to the party?

Writing Application: An Interview

You are a reporter for your school paper. The school show is tonight. Write five questions to use in interviewing the performers and the audience. Use the pronoun *who*, *whom*, or *whose* in each question. Use each word at least once.

For Extra Practice, see p. 381.

7 | Using *we* and *us* with Nouns

The pronouns *we* and *us* are often used with nouns for emphasis. Use the subject pronoun *we* with a subject or after a linking verb. Use the object pronoun *us* with a direct object.

WITH A SUBJECT: We girls are the state champions.

AFTER A LINKING VERB: The winning players were we boys.

WITH A DIRECT OBJECT: The team needs us fans.

Guided Practice Which pronoun is correct?

Example: (We, Us) students are learning about computers.   *We*

1. The learners are (we, us) sixth graders.
2. The most confused students were (we, us) beginners.
3. Our instructor watched (we, us) students patiently.
4. Ms. Gale put (we, us) beginners in front of the terminal.
5. (We, Us) students were surprised at its speed.

Summing up

▶ Use *we* with subjects or with nouns after linking verbs.
▶ Use *us* with nouns used as direct objects.

Independent Practice Write the correct pronouns.

Example: A boat took (we, us) people around New York Harbor.   *us*

6. (We, Us) tourists saw the Statue of Liberty.
7. The statue impressed (we, us) children because of its size.
8. (We, Us) girls took a close-up picture of the torch.
9. Our guide took (we, us) boys up to the crown of the statue.
10. The most excited tourists were (we, us) students.

Writing Application: A Paragraph

Write a paragraph about a place that you and your friends like. Use *we* with a noun and *us* with a noun at least once.

For Extra Practice, see p. 382

8 | Indefinite Pronouns

You have learned that pronouns take the place of nouns. The nouns that they replace are called antecedents. However, pronouns called **indefinite pronouns** do not have definite antecedents. An indefinite pronoun does not refer to a specific person, place, or thing.

Someone left a book on the desk.

Does anybody need a pencil?

Some indefinite pronouns are singular and always take a singular verb. Other indefinite pronouns are plural and always take a plural verb.

SINGULAR: Everybody <u>is</u> waiting for the teacher.

PLURAL: Many <u>are</u> excited about the lesson.

The chart shows the most common singular and plural indefinite pronouns.

Indefinite Pronouns				
Singular			**Plural**	
anybody	everybody	nothing	all	others
anyone	everyone	somebody	both	several
anything	everything	someone	few	some
each	nobody	something	many	

Guided Practice What is the indefinite pronoun in each sentence?

Example: Does anyone know the answer? *anyone*

1. Nobody is talking during the test.
2. Several have finished the test.
3. Others are still working.
4. Each of us needs help.
5. All of the students are hoping for a good grade.

Independent Practice Write each indefinite pronoun. Then write the verb in parentheses that correctly completes each sentence.

Example: Everyone (is, are) in the auditorium.   *Everyone   is*

6. All of us (is, are) learning about folk dancing.
7. Several of the dances (is, are) traditional folk dances.
8. Many (takes, take) practice and skill to perform.
9. Nobody (learns, learn) the dances quickly.
10. Everybody (is, are) clapping time to the music.
11. Few of the students (has, have) ever danced the Irish jig or the Highland fling.
12. Both (requires, require) a lot of energy.
13. All of us (wants, want) a chance to learn a square dance.
14. Someone (was, were) not listening to the instructions.
15. Now everyone (is, are) making mistakes.
16. Something (has, have) to be done quickly.
17. Nobody (is, are) following the leader.
18. Some of us (has, have) stopped for a rest.
19. Several of the dancers (is, are) still trying.
20. (Does, Do) anybody know the steps to the square dance?
21. Everybody (wants, want) another try.
22. This time nothing (is, are) going wrong.
23. All (is, are) in step.
24. Each of us (is, are) following the instructions carefully.
25. (Is, Are) anything more fun than this?

Writing Application: A Story

Imagine that you have discovered a strange planet. Write a story about what you see and hear. Use indefinite pronouns in some of your sentences and underline them.

For Extra Practice, see p. 383.
Indefinite Pronouns

Grammar-Writing Connection

Combining Sentences with Pronouns

You have learned that pronouns are words that replace nouns. You can use pronouns to avoid repeating a noun and to make your writing clearer and more interesting. You can also use pronouns when you combine sentences.

The earth and the moon are solid objects. The earth and the moon cast shadows.

→ The earth and the moon are solid objects, and they cast shadows.

The moon revolves around the earth. The moon's shadow sometimes falls on the earth.

→ The moon revolves around the earth, and its shadow sometimes falls on the earth.

Revising Sentences

Rewrite the sentences, using pronouns and the conjunctions *and* or *but* to combine the sentences in each item.

1. The people in the moon's shadow cannot see the sun. The people see an eclipse of the sun.
2. Sometimes the earth's shadow falls on the moon. The shadow makes the moon look dark or disappear.
3. The moon is covered with dust. The moon's surface cools during an eclipse.
4. Some ancient people did not know what caused eclipses. Some ancient people were afraid of them.
5. Other ancient people thought that eclipses were important. The people kept careful records of the events.
6. Eclipses are understood today. Eclipses can be predicted in advance.

Creative Writing

What does the letter to the girl say? If only we knew! But the mystery is locked forever in this painting and in the mind of the artist, who died over 300 years ago. Like the letter's contents, Jan Vermeer was something of a mystery. Little is known of his life, except that he was a master at painting hushed, glowing scenes such as this.

- How does the artist give the room a sense of space? of light?
- What is this painting's mood? How do its colors and the girl's expression add to that feeling?

Lady Reading at Open Window
Jan Vermeer
Gemäldegalerie Alte Meister-Staatliche
Kunstsammlungen
Dresden

Activities

1. **Write a letter.** Imagine that you are the writer of the mysterious letter. Perhaps you are the girl's brother, sister, or friend. Are you telling happy or sad news? You decide. Then write the letter, addressing it to Catherina and dating it 1659.
2. **Describe what lies out of sight.** This painting contains more than one mystery. What lies beyond the open window? What—or who—stands behind the half-closed curtain? Use your imagination to describe what lies just out of view.

Check-up: Unit 11

Pronouns and Antecedents (p. 356)
Write each pronoun and its antecedent. The antecedent may not be in the same sentence as the pronoun.

1. Rosa raises pigeons on the roof of the building where she lives.
2. They are specially trained to deliver messages.
3. Rosa rolls up the message that she has written.
4. Then she ties it to the leg of one of the pigeons.
5. She watches it fly sixty miles an hour to deliver the message safely.
6. She is pleased with the success of the pigeons' training.
7. They return to the cages faster than she had expected.

Pronouns as Subjects and Objects
(p. 358) Write each pronoun in these sentences. Write *subject* if the pronoun is a subject and *object* if it is a direct object.

8. Today we cleaned the entire house.
9. Dad and I dusted and polished the furniture.
10. Next, Kay washed the curtains and hung them.
11. She used the vacuum cleaner on the rugs and carpets.
12. I washed the kitchen floor and waxed it.
13. Dad took us out for a hearty dinner afterward.

Possessive Pronouns (p. 360) Write the sentences, using the correct words in parentheses.

14. I'm glad that you let me use (your, you're) telescope.
15. (Its, It's) lens is very clear but not too powerful.
16. (My, Mine) has lost (it's, its) cover.
17. Shall we use (my, mine) telescope to watch the eclipse of the moon?
18. Liz will bring (her, hers) too.
19. Bring (your's, yours) to (their, they're) observatory.
20. I wish that we could combine (their, they're) power.

Pronouns After Linking Verbs
(p. 362) Write the sentences, using the pronoun in parentheses that is correct.

21. The first person to bowl will be (she, her).
22. Our scorekeeper for the last game was (he, him).
23. That is (he, him) in the blue shirt.
24. The highest scorers will be (she, her) and (I, me).
25. Was it (them, they) who won last year's bowling trophy?
26. The person who will bowl next is (I, me).
27. Those who bowled strikes were (she, her) and (he, him).
28. The winners were (us, we), not (they, them).

Pronouns in Compound Subjects and Objects *(p. 363)* Write each sentence, using the compound subject or compound object that completes each sentence correctly.

29. Sue and (her, she) showed slides of London.
30. (He and I, Him and I) watched carefully.
31. The Tower of London fascinated them and (I, me).
32. Big Ben impressed (him and me, him and I) too.
33. (She, Her) and Joan had walked along the Thames River.
34. Friends and (they, them) had seen the Parliament buildings.
35. A guide told (they and she, them and her) about British government.
36. (Them and us, They and we) want to visit Shakespeare's birthplace.
37. My family and (I, me) saw the famous theater too.
38. The play impressed (my brother and I, my brother and me).
39. (Him and me, He and I) saw *Romeo and Juliet*.
40. The ending made (he and I, him and me) sad.
41. (They and we, Them and us) watched the slides for several hours.
42. Those slides made (them and us, they and we) eager to travel.
43. Sue and (I, me) want to visit Scotland some day.
44. (He, Him) and Joan want to see Ireland and Wales too.

Using *who, whom, whose* *(p. 365)* Write each sentence, using the correct word in parentheses.

45. (Whose, Who's) at the party?
46. (Who, Whom) should I thank for this present?
47. (Who, Whom) did you see?
48. (Whose, Who's) bracelet is this?
49. (Who, Whom) gave you the pen?
50. (Who, Whom) found the photos?
51. (Whose, Who's) pictures are these?
52. (Whose, Who's) going home now?
53. (Whose, Who's) on the telephone?

Using *we* and *us* with Nouns *(p. 367)* Write each sentence, using the pronoun *we* or *us*.

54. Mrs. Jones allowed (we, us) players to use her basketball court.
55. (We, Us) teammates raised money to rent a court.
56. (We, Us) parents had a bake sale.
57. Everyone helped (we, us) workers.
58. The hardest workers were (we, us) leaders.

Indefinite Pronouns *(p. 368)* Write each sentence, using the correct verb in parentheses. Underline the indefinite pronouns.

59. Everyone (enjoys, enjoy) painting.
60. Does someone (needs, need) paint?
61. Somebody (has, have) blue paint.
62. Few (likes, like) to paint with black and brown.
63. Others (uses, use) red paint more.
64. Everything (is, are) on the easel.

Enrichment

Using Pronouns

Giving Orders

Imagine that you are working in a take-out restaurant that serves a large variety of healthy foods. You have just prepared a number of orders and must give instructions to the counter person. Write a series of statements, using as many possessive pronouns as possible that identify the orders. Make sure the dishes that you mention are healthy. Underline all possessive pronouns.

The spinach salad is <u>his</u>.

DISCOVERIES

Find an example of a scientist or an inventor who came up with a startling invention. Now design and write a comic strip that shows how the public reacted to this invention. Do this by taping several sheets of paper together. Divide the paper into sections or frames. Draw a large picture in each frame, leaving enough room for the speech bubbles. Use pronouns in the dialogue and underline each one. Then exchange your comic strip with a classmate.

Order in the Court

Imagine that you are the script writer for a popular television show that dramatizes minor court cases. Find a newspaper or magazine article about a court case. Read the article and write questions that the judge in your show might ask. Use the pronouns *who*, *whom*, and *whose* correctly and underline each one.

⊞ Cross the Pronoun

Players—2. **You need**—graph paper, or divide a sheet of regular paper into one-half-inch squares.

How to play—The first player writes a pronoun horizontally or vertically, placing one letter in each square. The next player adds letters to write another pronoun that shares a common letter with the first pronoun. Continue taking turns and writing pronouns that cross each other until you run out of pronouns. Remember that whenever letters are beside each other, they must spell a pronoun.

Scoring—5 points for each pronoun. The person with the most points wins.

Extra Practice: Unit 11

1 | Pronouns and Antecedents (p. 356)

● Write each sentence and underline the pronoun.

Example: She is a good player.   *She is a good player.*

1. We can sit next to Nancy and Ben in the second row.
2. Where are they sitting?
3. He is wearing a red scarf and a dark blue sweater.
4. Do you have an extra ticket to the basketball game?
5. Fortunately, I do have an extra ticket.
6. Here it is.
7. You will certainly enjoy the next basketball game.

▲ Write each pronoun and its antecedent.

Example: Soccer is a very big sport in Glen Falls.
   It has replaced baseball in popularity.   *It—Soccer*

8. Erin likes the two sports equally.
   She decided to play baseball and soccer.
9. Marty scored the winning goal on Saturday.
   He made a perfect shot over the goalie's head.
10. Edie and Lee were talking about a school project.
   They missed all the excitement.

■ Write pronouns to complete the sentences. Then write the antecedents of the pronouns.

Example: The girls on Fourth Avenue decided to publish a newspaper. ____ had a meeting at Josie's house.   *They—girls*

11. Carla had the idea for the newspaper in the first place. ____ wanted the paper to have only two pages.
12. Her friends disagreed. ____ had many ideas for the paper.
13. Pamela wanted to write one story. ____ would be about sports.
14. Carla's father offered to print the newspapers. ____ could print ____ in his shop downtown.
15. Carla and Josie thought of a name for the newspaper. ____ named ____ the *Town Crier*.

2 | Pronouns as Subj. and Obj. (p. 358)

● Write each sentence. Label the pronoun *subject* or *object*.

Example: I helped Grandmother plant a small garden.
I helped Grandmother plant a small garden.   **subject**

1. Grandmother taught <u>me</u> a lot about gardening.
2. <u>She</u> prepared the soil.
3. Grandmother fertilized <u>it</u>.
4. <u>We</u> shopped for vegetable plants in the afternoon.
5. Mr. Hanscom sold <u>them</u> to Grandmother for half price.
6. <u>He</u> offered some good advice.
7. Grandmother thanked <u>him</u> for the plants and the advice.
8. Mr. Hanscom told <u>us</u> to come back again.

▲ Write these sentences, using the correct pronouns.

Example: (They, Them) added a small greenhouse off the kitchen.
They added a small greenhouse off the kitchen.

9. On Sunday (us, we) went to see the new addition.
10. Granddad showed hundreds of flower seedlings to (we, us).
11. (Him, He) was experimenting with different varieties.
12. Grandmother gave three seedlings to (I, me) to take home.
13. She always treated (they, them) with love.
14. (I, Me) promised to take special care of the plants.
15. (I, Me) will water (they, them) often.
16. (They, Them) will bloom for (we, us) soon.

■ Write a pronoun to complete each sentence. Label each pronoun *subject* or *object*.

Example: Dad drove _____ to the apple orchards. *us*   **object**

17. _____ are near Lake Fairlee.
18. _____ climbed a ladder to pick the apples.
19. Two apples hit _____ on the shoulder.
20. _____ fell from the branches onto the ground.
21. I put _____ in a big wooden basket.
22. _____ will make applesauce with most of _____.
23. Dad and _____ worked side by side.
24. Sarah told _____ to pick the biggest apples.

3 | Possessive Pronouns (p. 360)

● Write the possessive pronouns in these sentences. Remember that a possessive pronoun never has an apostrophe.

Example: Your coat is not in my locker. *Your my*

1. Maybe it's in his locker.
2. Your coat is hanging over her chair.
3. John can borrow mine during the lesson.
4. They're cleaning out their desks now.
5. Sophy put her red pen in her special blue folder.
6. Jeff will collect our workbooks after the quiz.
7. His math book is missing its back cover.
8. Your book is newer and in better shape than mine.

▲ Write these sentences, using the correct words in parentheses.

Example: Did Mary leave (her, hers) bike on the Baileys' lawn?
Did Mary leave her bike on the Baileys' lawn?

9. (They're, Their) not going to be pleased.
10. Is it (your, you're) bike?
11. I don't think that the bike is (hers, her's).
12. Mrs. Bailey spends hours tending (her, hers) flowers.
13. (You're, Your) dog trampled (their, they're) roses.
14. I'm glad that Chip is (yours, your) and not (mine, my).
15. Please keep (you're, your) dog on (its, it's) leash.

■ Write the following sentences correctly. Then underline only the possessive pronouns in the corrected sentences.

Example: Their working together on they're models.
They're working together on their models.

16. You're projects should be on they're desks by Friday.
17. Our's needs it's final coat of black paint.
18. Her's has yellow blinking lights.
19. Its not mine; it's her.
20. They're model is stuffed with rags like my.
21. Her's has a beeping sound when its running.
22. You're imaginations have soared beyond they're limits.

4 | Pronouns After Linking Verbs (p. 362)

● Write these sentences and underline the pronouns.

Example: The first-place runner was she.
The first-place runner was <u>she</u>.

1. The track and field judges were they.
2. The assistant coaches of the team were she and he.
3. The official starters for the games were he and I.
4. The stars of the afternoon were they.
5. The planners of the most difficult event were she and I.
6. The youngest runner was he.
7. The prize winners were he and she.
8. The one who handed out the prizes was he.

▲ Write the pronouns that complete the sentences correctly.

Example: It was (he, him) who jumped the longest distance.   *he*

9. The fans who cheered the loudest were (they, them).
10. The athletes who got sick were he and (I, me).
11. The gate attendants in the white caps were (they, them).
12. The flag bearers with the school colors were (they, them).
13. Was it (they, them) who recorded the scores?
14. The finalists were (she, her) and (I, me).
15. The band members with drums were (they, them) and (we, us).
16. It was (they, them) who led the parade.

■ Write the following sentences. Complete each one by adding a subject pronoun.

Example: The woman who built the space rocket was ____.
The woman who built the space rocket was she.

17. The astronauts who operate the controls are ____.
18. It was ____ who landed the craft safely.
19. The first reporter on the scene was ____.
20. The last people to leave the craft were ____ and ____.
21. It was ____ and ____ who made the final check.
22. The reporter who interviewed them was ____.
23. Those who wrote the most complete stories were ____ and ____.
24. The astronaut who appeared in the photograph was ____.

5 | Pronouns in Compounds (p. 363)

● Write the compound subject or compound object in these sentences. Include the conjunctions. Underline the pronouns.

Example: She and I walked on the nature trail.   *She and I*

1. The bus left Lena and me by the entrance.
2. You and they should not leave the path.
3. Mrs. Sanchez took George and me across the brook.
4. He or I can carry the camera.
5. Mary and I found a wounded bird.
6. The park ranger rewarded her and me.
7. We thanked Mrs. Sanchez and him.
8. Mrs. Sanchez and he took the bird to a safe place.

▲ Write each sentence, using the correct pronoun in parentheses.

Example: Carolyn and (I, me) stopped to eat lunch.
   Carolyn and I stopped to eat lunch.

9. We asked Ken and (he, him) to join us.
10. You and (me, I) will lead the others.
11. The snake did not scare Steve or (her, she).
12. The rain soaked Cora and (they, them).
13. Emily and (her, she) ducked into a small cave.
14. The huge oak tree sheltered Nicky and (me, I).
15. She and (them, they) ran back to the bus.
16. Did you and (she, her) catch a cold?

■ Write each sentence, using a pronoun that completes each sentence correctly. Label each new pronoun *subject* or *object*.

Example: Juan and ____ hiked down the steep path.
   Juan and I hiked down the steep path.   **subject**

17. ____ and I followed Luisa and Mark.
18. I asked ____ and Mark to wait.
19. Mark cautioned Juan and ____ to be careful.
20. Luisa and ____ had slipped and nearly fallen at the curve.
21. Luisa informed Juan and ____ that Cashman Falls was only a short distance away.
22. ____ and ____ were eager to see the waterfall.

6 | Using *who, whom, whose* (p. 365)

● Write each sentence, using the correct word in parentheses.

Example: To (who, whom) did he speak?   *To whom did he speak?*

1. (Who, Whom) called the store?
2. (Who's, Whose) ice skates are in the hall closet?
3. (Who, Whom) will drive you to the rink on Saturday morning?
4. (Who's, Whose) skis are here?
5. (Who, Whom) did you cheer at the game last night?
6. (Who, Whom) won the first two games of the season?
7. (Who's, Whose) that great goalie on our team?
8. (Who, Whom) do you know on the other team?

▲ Write *who, whom,* or *whose* to complete each sentence.

Example: ____ brought the basketball?
Who brought the basketball?

9. ____ will be the forward for our game today?
10. ____ is the best guard on the high school team?
11. ____ did she replace?
12. ____ wants to take a break between games?
13. ____ should we ask about the next game?
14. ____ volleyball net is this?
15. ____ takes the net down after every game?
16. ____ coaches the other two teams?

■ Write a question that each sentence below might answer. Use *who, whom,* or *whose* in each question.

Example: I would like to know.   *Who would like to know?*

17. He may come with the Jackson brothers.
18. That is my raincoat on the empty seat.
19. Ms. Greene is carrying the tickets.
20. Elena sat in the bleachers.
21. This is Barry's newspaper story.
22. He called the editor of the sports page.
23. Grace asked Pete for his autograph.
24. This is her special notebook.
25. It was a gift from her Dad for her birthday.

● ▲ ■ **Three levels of practice   381**

7 | Using *we* and *us* with Nouns (p. 367)

● Write each sentence, using the correct pronoun in parentheses.

Example: Mr. Dunn gave (we, us) students a treat.
Mr. Dunn gave us students a treat.

1. (We, Us) friends took a trip to New York.
2. The bus took (we, us) girls to a boat.
3. Then (we, us) boys took the boat to an island.
4. (We, Us) sixth-graders saw the Statue of Liberty.
5. The only group was (we, us) students.
6. The guide showed (we, us) visitors the museum.
7. (We, Us) people have fixed up the statue.
8. Supporters of the repairs included (we, us) students.
9. (We, Us) students learned that the statue's full name is Liberty Enlightening the World.

▲ Write each sentence, using *we* or *us*.

Example: The Statue of Liberty was given to ＿＿ Americans.
The Statue of Liberty was given to us Americans.

10. ＿＿ French sent it as a gift.
11. The lucky ones were ＿＿ citizens.
12. Were ＿＿ children the most excited tourists?
13. ＿＿ people know what the face looks like.
14. ＿＿ tourists see the face of the artist's mother.
15. The statue is a symbol of freedom to ＿＿ immigrants.
16. The statue belongs to ＿＿ supporters of freedom.
17. ＿＿ visitors read the poem on the statue.
18. The Statue of Liberty always welcomes ＿＿ travelers home.

■ Write a complete sentence for each group of words.

Example: We singers
We singers in the band write many of our own songs.

19. us experienced hikers
20. are we children
21. We artists and musicians
22. are we athletes
23. us newspaper reporters
24. are we visitors
25. We teammates
26. We brave explorers
27. us scientists
28. are we volunteers

8 | Indefinite Pronouns (p. 368)

● Write each sentence. Underline each indefinite pronoun.

Example: Everyone in my class enjoys field trips.
Everyone in my class enjoys field trips.

1. Each of us has a memory of a favorite field trip.
2. Some like trips to museums best.
3. Others prefer trips to factories or office buildings.
4. Today all of us are going to a pet store and an animal hospital.
5. Both are interesting places to visit.
6. Everybody is getting on the school bus at nine o'clock.
7. Nobody wants to be late!
8. Several of us are looking forward to the trip.

▲ Write each indefinite pronoun. Then write the verb in parentheses that completes each sentence correctly.

Example: All of the campers (loves, love) Longacre Farm.   *All   love*

9. Many (comes, come) from faraway places every summer.
10. Someone (drives, drive) all the way from California!
11. Some (gets, get) on the camp bus in New York City.
12. Something (is, are) always happening at Longacre Farm.
13. Today each of the campers (is, are) putting on a play.
14. Others (is, are) building a pen for the goats.
15. Everybody (stays, stay) busy the whole day.

■ Complete each sentence by writing an indefinite pronoun that makes sense in the sentence and agrees with the verb.

Example: _____ of my friends have interesting hobbies.
Many of my friends have interesting hobbies.

16. _____ enjoy learning computer games.
17. _____ of these is an interesting hobby.
18. _____ in my neighborhood collects maps of foreign countries.
19. _____ collects postage stamps from around the world.
20. _____ of the stamps are colorful.
21. _____ of these friends learn through their hobbies.
22. Has _____ in your neighborhood found an interesting hobby?

Until recently, plain survival at sea was hard enough. In the years from 800 to 1050, for instance, the Vikings were the world's greatest sailors. . . . But these master sailors crossed oceans the way drivers today handle long highways on sleety nights, by gritting their teeth and keeping their eyes straight ahead.

Jonathan Weiner
from *Planet Earth*

Research Report

Getting Ready When you were very little, you expected a grown-up to answer all your questions. Adults would explain to you why birds could fly, but you couldn't find out for yourself. Now you are old enough to discover the answers to questions. You can do the research to learn about machines, animals, sports, natural resources, historical events, in fact, almost anything! Write down some questions or ideas you would like to investigate. In this unit, you will have the chance to research and then write a report on the answers to those questions.

ACTIVITIES

Listening Listen as the quotation on the opposite page is read. What information does it give you?

Speaking Look at the picture. Make up as many questions about it as you can: Where do waves come from? What kind of rocks are these? Have a class secretary record all your questions. Circle the ones that are good ideas for a report.

Writing What risks do we take today that threaten our "plain survival"? List some ideas in your journal.

LITERATURE

What would it feel like to be thrown into the ocean in the middle of a raging storm?

Robinson Crusoe

By Daniel Defoe

Robinson Crusoe, one of the first novels ever written, is based on the real-life adventures of a Scottish seaman. When their ship is stranded in a storm, Crusoe and ten sailors set off in a rowboat to reach the safety of an island. Before they can make it, their rowboat overturns.

The wave that came upon me again buried me at once twenty or thirty feet deep in its own body, and I could feel myself carried with a mighty force and swiftness towards the shore a very great way; but I held my breath, and assisted myself to swim still forward with all my might. I was ready to burst with holding my breath, when as I felt myself rising up, so, to my immediate relief, I found my head and hands shoot out above the surface of the water; and though it was not two seconds of time that I could keep myself so, yet it relieved me greatly, gave me breath and new courage. I was covered again with water a good while, but not so long but I held it out; and finding the water had spent itself, and began to return, I struck forward against the return of the waves, and felt ground again with my feet. I stood still a few moments to recover breath, and till the waters went from me, and then took to my heels, and ran with what strength I had, farther towards the shore. But neither would this deliver me from the fury of the sea, which came pouring in after me again; and twice more I was lifted up by the waves and carried forwards as before, the shore being very flat.

The last time of these two had well-nigh been fatal to me; for the sea having hurried me along, as before, landed me, or rather dashed me, against a piece of a rock, and that with such force as it left me senseless, and indeed helpless as to my own deliverance, for the blow taking my side and breast, beat the breath as it were quite out of my body, and had it returned again immediately I must have been strangled in the water. But I recovered a little before the return of the waves, and seeing I should be covered again with water, I resolved to hold fast by a piece of the rock, and so to hold my breath, if possible, till the wave went back. Now, as the waves were not so high as

387

at first, being nearer land, I held my hold till the wave abated, and then fetched another run, which brought me so near the shore that the next wave, though it went over me, yet did not so swallow me up as to carry me away; and the next run I took I got to the mainland, where, to my great comfort, I clambered up the clifts of the shore, and sat me down upon the grass, free from danger, and quite out of the reach of the water.

I was now landed, and safe on shore.

Think and Discuss

1. What sensations and emotions did Robinson Crusoe experience in this passage? Back up your answer with examples from the story.

2. The sentences in this passage are very long, and the words are put together in unfamiliar ways. In the eighteenth century, when *Robinson Crusoe* was written, this **style** was not unusual. Here is the first sentence of the piece, rewritten in the way that people today write.

   "A huge wave swallowed me up. I must have been twenty or thirty feet inside it. I could feel myself being flung a long way towards the shore, but I held my breath and swam with the wave as hard as I could."

   How would you change the next sentence to make it sound like today's style?

3. What does this passage show you about the character of Robinson Crusoe? What adjectives would you use to describe him?

What would you do if you had to live for years on a desert island with only goats, crabs, and seabirds for company? How did Selkirk manage to survive?

The Real Robinson Crusoe

By Donald J. Sobol

In 1703 Alexander Selkirk, a Scottish seaman, sailed from England as first mate aboard the *Cinque Ports*.

While at sea, Selkirk fell out with his captain, Thomas Stradling. In Stradling's opinion, Selkirk's freely voiced criticisms bordered on mutiny, but he bided his time.

In September, 1704, the *Cinque Ports* called at Juan Fernández, a group of three uninhabited islands off the coast of Chile. Stradling dispatched a longboat to pick up two sailors who had been accidently left behind on an earlier visit.

Selkirk unwisely chose that moment to be outspoken. He swore that he would rather stay on Juan Fernández than serve another day aboard the leaky *Cinque Ports*. Stradling gladly obliged him. In the days of piracy, it was not an uncommon practice to dump mutineers on a deserted island. Within an hour, Selkirk found himself on one of the Juan Fernández islands.

Standing on the beach, he had a change of heart. The realization of what he had brought upon himself overwhelmed him. He pleaded to be taken back. Stradling refused, and Selkirk was abandoned to the company of goats, crabs, and seabirds.

389

For the first eight months, his life was filled with the terror of being alone. He ate only when hungry and fell asleep watching the horizon. But he was intelligent, healthy, and young, and he was used to hardship. A lesser man might have broken. Selkirk adapted.

Captain Stradling had left him with his clothes, bedding, a gun, one pound of powder, bullets, a hatchet, a knife, a Bible, his mathematical instruments, and a few books. He made the most of them.

Out of pimento trees, he built two huts and roofed them over with long grass. The walls he lined with the skins of the goats that abounded on the island. The goats had been brought over by ships putting in for wood and water.

He started fires by rubbing two pimento sticks on his knee, and he used pimento logs for cooking and light. The logs burned with almost no smoke and gave off a refreshing odor.

In the beginning, he caught fish, but they disagreed with him. Thereafter, he ate no seafood except crawfish, which were as big as lobsters and very good. He broiled or boiled them, as he frequently did with goat's meat to make broth.

When his powder gave out, he developed a substitute: speed of foot. Chasing goats wore out his shoes. Forced to do without them, his feet toughened till he could run anywhere barefooted. After his rescue, it was some time before he could wear shoes again without having his feet swell up.

With a nail for a needle, Selkirk stitched clothing from goat skins. When his knife and hatchet gave out, he made others from iron barrel hoops he picked up along the shore. He pounded them thin with stones and sharpened them upon the rocks.

Goats formed the chief resource of his existence, providing him with food, clothing, and shelter. And yet it was a goat that nearly took his life.

He had chased it into some bushes, forgetting in his eagerness that the bushes concealed the brink of a cliff. Over and down went man and goat. Selkirk was knocked unconscious. When he came to his senses, he found the goat dead beneath him. He lay there twenty-four hours, bruised and aching, before he managed to crawl the mile to his hut. He did not stir outside for ten days.

To vary his diet of goat's meat and crawfish, he ate turnips that had been planted by earlier visitors and had overspread several acres. He also ate the leaves of cabbage trees and spiced his meat with the pepperlike fruit of pimento trees.

On February 2, 1709, two English privateers under Captain Woodes Rogers beached longboats. Four years and four months after Selkirk had been left on Juan Fernández, rescue had come.

The landing sailors were shocked to see coming toward them a bronzed and bearded figure in goatskins. It was Selkirk.

Selkirk resumed his career as if it had never been interrupted. William Dampier, his first commander, was captain of one of the privateers and took him on as a mate.

Captain Woodes Rogers penned an account of the buccaneering expedition. Published in 1712 under the title *Cruising Voyage Around the World,* the book included Selkirk's story.

It was from this account that Daniel Defoe probably drew the inspiration for his fictional work *Robinson Crusoe*. He may also have spoken with Selkirk, but that is unproved.

Robinson Crusoe was published on April 25, 1719. Selkirk lived long enough to see the world's imagination captured by the tale of the lonely island dweller.

Think and Discuss

1. What did Selkirk eat to survive on Juan Fernández? In what other ways did he adjust to life on the island?

2. How did Selkirk come to be alone on a desert island?

3. "The Real Robinson Crusoe" is biographical. A **biography** is a written account of a person's life. "Lost on a Mountain in Maine," which you read in Unit 2, is autobiographical. It was written by Donn Fendler about himself. An **autobiography** is an account of a person's life written by that person. It is therefore told in the first person. In what other ways is an autobiography different from a biography? Why isn't the novel *Robinson Crusoe* an autobiography?

4. Do you think that Captain Stradling was fair in his treatment of Selkirk? Why or why not?

RESPONDING TO LITERATURE

The Reading and Writing Connection

Personal Response Have you ever said something recklessly or made a statement you didn't mean, as Selkirk did? Did your pride make you stand by it, or did you back down? Write a short paragraph telling what happened.

Creative Writing Pretend you are Selkirk. Write three diary entries—one from your first day on Juan Fernández, one from about a year later, and one from the day you are rescued. Try to imagine how Selkirk felt at each stage of his adventure.

Creative Activities

Make a Map Draw an imaginary map of Juan Fernández. Label places that were important to Selkirk—where he was put ashore, where the goats lived, where his hut was, and where he fell off the cliff.

Act Out Write a script for the scene that led to Selkirk being left behind on the island. What did Selkirk say when he pleaded to be taken back aboard? Act out the roles of Captain Stradling, Selkirk, and the sailors.

Vocabulary

What do you think a desert island is? Is it like the Sahara Desert? Use a dictionary to find out.

Looking Ahead

Reports In this unit you will learn how to write good beginnings and endings for reports. Look at the first and last two paragraphs of "The Real Robinson Crusoe." How does the author capture your interest at the beginning? How does he wrap things up at the end?

VOCABULARY CONNECTION

Prefixes and Suffixes

A **prefix** is a word part that is added to the beginning of a word. A **suffix** is a word part that is added to the end of a word. Prefixes and suffixes have meanings of their own.

> . . . he caught fish, but they **dis**agreed with him.
>
> William Dampier, his first command**er**, was captain. . . .
> *from "The Real Robinson Crusoe" by Donald J. Sobol*

When the prefix *dis-* (not) is added to the base word *agreed*, the word's meaning changes to "not agreed." When the suffix *-er* (one who does) is added to *command*, its meaning changes to "one who commands."

Word Part	Meaning	Example
Prefixes pre- un-, dis-	before not	precook—to cook before uncommon—not common
Suffixes -less -able, -ible	without able to	senseless—without sense readable—able to read

Words like **unwisely** have both a prefix and a suffix.

Vocabulary Practice

A. Add a prefix, a suffix, or both to each of these words from "Robinson Crusoe." Write the meaning of the new word.

1. covered   **2.** comfort   **3.** courage   **4.** breath

B. Find six words with a prefix, a suffix, or both from the literature in this unit. Use each word in a sentence of your own. Use your dictionary if you need help.

Listening: Telling Fact from Opinion

Read the two statements below. Can you tell which statement is a fact and which is an opinion?

1. Alexander Selkirk was stranded on an island in 1704.
2. Selkirk deserved his fate.

If you said that the first statement is a fact and the second an opinion, you were correct. A **fact** is information that can be proved to be true. You can check the accuracy of facts about Selkirk by looking in books. An **opinion** is a judgment or a feeling. It cannot be proved by checking facts.

Now read the following statements.

1. In 1703 Alexander Selkirk sailed from England.
2. He was the first mate aboard the *Cinque Ports*.
3. Selkirk fell out with his captain, Thomas Stradling.
4. Selkirk was the worst sailor on the ship.

• Which statements are facts? Which statement is an opinion?

When you are gathering information for a report, it is important to be able to tell the difference between facts and opinions. A report is different from many other kinds of writing because it tells only the facts.

Guidelines for Telling Fact from Opinion

1. Determine whether the statement can be proved true.
2. Pay attention to words such as *should, I think, best, worst,* and *I believe.* They signal opinions.

Prewriting Practice

Number a paper from 1 to 8. Then listen as eight statements are read. After each one, write *F* for fact or *O* for opinion.

Thinking: Identifying Causes and Effects

Suppose you are standing in the ocean when a large wave comes along and knocks you down. Two events have taken place. The first event—the wave coming along—made the second event—your falling down—happen. The wave was the **cause,** and your fall was the **effect.**

The skill of identifying causes and effects can be helpful when you are collecting information for a research report. It can help to explain things that happen to you or things you read about. For example, you just read that Captain Stradling abandoned Alexander Selkirk on an island. What was the cause of the captain's action? Selkirk insulted him. What was one effect of Selkirk's adventure? It inspired Daniel Defoe to write *Robinson Crusoe.*

To identify causes and effects, ask questions such as:

TO IDENTIFY CAUSES: Why did that happen? What made it happen?
TO IDENTIFY EFFECTS: What was the result? What happened when . . . ?

Read the paragraph below. What cause is stated? What was the effect?

The landing sailors were shocked to see coming toward them a bronzed and bearded figure in goatskins. It was Selkirk.
from "The Real Robinson Crusoe" by Donald J. Sobol

The cause in this paragraph is Selkirk's appearance. The effect is that the sailors were shocked by that appearance.

Now read this passage. How many causes and effects can you find?

The wave that came upon me again buried me at once twenty or thirty feet deep in its own body, and I could feel myself carried with a mighty force and swiftness toward the shore. . . .
from Robinson Crusoe *by Daniel Defoe*

The passage states only one cause: the wave came upon Crusoe. However, two effects are stated: the wave buried Crusoe, and it carried him toward the shore. A cause may have more than one effect, and an effect may have more than one cause.

Causes and effects can also form a kind of chain, with one cause leading to another or with one effect leading to another. Read the paragraph below.

When his powder gave out, he developed a substitute: speed of foot. Chasing goats wore out his shoes. Forced to do without them, his feet toughened till he could run anywhere barefooted. After his rescue, it was some time before he could wear shoes again without having his feet swell up.

from "The Real Robinson Crusoe" by Donald J. Sobol

- What cause or causes are stated in the paragraph?
- What effects are stated? How are they related?

These guidelines will help you identify causes and effects.

Guidelines for Identifying Causes and Effects

1. To identify causes, ask *Why did it happen? What made it happen?*
2. To identify effects, ask *What is the result? What happened when . . . ?*
3. Look for more than one cause and more than one effect.

Prewriting Practice

A. With a partner, think of two possible causes for each event below. Use the guidelines above.

1. a shipwreck
2. a smoggy day
3. an oil spill in the ocean
4. a visit to the library

B. List two possible effects of each of the above. Use the guidelines. Then compare your list with your partner's.

Composition Skills
Research Report

Finding Facts ☑️

Suppose you wanted to know whether the Juan Fernández Islands were still uninhabited. Would you know how to find that information? The answer to almost any question you can think of is available in printed form somewhere in your library, but you have to know where to look.

Libraries have three kinds of books: **fiction, nonfiction,** and **reference books.** Libraries also have current and back issues of newspapers, magazines, and other periodicals.

Nonfiction books contain factual information about real people and events from the past and present. They also contain information about subjects like wildlife, carpentry, and physics. To find nonfiction books, use the card catalog in a library. See Study Strategies in the back of the book for information on using the card catalog to find the book you want.

Reference books are a special kind of nonfiction. They are books of general facts, such as dictionaries, encyclopedias, atlases, and almanacs.

1. A **dictionary** contains more information than the spellings, definitions, and pronunciations of words. A dictionary may include information about famous people, such as the dates of their birth and death, their nationalities, and why they are famous. Entries for places will give the locations, populations, and geographic or historical importance. Some dictionaries may include maps.

2. An **encyclopedia** is a set of books containing articles on hundreds or even thousands of subjects. The articles are arranged in alphabetical order. You use an encyclopedia when you want general information about a subject.

3. An **almanac** is a book of facts that is published yearly. It contains many short articles, lists, and tables that give information on subjects from American cities to Nobel Prize winners to the solar system. It also has many facts about one particular calendar year. A 1991 almanac would have many facts about 1990. You use an almanac when you want up-to-date information on a subject.

4. An **atlas** is a book of maps and tables that give information about places. There are many different kinds of atlases. A *world atlas* gives information about all the nations. A *regional atlas* has information about various sections of a nation or state. A *road atlas* shows highways, streets, and roads in a given area. Although you can find maps in an encyclopedia, atlas maps are usually much more detailed.

Newspapers and **magazines** contain the most up-to-date information you can find. If you want information on a very recent event, check the newspapers that were published that day or the next and the following week's news magazines.

Because each type of reference book contains a specific type of information, you should become familiar with the different books. When you use reference books, follow these guidelines.

1. Choose the reference book that contains the type of information you want.
2. Check your facts in more than one source.
3. Use the most up-to-date book.

Prewriting Practice

A. Where would you look for the answer to each question: in an encyclopedia, an almanac, an atlas, or a newspaper?

1. What nation rules the Juan Fernández Islands?
2. What is the distance between England and the Juan Fernández Islands?
3. Where was Daniel Defoe born?
4. Who is the governor of South Dakota?
5. What language is spoken in the Juan Fernández Islands?
6. Which nation borders Scotland?
7. What are the names of the three Juan Fernández Islands?
8. Who won last night's high school swim meet?
9. What is the best route from New York City to Boston?

B. Choose five of the questions from Practice A. Using a public or a school library, find the answers to the questions. Give the sources where you found the answers.

Taking Notes ☑

Note-taking is one of the most important skills you can learn. It is a short cut for writing down information you want to remember. You can take notes to help you study a subject like science or history. You can also take notes to help you write a report. Decide the questions you want to find answers to, and take notes on that information. Skim the material, looking for the specific facts you want.

Suppose you wanted to find out what a crawfish looks like. When you read, you would take notes to tell you that information. Read the encyclopedia entry and notes below.

> **crawfish** or **crayfish** fresh-water crustacean similar to but smaller than a lobster. Crawfish are native to every continent but Africa and are usually found in ponds and streams. Some are partially terrestrial. They eat small aquatic animals. Crawfish are usually a dull, brownish-green color. A red-clawed variety is eaten in Europe.

What does a crawfish look like?
—shaped like a lobster but smaller
—dull, brownish green
—some have red claws

- Do the notes answer the question?
- What facts were left out of the notes? Why?

Prewriting Practice

Alexander Selkirk was marooned on an island that is now named Robinson Crusoe. Read the following paragraphs. Take notes that answer the question, "What is the island Robinson Crusoe like?"

The Juan Fernández Islands are a group of three islands off the coast of Chile. The islands are called Robinson Crusoe, Santa Clara, and Alejandro Selkirk. The natural beauty of the rugged mountains, green valleys, and beautiful beaches make Robinson Crusoe an attractive place for tourists. Striking, nearly vertical cliffs of up to 1,000 feet ring the island. The island's highest peak is 3,000 feet, and is always covered by clouds. The main industry of the island is lobster fishing.

Unfortunately, the island's fragrant sandalwood trees have all been chopped down by traders. The government now protects the hardwood trees from that same fate. However, the giant fern still grows on the island. More than forty varieties of ferns can be found here. Some ferns even grow to tree size in the warm climate, where the temperature is a constant 67 degrees F (19°C).

Writing an Outline ☑

When you have finished doing the research for your report, you may have several pages of notes. These notes answer your three or four major questions. How do you begin turning these bits of information into a well-written report? The first step is to make an outline. An outline is a framework for organizing the information you have gathered. It has several parts.

1. Every outline has a **title**.
2. **Main topics** tell what each section of the outline is about. They are marked with Roman numerals. Each of your major questions becomes a main topic.
3. **Subtopics** are facts and ideas that support the main topics. They are marked with capital letters. The answers to the questions become the subtopics.

➡

4. Details give more information about the subtopics. They are marked with numbers.

How do you turn your notes into an outline? Study the following notes and outline.

What are the facts about Daniel Defoe's early life?
—born London, 1660
—married Mary Tuffley, 1684
—from a family of religious dissenters
—father was a butcher
What did he do for a living?
—retail merchant
—at first successful, later bankrupt
—owned a tile factory
—pamphlet writer for government
—friendly with William III
—imprisoned for political reasons

Daniel Defoe

I. Early life **main topic**
   A. Born in London, 1660 **subtopic**
   B. Family were religious dissenters
   C. Father was a butcher
   D. Married Mary Tuffley, 1684
II. How he made a living **main topic**
   A. Retail merchant **subtopic**
      1. At first successful **detail**
      2. Later went bankrupt
   B. Owned tile factory
   C. Pamphlet writer for government
      1. Friendly with the king
      2. Later imprisoned for political reasons

• Which parts of the notes became main topics? subtopics? details?
• Has the order of any of the facts been changed? Why or why not?

Prewriting Practice

Using the notes below, complete the outline. Rewrite the questions as main topics. Write the notes that answer the questions as subtopics. Put them in an order that makes sense. Remember to capitalize the first word of each main topic, subtopic, and detail.

What does a wild goat look like?
—1½ to 4 feet tall
—body covered with wool
—may have horns
—may have a beard
—short tail that stands straight up
—cloven hoofs

What are a wild goat's habits?
—prefers to live in rocky, mountainous area
—eats bushes, leaves, tree bark
—chews food only slightly
—uses horns in fighting
—doe or kid lives in a herd
—buck lives alone

Wild Goats

I. Appearance
  A. Measures 1½ to 4 feet tall
  B.
  C.
  D.
  E.
  F.
II.
  A.
  B. Living habits
    1.
    2.
    3.
  C. Eating habits
    1.
    2. Chews food only slightly

Writing a Paragraph from an Outline ☑

An outline is the skeleton of a paragraph. Once you have your information in outline form, you are ready to expand it in paragraph form. You expand each section of the outline into a full paragraph by adding words and phrases that explain, describe, and give interest to the facts.

The Topic Sentence How do you write a topic sentence from an outline? First, read over the main topic, subtopics, and details of one outline section. Think about the main idea. Then write a topic sentence that states the main idea.

> The Last Voyage of the *Bounty*
> II. Mutiny
>   A. Occurred April 27–28, 1789
>   B. *Bounty* was in South Pacific
>   C. Mutineers led by Fletcher Christian
>   1. Disarmed the captain
>   2. Most of the crew sided with Christian
>   3. Eighteen men remained loyal to Bligh
>   D. Bligh and followers forced off ship
>   1. Put into ship's longboat
>   2. Set adrift

Now look at these topic sentences.

> 1. On April 27, 1789, the crew of the *Bounty* mutinied.
> 2. On April 27, 1789, the *Bounty*'s desperate crew rose up and seized the ship.

Both topic sentences state the main idea of the paragraph. The first sentence states only the bare facts. The second sentence is more interesting because it gives more information. Its language is more vivid.

The Paragraph The rest of the sentences in the paragraph give the supporting details. The supporting details are the facts in the outline that you have not included in the topic sentence. Add words and phrases to expand these facts into clear, interesting sentences.

Read the paragraph below. It was written from the outline about the mutiny on the *Bounty*.

On April 27, 1789, the *Bounty*'s desperate crew rose up and seized the ship. Led by Fletcher Christian, the mutineers disarmed Captain Bligh and informed him that they were taking command of the ship. Most of the crew sided with Christian, but eighteen remained loyal to Bligh. The mutineers forced Bligh and his men into the ship's longboat, an open rowboat, and set them adrift in the South Pacific.

- Which sentence combined facts from two subtopics?
- What words and phrases were added that help you picture this even more clearly?

Prewriting Practice

Read the outline section below. Use it to write two topic sentences. Choose the topic sentence you like better. Then write a paragraph. Make the subtopics into complete sentences that will serve as strong supporting details for your topic sentence. Try to use words and phrases that will make your sentences interesting.

Sailing Ships of Selkirk's Time
I. Some kinds of ships
  A. Galleons
    1. First appeared in mid-1500s
    2. About 140 feet long
    3. Served as warships and merchant ships
    4. Elaborate living quarters
    5. Used by Spain to carry New World treasure

  B. East Indiamen
    1. First built during 1600s
    2. About 170 feet long
    3. Used for trade with India and the Far East
    4. Carried ivory, silks, and spices
    5. Had cannons and guns to fight pirates

Writing Good Introductions and Closings ☑

1. In December, 1787, the *Bounty* set out from England and headed for the South Pacific.

2. In December, 1787, the *Bounty* set out on what would be her final voyage.

If you did not know the story of the *Bounty,* which opening sentence would make you want to read on? The second sentence makes a better introduction to a report on the *Bounty.* It makes the reader want to know what happened that made this voyage the *Bounty*'s last. It hints that the report will include exciting events.

When you write a report, you should pay special attention to how you begin and end it. The introduction to your report should capture the reader's interest. It may do this by giving a hint as to what will follow, as in the above example, or by stating the main idea in an unusual way:

> If you had sailed on a merchant vessel three hundred years ago, you probably would have met a pirate.

You can state a surprising fact:

> British sailors got the nicknames *limeys* because they drank lemon juice to avoid getting scurvy, a disease caused by a lack of Vitamin C.

Can you think of other ways to begin a report that would capture the reader's attention?

A good closing is as important as a good introduction. A good closing finishes the report. It does this by summing up the main ideas of the report:

> Because of unrestricted hunting of whales a hundred years ago, some types of whales nearly became extinct. Today an international commission regulates the hunting of these mammoth creatures of the sea.

Your closing can tie different strands of the report together:

> *Robinson Crusoe* was published on April 25, 1719. Selkirk lived long enough to see the world's imagination captured by the tale of the lonely island dweller.

You can show how the information in the report is related to the reader's everyday life or to the wider world:

> So the next time you are wondering whether to go sailing, check the clouds. Cumulus? Cirrostratus? Cumulonimbus? Each contains a clue to the coming weather.

Can you think of other ways to end a report?

Prewriting Practice

Write a new introduction and closing for "The Real Robinson Crusoe." Make sure that your introduction will capture your reader's attention and that your closing wraps things up in an interesting way.

The Grammar Connection

Pronouns and Contractions

Do not confuse the possessive pronouns *its, your,* and *their* with the contractions *it's, you're,* and *they're. It's* means it is; *you're* means you are; *they're* means they are. Read the following sentences.

> Reporters have interesting careers. You're always on the go, interviewing people, checking your facts, and writing stories. Your stories and articles are read by thousands of people, so it's important to be accurate. It's a difficult job at times. You're required to get your stories written on time. A newspaper doesn't include old news in its latest edition.

Practice Rewrite the above paragraph, changing *your* and *you're* to *their* and *they're.*

The Writing Process
How to Write a Report

Step 1: Prewriting—Choose a Topic

Nicole made a list of things she was curious about. Then she thought about which one would make the best report topic.

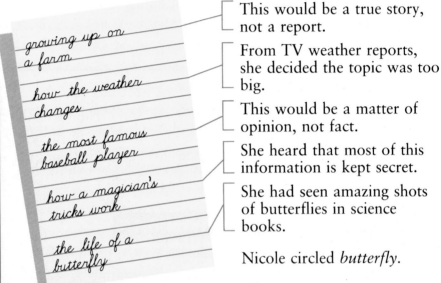

growing up on a farm — This would be a true story, not a report.

how the weather changes — From TV weather reports, she decided the topic was too big.

the most famous baseball player — This would be a matter of opinion, not fact.

how a magician's tricks work — She heard that most of this information is kept secret.

the life of a butterfly — She had seen amazing shots of butterflies in science books.

Nicole circled *butterfly*.

On Your Own

1. **Think and discuss** List some topics you would like to know more about. Turn to the Ideas page. Each topic can be narrowed to cover a smaller area. See "Narrow Your Topic" for help.
2. **Choose** Ask yourself these questions about each topic.
   Can I find enough information?
   Can I cover the topic in a two- or three-page report?
   Does this topic really interest me?
   Circle the topic you want to write about.
3. **Explore** Before you begin writing, do *both* activities under "Exploring Your Topic" on the Ideas page.

Ideas for Getting Started

Choosing Your Topic

Topic Ideas

Finding a sunken ship
Life on a desert island
Training for the
   Olympic marathon
Volcanos
Great Wall of China
Birds that talk
Underwater tunnels
Gold rush of 1849
Solar heating
The Pulitzer Prize

An Idea File

Have everyone in your class pick a different letter of the alphabet. Look in the index of an encyclopedia or in a library's card catalog under your letter. Jot down ten interesting topics. Meet in small groups to share and discuss these ideas. Then pool all your cards into a class idea file.

Exploring Your Topic

Plan Your Research

What do you want to find out about your topic? Think of five questions. Here is an example.

Topic: The Life of Martin Luther
   King, Jr.
Where and when was he born?
What was his youth like?
How did he become a leader?
What did he achieve?
How and when did he die?

Write five questions that you would like your own report to answer.

Narrow Your Topic

Sometimes a narrower topic makes a better report. With a partner, discuss whether any of your five questions would make a good report in itself. Decide if you would rather write on that narrower topic.

Step 2: Plan Your Report

Nicole asked herself what she wanted to find out about butterflies. She wrote down five questions.

```
How large and how small can butterflies be?
How are they born?
What and how do they eat?
Where do they live?
How long do they live?
```

Nicole looked in library books and encyclopedias for the answers to these questions. When she found a fact she needed, she wrote it on a note card.

Nicole wrote only one fact on each note card. Above the fact, she wrote the question the fact answered. Below the fact, she wrote where she found the fact.

Nicole wrote down the title, the author, and the page number. Later she would put these sources in a **bibliography** at the end of her report. A bibliography lists alphabetically, by the authors' last names, all the sources used in the research.

Here is one of Nicole's note cards.

How large and small?

Largest has wing spread of about eleven inches (p.19)

Stone, Janet. Butterflies. Boston: Mifflin Company, 1985.

This is the question the fact answers.

This is the fact.

This is where Nicole found the fact.

Nicole wrote an outline from her note cards.

1. She put all the cards for each question into a separate pile. She made five piles.
2. Nicole read through one pile. She put the cards in order so the facts made sense. She did the same for the other piles.
3. She made each question into a main heading for her outline.
4. She wrote facts that answered each question as subtopics.
5. She wrote any facts that told about the subtopics as details.

Part of Nicole's outline

I. How butterflies are born

    A. Start as eggs

    B. Hatch into caterpillars

    C. Caterpillars make cocoons

    D. Caterpillars turn into butterflies

II. The sizes of butterflies

    A. All butterflies born full grown

    B. Largest, eleven-inch wing spread

        1. Called Queen Alexander

        2. Lives only in New Guinea

    C. Smallest, ten millimeters

        1. Called the Western Pygmy Blue

        2. Lives in and near Nebraska

Think and Discuss ✓

- What are Nicole's main topics? subtopics? details?
- How did she change her main topics? Why?
- Where might Nicole need more facts?

On Your Own

1. **Do research** Use the five questions you wrote in "Exploring Your Topic." Look in books and encyclopedias to find the answers to your questions.
2. **Take notes** When you find a fact you need, write it on a note card. Write one fact per card. Include the question it answers and where you found the fact.
3. **Put your notes in order** Put together all the cards that answer the same question. You will have five piles. Put the cards in each pile in order so that the facts make sense.
4. **Write an outline** Write each of your questions as a main topic heading. Write the facts that answer each question as subtopics. Write any details that tell about the subtopics.

Step 3: Write a First Draft

Nicole decided to write her report for her summer camp counselor, Susan. Susan knew a lot about interesting insects.

Nicole wrote her first draft. She did not stop to correct her spelling and grammar. She would be able to make those corrections later.

The beginning of Nicole's first draft

Think and Discuss ✓

- What is the topic sentence of her second paragraph? What are the subtopics?
- What details could be clearer?

Butterflies are interesting insects.
There is much to learn about them.

A butterfly's life has four stages.
Butterflies ~~begin~~ come into the world as
eggs. The eggs hatch into caterpillars.
~~They~~ The caterpillars make cocoons. Then
they turn into butterflies.

A butterfly does not grow any bigger.
The world's largest kind of butterfly has
a wing spread of eleven inches. It

On Your Own

1. **Think about purpose and audience** Ask these questions.
   What do I want my reader to learn? How much detail should I include?
   Who will my reader be? What facts need explanation?
2. **Write** Write your first draft. Remember to follow your outline. Write on every other line to leave room for changes. Write down all your facts without stopping to correct spelling and grammar. Save those changes for later.

Step 4: Revise

Nicole read her first draft. She decided to write a better opening for such an interesting topic.

Nicole read her report to Heather.

Reading and responding

Nicole checked through her report for any more terms or facts that might be unclear. She added words to explain them. She added that a butterfly comes out of a cocoon fully grown.

Part of Nicole's revised draft

Most people know that butterflies are beautiful,
^~~Butterflies are interesting insects.~~
but they might not know how interesting they are.
There is much to learn about them.

A butterfly's life has four stages.

Butterflies ~~begin~~ come into the world as
wormlike creatures called
eggs. The eggs hatch into ^caterpillars.

~~They~~ The caterpillars make ^~~cocoons~~. Then
they turn into butterflies.

a sticky thread and wind it around
themselves. This wrapping is called a cocoon.

Think and Discuss ✓

• Why did Nicole change the opening of her report?
• What terms did she explain?
• What fact did she make clearer?

On Your Own

Revising Checklist

☑ Will the opening make my reader want to know more?
☑ Does each paragraph begin with a topic sentence?
☑ Have I included details that support my main ideas?
☑ Have I explained each fact clearly?
☑ Does my closing sum up the report?

1. **Revise** Make changes in your first draft. Make your sentences interesting to your readers. A thesaurus can help you find clearer words.

2. **Have a conference** Read your report to a classmate.

WRITING CONFERENCE

Ask your listener:	**As you listen:**
"How could I make the opening more interesting?" "What parts seemed unclear or out of order?" "How could I improve the closing?"	I must listen closely. Did the opening catch my interest? Is this easy to follow? Are the facts clear? What would I like to know more about?

3. **Revise** Can you use any of your partner's suggestions? Do you have other ideas? Make those changes on your paper.

Thesaurus

careful cautious, watchful
change vary, alter, transform, convert
common ordinary, normal, general, regular
conclusion end, outcome, decision, deduction
doubt distrust, question
explore study, probe, investigate

grow raise, produce, become, mature
learn discover, memorize, pick up
rewarding worthwhile, enriching
search seek, examine
succeed achieve, gain
unreasonable illogical, irrational, nonsensical

Step 5: Proofread

Nicole proofread her report for mistakes in spelling, grammar, capitalization, and punctuation. She checked her spellings in a dictionary. She used proofreading marks to make changes.

Here is the way the end of Nicole's proofread report looked.

Nicole's proofread ending

Like most insects, butterflies do not

live v~~a~~ery long, ℓ̸ompared with people and

animals. Some kinds live almost a year☉

live only a few weeks.

many other kinds ∧ ~~die sooner.~~ ¶Although much

there

is known about butterflies, ~~their~~ is more

discovering new

to find out. S̲c̲ientists are still ∧ ~~learning~~

kinds of butterflies and new facts about them.

~~things about butterflies.~~

Think and Discuss

- How did Nicole correct a sentence fragment? run-on sentence?
- What words did she correct for spelling?

On Your Own

1. **Proofreading Practice** Proofread this paragraph. Correct the mistakes in grammar and spelling. There are three incorrect pronouns, two missing punctuation marks, and one misspelled word. Write the paragraph correctly.

   Today there are few science fiction fans to who the name Ray Bradbury is unfamilier. Bradbury an American author was not someone who's success came easily. After finishing high school, he sold newspapers during the day and wrote at least 2,000 words every night. If anyone deserved success, it was him.

Proofreading Marks

¶	Indent
∧	Add
⋏	Add a comma
⌦⌦	Add quotation marks
☉	Add a period
ℓ	Take out
≡	Capitalize
/	Make a small letter
∩	Reverse the order

2. **Proofreading Application** Now proofread your report. Use the Proofreading Checklist and the Grammar and Spelling Hints below. Check your spellings in a dictionary. You may want to make your corrections with a colored pencil.

Proofreading Checklist

Did I

☑ **1.** indent the first line of every paragraph?

☑ **2.** use capital letters and punctuation marks correctly?

☑ **3.** correct any run-on sentences or sentence fragments?

☑ **4.** use the correct form of every verb?

☑ **5.** use the correct form of every pronoun?

☑ **6.** spell all words correctly?

The Grammar/Spelling Connection

Grammar Hints

Remember these rules from Unit 11 when you use pronouns.

• Use *who* as the subject. (*Who is coming to the party?*)

• Use *whom* as the direct object. (*Whom are you inviting?*)

Spelling Hint

Remember this spelling hint.

The vowel and (r) sound can be spelled in different ways.

The (är) sound can be spelled **ar**. (*chart, guitar, march*)

Step 6: Publish

Here is the way Nicole shared her report with her camp counselor. She painted the world's largest and smallest butterflies, showing their true colors and their actual size. She attached her report below them.

On Your Own

1. **Copy** Write or type your report as neatly as you can.
2. **Give it a title** Think of a title that will catch your reader's interest.
3. **Make your bibliography** For books, follow the model on Nicole's note card. For articles, also include the name of the magazine or encyclopedia.
4. **Check** Read over your report again to make sure you have not left out anything or made any mistakes in copying.
5. **Share** Think of a special way to share your report.

Ideas for Sharing

- Make a chart, drawing, or model that helps explain something in your report.
- Make a class "book of knowledge" with your reports. Include a table of contents.
- Give a talk, using the information in your report. See page 215 for guidelines on how to give a talk.

Applying Research Reports

Literature and Creative Writing

The passage from *Robinson Crusoe* told how Crusoe fought his way out of the stormy sea into which he had been thrown. "The Real Robinson Crusoe" was the story of Alexander Selkirk, who, through his own folly, spent four years on a desert island. His experiences inspired the novel *Robinson Crusoe*.

Use what you have learned about writing reports to complete one or more of the following activities.

> **Remember these things** ☑
>
> Take notes that answer your main questions.
>
> Turn your questions into topic sentences.
>
> Make your opening capture the reader's attention.
>
> Sum up the main points in your closing.

1. **What is it like to be shipwrecked?** Do research and write a report on a twentieth-century person who has been stranded at sea, or on someone who undertook a harrowing raft or boat trip on the ocean.

2. **Danger on the high seas!** Do research and write a report on one of the following topics: (1) the sinking of the *Titanic,* (2) the mutiny on the *Bounty,* (3) the sinking of the *Lusitania,* (4) the hijacking of the *Achille Lauro.*

3. **Write an April Fool's report.** Pretend you are reporting a news story about the sighting of a sea monster or some other unlikely event at sea. Interview imaginary scientists, eyewitnesses, and other experts. Make your "report" as convincing as possible.

Writing Across the Curriculum
Geography

Geographers study all the features of the earth and everything that can change it, such as wind and rain, and plants, animals, and people. Not all geographers travel to faraway places. They may study the land features and plant and animal life in your nearby woods.

1. **Discover your own area.** Write a geographic report about the area where you live. Use maps and other resources to describe the climate, average rainfall, topography, and population. A hike through some woods can tell you about the land features and plant and animal life.

2. **Travel in time.** Write a report about what the area you live in was like one hundred years ago. What was the population? What kinds of crops were grown? Was there a large city or town, or did people live on farms?

3. **Run the Colorado.** The Colorado River is one of the most exciting rivers in America. Write a report on the main uses of the river. Why is the river so important?

Writing Steps
1. Choose a topic
2. Write a first draft
3. Revise
4. Proofread
5. Publish

Word Bank
source
rapids
irrigation
recreation
agriculture

Roberto really enjoyed reading about "The Real Robinson Crusoe." He was surprised that Crusoe never tried putting an SOS note in a bottle! Roberto read the other twenty sea adventures in the same book, which was called *Great Sea Stories*, by Donald J. Sobol. He decided to share the book with his classmates by writing a newspaper article about one of the incidents. Here is what Roberto wrote.

Money Mail Washed Up in Morocco

A French woman in Saffi, Morocco, spotted a bottle on the waterfront and fished it out to find a message and a check, reports Donald J. Sobol in "The Bottle Post," one of many true stories found in his book Great Sea Stories.

The message read "Hurrah for Lindbergh!" Investigation showed that the bottle came from an ocean liner, the President Roosevelt, and had been dropped overboard in 1927 by a passenger excited by Lindbergh's successful flight across the Atlantic.

No dates are available for this incident, but the check was still good.

This is just one of many incidents in which bottles have carried messages for many miles and many years. Bottles do not break as easily as you might think. Read more fascinating cases of bottle messages in the account in Great Sea Stories by Donald J. Sobol.

Think and Discuss
- What did you learn from this article?
- What other kinds of stories do you think the book contains?
- Why is this a good way to share a book?

Share Your Book

Write a Newspaper Story

1. Choose one exciting or interesting event from your book. Jot down who was involved in the event, when it happened, where it happened, and how and why it happened.
2. Write the news story using the facts you listed. You may want to include background information to help make the incident clear to your readers.
3. Write three different headlines for your story, and choose the best one. Headlines should catch the readers' attention in as few words as possible.
4. Include the title of the book and the name of the author.

Other Activities

- Sometimes photographs are used to help tell a news story. Use a picture or a photograph to illustrate your story.
- Write a message that someone in your book might have put in a bottle. It could be a cry for help, or it might simply tell about the character and ask for a reply.
- Plan a radio news program for another class. Choose several articles written by members of your class, and present them in a "broadcast."

 # The Book Nook

The Cay	**Call It Courage**
by Theodore Taylor	*by Armstrong Sperry*
When Philip and his mother flee Curaçao during World War II, their ship is sunk. Philip, blinded, is marooned with a cat and an old sailor.	A Polynesian boy who fears the sea is cast on an island where he must find food, clothing, and shelter alone.

Language and Usage

This cat
Walks into the room and across the floor,
Under a chair, around the bed,
Behind the table and out the door.
I'm sitting on the chair
And I don't see where he is.

Karla Kuskin
from "This Cat"